Created and Directed by Hans Höfer

INSIGHT GUIDES
GREEK ISLANDS

Edited by Martha Ellen Zenfell

Editorial Director Brian Bell

HOUGHTON MIFFLIN COMPANY

APA PUBLICATIONS

GReek IslAnds

Third Edition (3rd Reprint)
© **1993 APA PUBLICATIONS (HK) LTD**
All Rights Reserved
Printed in Singapore by Höfer Press Pte. Ltd

Distributed in the United States by:	Distributed in Canada by:	Distributed in the UK & Ireland by:	Worldwide distribution enquiries:
Houghton Mifflin Company	**Thomas Allen & Son**	**GeoCenter International UK Ltd**	**Höfer Communications Pte Ltd**
2 Park Street	390 Steelcase Road East	The Viables Center, Harrow Way	38 Joo Koon Road
Boston, Massachusetts 02108	Markham, Ontario L3R 1G2	Basingstoke, Hampshire RG22 4BJ	Singapore 2262
ISBN: 0-395-66261-3	ISBN: 0-395-66261-3	ISBN: 9-62421-081-0	ISBN: 9-62421-081-0

ABOUT THIS BOOK

Writing about Greek Islands is the opposite of visiting Greek Islands. The qualities which make destinations such as Mykonos shimmering holiday centres are the very qualities which give journalists sleepless nights. Deadlines on a Greek Island? Dedicated accuracy from a shepherd tending his flock? An island that spells its name three different ways and has a ferryboat only once a week?

As a veteran of several travel guides to the islands, project editor **Martha Ellen Zenfell** was aware of the logistical problems. For her own book, *Nicholson's Guide to the Greek Islands*, she travelled to more than 50 of them, armed only with a typewriter, a notebook and a waterproof pen. The memories are still clear. She was severely bitten by mosquitos on Zakynthos and ate grey gruel for days when fresh food ran out on Telendos. Her motorbike broke down in a storm on Skopelos and tears were shed in the Dodecanese when the third ferry in as many days was, again, six hours late. "But why do you want to leave Leros?" asked a fishman who found her weeping on the beach. "Is this not the most beautiful island in the Aegean? Come and stay with my family, and write your book here."

It was memories like this one which prompted Zenfell to contact **Brian Bell**, Apa Publications' London-based editorial director, about the possibility of another book on the Greek Islands. The kindness of strangers is the flip side of travelling alone and extensively in Greece: the unknown man who lent 2,000 drachmas from his own pocket when stranded on Halki; the farmer's wife on Naxos whose invitation prompted a short-term stint as a wailer at an island funeral. Zenfell and Bell settled down to assemble a crack team of reporters and photographers to share the tribulations and the satisfactions of producing a book on the islands.

Rowlinson Carter was one of the first to be recruited. He writes now and again, and sometimes quite frequently, for the *Spectator*, the *Sunday Times Magazine*, the *Guardian*, the *Daily Telegraph*, *Tatler* and *Harper's & Queen*. His journal of a year-long stay in the Sporades forms the basis for several of the essays on contemporary island life.

Mark Mazower, who wrote the history section, was born in 1958 and educated at universities in Oxford and Bologna. He has lived in Athens and contributed substantially to *Insight Guide: Greece*. At present, Mazower is a Research Fellow of Christ Church, Oxford, where he is working on 20th-century Greek history.

Marcus Brooke, whose major written contribution is the Crete section and who also supplied many of the photographs, is a Scot who wanders around the world with typewriter and cameras. Aeons ago, when leading a less peripatetic life and when on vacation in Italy, Brooke tossed a coin to decide whether to remain in Positano or to explore new countries. The coin said Greece, which was then the Levant, and Brooke was seduced hook, line and sinker. Since then he has lived, on various occasions, on Crete, Rhodes and Hydra.

Freelance journalist **Stephanie Ferguson** has been a regular traveller to Greece for over 10 years. She sees herself as a visitor rather than a tourist, and likes to get involved, from learning to belly-dance on Lesvos to sharing snails and chips with the shepherds of Halki, or staying in the monastery on Symi. Born and brought up in Cardiff, she has written for

Zenfell

Carter

Mazower

the *Daily Mail*, the *Sunday Times Magazine*, the *Guardian*, and *You* magazine. Currently she contributes travel articles, mainly on Greece, to the *Independent* newspaper.

Anita Peltonen was born to travel. Montreal, Manhattan, Helsinki and London couldn't hold down American-born Peltonen, who has been published in several British national newspapers. She writes: "There is no middle ground when travelling in Greece; it's an experience always imbued with passion. It's a place to find exotic husbands—and diseases. The islands are not the neatly wrapped touristic trinkets they appear to be, and this is what I love about them. You can be in the throes of shamelessly European gratification one day and pitched into an unforgiving wilderness the next. All it takes is a few steps off the beaten path."

John Carr's contributions combine two of his specialities. As Athens correspondent of the *Wall Street Journal,* Carr was in an informed position to write the essay on shipping and cruising called "Ships in the Night". As a drummer in a reasonably successful rock band when he first arrived in Athens, he studied the cadences of Greek folk music and contributed to *Billboard* magazine; he was the natural person, therefore, to approach for the article on island music. He has lived in Athens for two decades (Carr's elegant mother is Greek).

David Glenn is also a specialist: his job is sailing. As deputy editor of the glossy magazine *Yachting World,* there is little Glenn doesn't know about yachts. His article on cruising the Med, with its pitfalls and pleasures, should be read by anyone contemplating hoisting a sail.

Kerin Hope, who wrote the sections on Athens and Piraeus, was at the time the Athens correspondent for the Associated Press. An erstwhile archaeologist and contributor to numerous publications (including *Insight Guide: Greece*), she now represents the *Financial Times* in Athens.

Rhoda Nottridge, a writer from Brighton, England, gave up her holiday time to cover the dubious delights of Corfu. Her plea to save the turtles on Zakynthos is a reminder that tourists can play an active, rather than a passive role, in preserving the islands.

It fell to **Carol Reed**, a hard-working freelance writer based in Athens, to put the tourism question into perspective. What can we expect from the islands not only now, but well into the 21st century? Read her article and find out.

Anthony Wood spent over a year studying traditional agricultural farming, specifically related to a Greek island. **Jane Cocking**, who wrote the piece on island crafts, is a research fellow of Darwin College, Cambridge. Her Ph.D was on the folk textiles of Crete. **Nile Stanton**, an American-born lecturer at the Faltaits Museum was, during his first winter on Skyros, the only English-speaking person on the island.

As more than a dozen photographers contributed to this book, they cannot, unfortunately, all be singled out by name. Special thanks, however, go to **Pierre Couteau**, **Markos G. Hionos** and **Michele Macrakis** in Greece, and to **David Beatty** in England.

Thanks, too, must be extended to **Olympic Holidays**, for flying several of us to the islands and ensuring our safe return, to the **National Tourist Organisation of Greece**, and to **Elizabeth Boleman-Herring**, editor of the literary magazine *The Southeast Review*, who proof-read the manuscript and generally smoothed the way:

Brooke

Ferguson

Peltonen

Carr

Beginnings

23 **The Island Mentality**
—by Rowlinson Carter

31 **Beginnings**
32 **Waves of Invaders**
43 **The Islands Today**
—by Mark Mazower

49 **Portrait of an Island Family**
—by Stephanie Ferguson

57 **Coping with Tomorrow's Tourism**
—by Carol Reed ·

58 *Island Hopping*
—by Martha Ellen Zenfell

Places

73 **Athens Stopover**
—by Kerin Hope

74 *Coping with Piraeus*
—by Kerin Hope

83 **Corfu**
—by Rhoda Nottridge

87 *Traditional Agriculture*
—by Anthony Wood

89 **The Southern Ionian Islands**
—by Martha Ellen Zenfell

95 *Turtles under Threat*
—by Rhoda Nottridge

99 **The Saronic Gulf Islands**
—by Martha Ellen Zenfell

107 Plumbing and other Problems
—by Stephanie Ferguson

113 The Cyclades Islands
—by Anita Peltonen

129 Pelican Power on Mykonos
—by Anita Peltonen

130 Ancient Delos
—by Marcus Brooke

149 The Sporades Islands
—by Rowlinson Carter

154 The Faltaits Museum
—by Nile Stanton

163 The Northeast Aegean Islands
—by Anita Peltonen

170 Literary Lesvos
—by Stephanie Ferguson

183 Rhodes
—by Stephanie Ferguson

194 Leisurely Lindos
—by Marcus Brooke

199 The Southern Dodecanese Islands
—by Stephanie Ferguson

205 The Northern Dodecanese Islands
—by Martha Ellen Zenfell

210 Festive Occasions
—by Stephanie Ferguson

223 Crete
228 Knossos
231 Zorba's Legacy
234 Samaria Gorge
238 A Cretan Custom
—by Marcus Brooke

Features

251 Sailing the Seas
—by David Glenn

257 Sun, Sea, Sand and Sex
—by Rowlinson Carter

263 Man, Myth and Music
—by John Carr

269 Crafts and Customs
—by Jane Cocking

275 Ships in the Night
—by John Carr

281 Catering for All Tastes
—by Rowlinson Carter

285 Island Elections
291 Writing the Great Novel
297 Islands Out of Season
—by Rowlinson Carter

Maps

70 The Greek Islands
83 Corfu
90 The Ionian Islands
101 The Saronic Gulf Islands
115 Santorini
118 The Central and Eastern Cyclades Islands
138 The Western Cyclades Islands
152 The Sporades Islands
166 The Northeast Aegean Islands
183 Rhodes
200 The Southern Dodecanese Islands
206 The Northern Dodecanese Islands
224 Crete
226 Iraklion

TRAVEL TIPS

306 *Getting There*

307 *Travel Essentials*

309 *Getting Acquainted*

313 *Communications*

315 *Emergencies*

316 *Getting Around*

319 *Where to Stay*

322 *Food Digest*

325 *Things to Do*

326 *Culture Plus*

329 *Nightlife*

330 *Shopping*

330 *Sports*

331 *Special Information*

331 *Language*

333 *Further Reading*

334 *Useful Addresses*

**For detailed Information
See Page 305**

THE ISLAND MENTALITY

"Island" is one of those words which psychiatrists might use to trigger an automatic response from patients stretched out on the couch. The response may be influenced by childhood recollections of Robinson Crusoe, in which case islands are possibly associated with the idea of escape from a complex universe into a private, more manageable world which offers individuals control over their own destiny. Crusoe becomes comfortable in his reconstructed womb, and it is a surprise, when rescue is at hand, that he doesn't tell his saviours to push off.

"Greek island" would probably add some specific touches to the imagery: a cluster of blisteringly white buildings against a shimmering sea, donkeys with a backdrop of olive groves, weather-beaten fishermen repairing nets, and tavernas full of retsina, moussaka, shattered plates and an endless supply of "Never on Sunday" and "Zorba the Greek." Accurate as far as it goes, but any worthwhile generalisation about the Greek islands—anything, that is, more adventurous than the staringly obvious—would almost certainly be wrong.

Inter-island relations: Although the islands are classified as members of one group or another, they have a strong sense of separate identity and invariably an idiosyncratic history to back it up. Often, the feeling between neighbouring islands is mutual suspicion bordering on loathing, although this is something visitors would seldom be aware of unless they made a point of going down to the local *ouzerie* and chatting to the old boys entrenched there. Conditioned by long winter nights when nothing much happens, the old boys have developed the knack of waffling on about any subject under the sun, and a new face in the audience is welcome.

As an example of inter-island relations, Skiathos and Skopelos in the Sporades have never been able to see eye to eye on the matter of ice. The origins of the dispute are

Preceding pages: the secret key to the islands; welcome to Greece; a rural retreat; a church in the Cyclades; a priest on his way to work; a donkey goes shopping; sailing into the sun. Left, men playing cards on Hios. Right, a boatman beckons.

buried in history, but it may spring from days when making ice depended on clanking contraptions which were partly home-made and therefore the focus of parochial pride. Neither side in the respective *ouzerie* will volunteer what is wrong with the other island's ice. Uncharacteristically, questions are turned aside, but hopeless shaking of grey heads hints at a truth so awful that they cannot bring themselves to utter it.

The telephone directories on Skiathos and Skopelos reveal some of the same surnames.

Could the families by any chance be related? The inquiry seems to hit a nerve as painful as the ice business.

Only in one area, if the old boys are to be believed, are the two islands in full agreement, and that concerns Skyros, the largest island in the chain. Skiathos and Skopelos are within full view of one another, a distasteful but undeniable fact, whereas Skyros lies below the horizon. According to the miraculously united old boys, that means, luckily, that Skyros may not exist.

Such theories are expounded with twinkling eyes and guffaws; even if they should not be taken too literally, they are great fun, and the opportunity to move among neighbouring islands in order to compare notes should not be missed.

It is sometimes said that if against the odds two islands struck the curious visitor as being practically identical, those islands would necessarily be at opposite ends of the Aegean. Apart from the natural tendency for small island communities to be staunchly independent, there is a historical basis for their individualism. From the Phoenicians onwards, the islands have been tossed around like loose pebbles in the cultural tides which have surged backwards and forwards through the eastern Mediterranean, and none has emerged from that experience quite like

if the traces today would require more diligent research than most visitors would be inclined to conduct while on holiday.

Beginning in the 11th century, Corfu was invaded by Normans, Sicilians, Genoese, Venetians, Greeks ("the despotate of Epirus"), more Sicilians, Neopolitans and the Venetians again. On this occasion they stayed for 400 years, then the procession resumed: France, Russo-Turks, Britain, Greece, Serbia (80,000 Serbs descended on the island and it became the seat of the Serbian government in exile), Greece, Italy, Germany and, finally after World War II, Greece again.

Dedicated scholars could probably as-

any other.

Momentous events were taking place on Crete and some of the Cyclades as early as 3000 B.C. The golden age of Athens under Pericles lay as far in the future then as, for us, it now lies in the past—more than two millennia either way. Settlers from Mesopotamia landed with the skills which developed into the Minoan civilisation.

Intruders: To look at the history of Corfu merely from the 11th century is therefore to pick up that particular story a long way down the line. Nevertheless, the record from that date shows an amazing cavalcade of intruders, all of whom must have left a mark, even

semble a jigsaw, with pieces extant in Corfu, that would reflect each and every one of these waves. The evidence does not necessarily consist of archeological ruins or excavated objects. Corfu extrapolated from one small chapter of its convoluted history an abiding passion for cricket. It is still played on the square in the middle of the town, albeit with local variations which would raise the eyebrows of traditionalists in England.

Other islands got almost as much unwanted outside attention as Corfu. Piracy was a perennial problem, and that accounts for the number of citadels *(kastra)* on high ground to which the island population retreated when danger threatened, which in some cases meant they were holed up for years—even centuries—on end.

Determined pirates: The defences did not always keep determined pirates like Barbarossa out, but they did mean that the pirates had to summon the effort instead of lazily helping themselves to everything of value when they happened to be cruising by.

Crete and Rhodes have by far the richest and most thoroughly documented sites for historically-minded visitors, but on any island there is bound to be something to pick over, even if it isn't marked on the map. A good tip for amateur archaeologists would be to ask themselves where, taking into

they are not remotely connected with their distinguished ancestors.

It is not to become embroiled in that argument to observe, however, that the "Greekness" of the islands is variable. Italy did not cede the Dodecanese to Greece until 1947, and the inclusion of Crete as part of Greece was once an issue nearly as hot as the present one over Cyprus. Some islands were deeply affected in the 1920s when Greece and Turkey exchanged large numbers of their respective ethnic expatriates.

The topographical differences among the islands are worth considering. If some of the islands look like mountain peaks, it is because much of the area now covered by the

account security, prevailing winds, terrain, water supply etc., they themselves would have chosen to build something—and then start looking.

Invasions of self-contained communities in the confined space of a small island would naturally be more disruptive than they would be on a relatively amorphous mainland. In extreme cases, invaders wiped out the existing population and started again. Modern Greeks are ultra-sensitive to the suggestion, usually emanating from Turkey, that the country has been overrun so many times that

Left and above, the church plays a social role.

Aegean was once a solid land bridge between Greece and Asia Minor, which eventually fractured and "sank". These islands are the tips of what used to be ranges encroaching from either side.

The largest mountain ranges in mainland Greece caused famous military bottlenecks at places like Thermopylae where, in Xerxes' time, there was only the narrowest of passages between the mountains and the sea. Since then the sea has receded, so what used to be a death trap, where Spartan defenders calmly bathed and combed their hair (according to Herodotus) while waiting for the Persian onslaught, is now a plateau three miles (five km) wide.

The contours of submerged mountains and valleys extending from the area around Thermopylae caused the seabed around the islands to drop precipitously to 6000 ft. On the Turkish side, the sea is generally much shallower, and it is the shallows which can cause the Aegean, quiet and bather-friendly one moment, to be transformed into a lethal cauldron within the space of an hour or two.

Anyone hiring a boat on holiday should never leave port without consulting the islanders. For thousands of years, lives have depended on accurate weather predictions, and local knowledge handed down is often more reliable than official forecasts carried

on the wireless or in newspapers.

If the purpose of a visit to the islands is nothing more than to settle on a stretch of agreeable beach and live cheaply, visitors should be lucky on both counts. Greece has about 2,000 islands altogether and these, plus the islets, add up to technically the longest coastline of any country in Europe. Basic commodities, including restaurant meals, are price-controlled. They may rise with inflation, but against major foreign currencies the Greek drachma usually goes down, so the net result for foreigners is constant good value for money.

Advanced androgyny: The one exception may be Mykonos, which in recent years seems to have cornered a market in advanced androgyny. The islanders used to ask themselves why there were so many churches on Mykonos (hundreds of them); they now tend to say (stoically, while pocketing the money) that the birds of paradise who descend on them in summer undoubtedly need every one of them. Mykonos would not have been allowed to develop its exotic reputation under the puritanical military junta, when even topless sunbathing was discouraged. Since the overthrow of the glum colonels, what bathers choose to wear or discard has been a personal decision, and there is usually at least one beach on an island where nudity is tolerated even if it is not official.

There is nothing ambivalent about the attitude towards drugs, however, and the more popular islands are subject to close undercover surveillance. Some humdrum medicines sold without prescription elsewhere may be illegal in Greece, and as the legal system seems to rest on the principle that the slightest suspicion warrants a spell in prison before the proceedings proper begin, it is wise to err generously on the side of extreme caution.

The best way to enjoy the islands is to arrive with a certain attitude of mind. By all means, begin by uncritically enjoying the cluster of blisteringly white buildings against a shimmering sea, donkeys with a backdrop of olive groves, etc.—the vista, indeed, seared into the senses by piles of island holiday brochures.

Do not shrink, either, from personally smashing a few plates. They are a special, unglazed type not intended for any other purpose. When the novelty wears off, or perhaps earlier, examine each island as if it were an onion, and start stripping off the skins. If not a long-standing dispute about ice, something else is certain to be revealed.

How to strip the onion is a large part of what this book is about. It hopes and tries to show by example. A book that says everything about 2,000 islands will never be written. The learned Helidorius once tried to set out all he had learned about the monuments of Athens—as they existed in the second century B.C. Fifteen volumes later…

Left, a man peels an apple for a snack. Right, women are responsible for preparing the meals.

BEGINNINGS

What distinguishes the course of Greek history from that of her Balkan neighbours is the impact of the sea. The sea diffuses cultures, transfers peoples and encourages trade—and until our own times it was invariably a swifter means of transmission than overland. Nowhere in Greece is the sea as inescapable as on the islands.

Foreign incursions: The poverty of the arid island soil has forced inhabitants to venture far afield for their livelihood. At the same time, the islands have been vulnerable to foreign incursions whether by Arab pirates, Italian colonists or modern tourists. All have played their part in transforming local conditions; some have had an even wider impact.

Phoenician traders, for example, appear to have brought some form of the Greek alphabet to Crete in the early archaic period, just as Egyptian influence was leading island sculptors to work in stone. It is no coincidence that the earliest examples of monumental Greek sculpture are all to be found on the islands.

On Crete, the Bronze Age had produced the first urban civilisation in the Aegean: this was the age of the Knossos and Phaistós palaces, erected in the centuries after 2000 B.C. Other islands, too, such as Santorini, flourished at this time. Thucydides' account of how King Minos of Crete established his sons as governors in the Cyclades and cleared the sea of pirates certainly suggests considerable Cretan control of the Aegean.

This control, if it ever did exist, disappeared with the destruction of Minoan society in the 15th century B.C. The Aegean was not to be dominated by a single sea power for another millennium until the rise of the Athenian empire.

Considerable wealth: Before this, however, communities of Greeks had begun to flourish on most of the islands, exploiting local quarries and mines, and developing indigenous political systems. Some communities achieved considerable wealth, notably on

Sifnos, whose gold and silver mines had made her inhabitants reputedly the richest citizens in the Cyclades by the sixth century B.C. Some reflection of this wealth can be seen in the ruins of the marble treasury which Siphniots dedicated to Apollo at Delphi.

It was in the sixth century, too, that the inhabitants of Santorini began to mint their own coinage, a physical manifestation of the island's powerful status in the Aegean. At one point Santorini's influence was to extend, not only to Crete, Milos, Paros, and Rhodes, but as far west as Corinth and as far east as Asia Minor.

During the fifth century B.C., the islands' independence was curtailed as Athens used anti-Persian fears to manipulate the Confederacy of Athenian leadership. The Confederacy had been formed in 478 B.C. as an alliance between equal partners to form a strong naval power in the Aegean. But Athens soon controlled the Confederacy and used its resources in a series of wars against rivals such as the naval power of Aegina.

Athenian intrigue: It was Athenian intrigues with the Corinthian colony on Corfu, however, that led to the second Peloponnesian War which was ultimately to cripple—and break—Athens forever.

In the Hellenistic period the islands remained turbulent backwaters, prone to internecine struggles which made them easy prey for their more powerful neighbours. By the middle of the first century B.C., Rome had established herself in the Aegean; Crete became the centre of a province which included large parts of Africa.

Under Roman guidance roads were laid, aqueducts constructed, new towns and grand buildings erected. It has been estimated that the islands' population in Roman times was probably greater than it is today.

Despite this prosperity, the Aegean as a whole remained in the background in Roman times. Little is known of conditions of life in the islands either then or after A.D. 395, when they passed under the control of the eastern Roman Empire. Only with the onset of the Arab raids in the seventh century does the historical record become more complete.

Preceding pages: statues from the Rhodes Museum: Ilios the Sun God, (second century B.C.) and Aphrodite bathing (first century B.C.). Left, statue from Early Cycladic II era.

With the decline of Roman power in the Mediterranean, the islands faced a long period of instability: for more than a millennium they were attacked by invaders from all points of the compass. From the north, briefly, came the Vandals and Goths; from the south, the Saracens, who established themselves on Crete in 827 and proceeded to plunder the rest of the Aegean for over a century; from the west came Normans in the 11th century, followed by the Genoese and Venetians; finally, from the east came the Turks, who succeeded in dominating almost all of the Aegean between the 15th and 18th centuries.

Other groups, too, played minor roles—quite apart from powers such as the English, French and Russians, who all shared an interest in the Greek islands. There were always pirates—a notoriously mixed bunch. A 13th century Venetian report on piracy mentions corsairs of the following backgrounds: Genoese, Venetians, Lombards, Sicilians, Provençals, Catalans, Spaniards, Greeks, and Slavs.

The impact of these various peoples on the islands was complex and tangled, making it awkward to generalise about the historical experiences of the islands themselves. Only by considering the main island groups individually may things fall into place.

The Ionian Islands: On the eve of the 1821 Greek uprising, an English traveller to Corfu noted that "The natural weakness and position of the Ionian islands, and all their past history, demonstrate that they must ever be an appendage of some more powerful state; powerful at sea and able to protect them as well as to command." Close to the Greek mainland, vital staging-posts on the voyage from western Europe to the Levant, it was inevitable that the Ionian islands should be a source of constant conflict.

Corfu had suffered brief attacks during the fifth century from Vandals and Goths, the destroyers of the Roman Empire in the West, but it was not until the eastern Empire lost its possessions in southern Italy that the Ionian islands once again became vulnerable.

This time the predators were the Normans. At the time when William the Conqueror was establishing Norman control over England, Robert Guiscard, Duke of Apulia, defeated the Byzantine army and its emperor, before dying of a fever at Cephalonia. His nephew Roger, King of Sicily, occupied Corfu in 1146 and held it for six years. As the Byzantine hold over the islands weakened, the Venetians were forced to come in as reluctant allies.

These allies soon proved to have territorial ambitions of their own. The islands lay on important trade routes to the eastern Medi-

terranean, and commercial interests led to the desire for political control. After the sack of Constantinople in 1204 during the Fourth Crusade, the islands were divided into fiefdoms among noble Venetian families. Not until 1387 however, were the islands brought under direct Venetian rule, which continued through a succession of Ottoman attacks down to 1797 when under the new order created by Napoleon's conquests, the islands were given up to France. During these four centuries, the islands were ruled by local nobility in conjunction with administrators sent out from Venice. The influence of the Republic was felt in the introduction of cash crops such as olives and currants, in the repressive regime under which the peasants worked and in the Italian language which the local nobility affected to speak.

At first Venetian rule was energetic—so that, for example, after Turkish raids had left Zakynthos virtually uninhabited in the early 16th century, vigorous resettlement policies soon created the basis for new prosperity. Zakynthos had only 36 families in 1485, but 752 families by 1516, and her revenues increased forty fold in 30 years thanks to the in-

usually of noble family and often of decayed fortune; men who undertook the office as a speculation of interest and executed it accordingly. Bribery and every mode of illegal practice were carried on openly; toleration for a crime might easily be purchased; and the laws, in many respects imperfect themselves, were rendered wholly null by the corruption of the judges."

The end of Venetian rule was bloodless: when the French invaders arrived they found the fortress guns rusting and the garrison

troduction of these valuable crops.

Corrupt: But by the 18th century Venice had lost her possessions in the Aegean and the Peloponnese; in the Ionian islands, her last remaining stronghold, Venetian rule was corrupt. The islands were ravaged by pirates based on Paxos and the Albanian coast; internally, blood feuds and political assassination made life precarious.

Henry Holland wrote in 1812: "the governors and other officers sent to the island were

Left, Dionysios Solomos, national poet and the Ionians' most famous son. Above, a watercolour of Ithaki harbour.

without powder. Napoleon himself had written in 1797 that "the great maxim of the Republic ought henceforth to be never to abandon Corfu, Zante..." But British troops established a foothold in the minor islands in 1809. After Napoleon's defeat this was extended and the new Septinsular Republic was placed under British protection.

The British found a backward society at least by their lights: wheeled transport was virtually unknown on several islands owing to the appalling roads; the superstition of the priests was such that they opposed the introduction of the potato into the islands on the grounds that this was the apple with which the serpent had tempted Eve in the Garden of Eden. Yet the inhabitants of these islands were demanding the most modern of political institutions. Sir Thomas Maitland, the first Lord High Commissioner—in the words of a Victorian historian—"reconciled these incongruities by establishing a Constitution which, possessing every appearance of freedom, in reality left the whole power in his hands."

Autocratic British rule brought the islanders the benefits of improved roads, drainage schemes and, not least, the game of cricket. But it could not satisfy the islanders' desire for freedom from foreign rule, a desire which intensified after the creation of the Kingdom of Greece in 1832.

The Cyclades, Sporades, Saronic Islands:
The Cyclades, unlike the Ionian islands, were a commercial backwater: main trade routes passed through Crete and the eastern Aegean islands to Smyrna and Aleppo. While they remained a lure to pirates, they were never of comparable interest to major powers. Until the rise of the seafaring Italian city-states in the 11th century, most trade in the Aegean was in the hands of Greeks.

However, the weakness of the Byzantine navy was underlined by a series of Saracen raids against the islands and the Greek mainland. By the 12th century a British chronicler noted that piracy had become the curse of the Aegean: many of the islands were abandoned, while others—Skyros in the Sporades, for example—became pirate lairs.

The sack of Constantinople in 1204, which brought the Ionian islands under Venetian control, also brought new masters to the Aegean. The unimportance of these islands meant that the Venetians were content to leave the task of occupying them to private citizens. Of these, the most successful was Marco Sanudo, a nephew of the Doge Dandolo, who equipped eight galleys at his own expense and sailed to the Aegean where in 1207 he founded the Duchy of Naxos.

Naxos itself became the capital of a fiefdom of some islands, and on it Sanudo built a castle, erected a Catholic cathedral and provided solid fortifications for the town. Other adventurers helped themselves to islands such as Andros and Santorini. The Ghisi family obtained Tinos and Mykonos, as well as the islands in the Sporades, establishing a dynasty which clashed with the

Sanudi until both were overwhelmed by the Ottoman navy in the 16th century.

Traces of the Venetian presence are to be found both in the Catholic communities which survive on Syros and Tinos, and also in local family names which betray a strong Italian influence. The Duchy of Naxos lasted over 350 years, and only ended with the death of Joseph Nasi, the Sephardic Jewish favourite of Selim II, upon whom the Sultan had bestowed the islands after their capture from the Sanudi.

But the exceptional longevity of the Duchy of Naxos should not be allowed to obscure the turbulence of life in the Aegean in these centuries. Piracy had increased in

the late 13th century, with Greek corsairs from Monemvasia or Santorini, Sicilians and Genoese—and had led, for example, to the inhabitants of the island of Amorgos to emigrating *en masse* to Naxos whose fertile interior was relatively inaccessible.

In the 14th century, Catalan mercenaries, brought in for the conflict between Venice and Genoa, ravaged some islands and raided others. Turkish troops landed on Naxos and took 6,000 captives. The Turkish forces often consisted of recent converts to Islam, and were led by renegade Aegean Greeks such as the notorious brothers from Lesvos, Khaireddin and Amrudj Barbarossa.

Local rulers began to complain of depopulation: Andros had to be resettled by Albanian mainlanders; Ios, virtually uninhabited, was replenished by families from the Peloponnese. Astipalea was repopulated in 1413, abandoned in 1473 and only inhabited once more after 1570. In the 16th century, the islands suffered a series of attacks by the Turkish navy and by mid-century Venetian influence was on the wane. Within 50 years, most of the islands had been brought under Ottoman rule, though the last, Tinos, only succumbed as late as 1712.

Conditions of life did not improve under Turkish rule. Piracy, famine and fatal disease remained the perennial problems. In the

18th century, the plague decimated the islands on four separate occasions, continuing into the next century, well after the disease had died out in most of Europe. Thus the Turks, like their predecessors, were forced to repopulate.

Early visitors: Often the new colonists were not Greeks. Tournefort reported in the early 18th century that most of the inhabitants of Antiparos were descended from French and Maltese corsairs. He also noted that villages on Andros were "peopled only by Albani-

Left, detail of Skyros embroidery, probably 17th-century. Above, watercolour of Naxos, 1795.

ans, dressed still in their traditional style and living their own way, that is to say with neither creed nor law."

It was the Albanians who were to play a major role in the struggle for Greek independence. Waves of Albanians had colonised the islands of the Aegean since the 14th century. They were concentrated on the Saronic islands—the eminent Koundouriotis family, for example, moved from Epiros to Hydra around the year 1580. By the late 18th century, Hydra, with a largely Albanian population, possessed one of the largest and most powerful shipping fleets in the Aegean, which played no small part in defeating the Turks after 1821.

The importance of these islands was underlined by the choice of Aegina, briefly, as the first capital of the new Greek state. Refugees flocked here when it was the seat of government, only to leave again when Nafplion replaced it. When Edouard About visited the town in 1839 he reported it "abandoned—the homes that had been built tumbled into ruins, the town once more became a village; its life and activity fled with the government."

The Northeast Aegean Islands: Although the east Aegean islands shared the experience of Arab raids with the Cyclades, the two areas developed differently as the rivalry between Venice and Genoa increased after the Fourth Crusade. As allies of the resurgent Byzantine Empire against her Latin enemies, the Genoese were given trading rights in the Black Sea and granted permission to colonise the eastern Aegean.

A Genoese trading company controlled the *mastic* plantations of Hios from the beginning of the 14th century. In 1333 Lesvos passed into the hands of the Gattiluso family, who eventually extended their control to Thassos and the other northern islands. However, as in the west Aegean, the power of the Ottoman navies simply overwhelmed these local potentates, and with the fall of Hios in 1566 all the islands of the east Aegean passed into Turkish hands.

On Lesvos, an early conquest, the Greek inhabitants were exiled or deported and their property given to the Janissaries. Some of the exiles colonised Samos which had remained deserted since its capture by the Turks in the late 15th century. Belon du Mans, who visited the island around 1546, wrote: "It is striking that an island like Samos must remain deserted. The fear of pirates has rendered her uninhabited so that now there is not a single village there, nor any animals."

Despite the islands' proximity to the mainland, they attracted only a small number of Moslem colonisers, and the bulk of the population remained Greek, supplemented by the inevitable Albanian immigrants. Only on Lesvos were Moslem settlers to be found farming the land; elsewhere they stayed close to the towns. The 1821 insurrection sent shock waves through the islands. Samos was first; the unrest then spread to Hios where, in 1822, the Turks brutally sup-

Elsewhere in the east Aegean, the changes were just as great. The Ottoman authorities were only able to suppress the rising with the aid of Mehmet Ali and his Albanian mercenaries who had as little respect for the local Moslem notables as they had for the Greeks: many Turkish landowners sold up and emigrated to Anatolia, while their properties were bought by middle-class Greeks who became an increasingly powerful force in the aging Ottoman Empire.

By the end of the century the Turkish hold had become tenuous: Samos, for example, had been granted autonomy under a traditionally Christian prince. And on Thassos the Oxford don Henry Tozer found in 1884

pressed a rather uncertain revolt. Fustel de Coulanges wrote in 1856 that "Any person aged more than 32 years whom one meets today on Hios was enslaved and saw his father slaughtered." It was little consolation to know that the massacre on Hios had aroused the attention of European liberals, and strengthened philhellene sentiment. Refugees fled westwards, transporting the island's traditional *loukoumi* industry (the making and selling of Turkish Delight candy) to Syros, in the Cyclades, which in turn became the busiest port in the new Greek state. Hiot colonies sprang up in Alexandria, Trieste, Marseilles and Amsterdam.

that there were no Moslems there apart from the governor himself and a few soldiers. Since the people had to pay neither the "head tax"—universal elsewhere in the Ottoman Empire—nor Ottoman trade duties, it is not surprising that they appeared content with their system of government.

The Moslem islanders, on the other hand, continued to leave for the mainland. Even before the Greco-Turkish population exchange in 1923, the Turkish communities on Hios and Lesvos had dwindled away. Their place was filled by a mass of Greek refugees from Anatolia, whose arrival underlined the Greek identity of these islands.

The Dodecanese Islands: The 14 or more islands, misleadingly known as the "Dodecanese", suffered as elsewhere from the collapse of Roman authority. Symbolic of this decline was the destruction of that wonder of antiquity, the Colossus of Rhodes, during the Saracen occupation of the island in A.D. 654. The Byzantine hold remained firmer here than in the west, but after 1204 these domains too were ceded to Frankish adventurers in return for nominal acknowledgement of Byzantine sovereignty.

By the beginning of the 14th century Venice had helped herself to those two crucial stepping-stones to the East, Kassos and Karpathos. At the same time, the Venetian

were outnumbered by a massive Ottoman force over 100,000 strong, and after a siege lasting several months the starving defenders were forced to capitulate. With the fall of Rhodes, the position of the neighbouring islands was undermined, and by 1537 they had all been incorporated into the formidable Ottoman Empire.

Although Ottoman rule was not notably harsh for the Orthodox community, it was not designed to foster economic growth. There were, for example, prohibitions on Christians living in major towns such as Rhodes. Since the land on many islands was difficult to farm, the islanders looked elsewhere for their livelihoods. Many became

nobles who held Rhodes handed it over to the Knights of St John, a military order which had been based in Cyprus since the loss of Jerusalem in 1291. Fulke de Villaret, the first Grand Master of Rhodes, reconstructed the city, which was further improved during the 15th century.

But, although the island had thus been able to withstand a siege by the Turks in 1480, not even the Knights of St John could hold off the Ottoman threat indefinitely. In 1521 they

Left, the sea battle of Samos; watercolour from 1824. Above left, the Colossus of Rhodes. Above right, 19th-century drawing of Kassos girl.

seamen, while on Kalimnos and Symi the tradition of sponge fishing prospered. In 1521 the islanders of Kalimnos paid homage to Suleiman II with sponges and white bread to show that "sponge fishers do not cultivate corn, but buy flour—and only of the best quality." During the 19th century, the sponge fishers opened agencies in London, Frankfurt and Basle.

Unexpected liberation: But these developments, typical of the growing Greek middle class, did not lead to union with Greece until late in the day. The islands had been intended for the new Greek state in 1830, but were retained at the last minute by Turkey in return for the mainland island Euboea. Liberation from the Ottoman Empire came unexpectedly through the occupation of the islands by the Italians during their war with the Turks in 1912.

The arrival of the Italians was at first welcomed by the islanders. A congress on Patmos passed a resolution thanking the Italian nation for delivering them from the Turkish yoke. However, another resolution at the same congress calling for unification with Greece was less satisfactory to the local Italian commander who broke up the congress and forbade further public meetings.

The Italians did not intend to hold the islands permanently but, with the dismember-

gans such as "Viva la Duce, viva la nuova Italia imperiale!" were daubed on the walls of recalcitrant shopkeepers.

But the process was brought to an abrupt halt by World War Two. Once Italy surrendered in 1943, the islands were taken over by the Germans who managed, in the course of their brief and very brutal occupation, to exterminate the ancient Jewish population, much against the evident wishes of the islanders, the Italians and even some of their own soldiers.

Today, only three survivors of the Jewish community remain on Rhodes. Just a few months after the Jews had been deported, the islands were occupied by the Allies, who

ΣΚΗΝΗ ΕΝ ΚΡΗΤΗ ΚΑΤΑ ΤΟ 1866.

ment of the Ottoman empire, their dreams of establishing a foothold in Asia Minor led them to renege on a promise made in 1920 to return the islands to Greece. Mussolini sent groups of reluctant administrators to turn the islands into a fascist colony. In the early 1930s, many islanders emigrated to the mainland, Egypt and Australia.

For those who remained life had to be endured under the farcical prohibitions of a totalitarian regime: an extensive secret police network guarded against nationalist activity; the colours of the Greek flag—blue and white—were prohibited in public; all shop signs had to be painted in Italian. Slo-

finally handed them over in 1947 to Greece.

Crete: The "Great Island" has had the most violent history of all: its strategic position, agricultural riches and, not least, its inhabitants' fierce and unbroken tradition of resistance to foreign oppression have all ensured this. From A.D. 823, when it was conquered by Saracen freebooters out of Alexandria, who made it the centre of the slave trade and a springboard for pirate raids throughout the Aegean, the strategic importance of Crete has been obvious.

Around 3000 B.C. a prosperous civilisation spread its influence throughout the Aegean. The Minoans, whose rituals have filtered down to us through the legend of Theseus and his labyrinthine struggle with the Minotaur, left proof of their architectural genius in the ruined palaces of Knossos and Phaistós. Daring soldiers, they appear to have preferred commerce to agriculture. They established outposts in the Peloponnese and made contact with the Egyptians.

By 1500 B.C., Cretan civilisation had reached its zenith. Yet barely a century later, for reasons which remain unexplained, most centres of their power were destroyed by fire and abandoned. The Minoan settlement in Santorini was annihilated by a violent volcanic eruption, but the causes of the wider disintegration of Minoan control remain a

became crucial after 1453 when the island gave refuge to exiles fleeing the Turks, and briefly became the centre of a renaissance of Byzantine culture: artists such as Dom. Theotokapoulos, otherwise known as El Greco helped pass on ideas from Crete to enrich the renaissance in western Europe.

Though the Venetians developed the towns and fortresses on the north coast, they knew how little they were loved by the Cretans. In 1615 a certain Fra Paolo Serpi had warned that "the Greek faith is never to be trusted", and he had recommended that the people "must be watched with more attention lest, like the wild beasts they are, they should find an occasion to use their teeth and

mystery. Only Knossos continued to be inhabited as Cretan dominance in the Aegean came to an end.

In the early 13th century Venice and Genoa tussled to wrest the island away from the waning Byzantine Empire. Though Venice ultimately turned Crete into her prize possession, Byzantine influence there remained strong. The old Greek noble families survived, while ties with Constantinople were reflected in church art and secular literature. This strong Byzantine tradition

Left, oil painting of the 1866 Cretan Revolt. Above, Iraklion at the turn of the century.

claws. The surest way is to keep good garrisons to awe them." Under such a regime the peasants were probably worse off than under the Turks on the mainland.

Occasionally, as in 1263 and 1571, there were major uprisings which the Venetians harshly put down. After one such revolt it was found necessary to execute more than 300 persons, and send many into exile, to burn and raze their villages, confiscate their property and exact other severe penalties. In 1538 the coasts were laid waste by the pirate Khayrad Din Barbarossa. On top of all this, the inhabitants faced other—natural—terrors such as the famine which in 1626 reduced the population of the island by one fifth. In these circumstances it is not surprising that the Venetian presence on the island remained small and that Catholicism never became widespread.

Venice held on to Crete long after most of her other Aegean possessions had been surrendered. But in 1645 Hania fell to the Turks and in 1669, after a siege lasting two years, Iraklion fell too and the entire island came under Ottoman rule. By this time the Turkish administration had lost much of its early vigour: in the early 18th century Iraklion was described as "the carcass of a large city...little better than a desert."

Cretan converts: In an effort to escape the

burdens of Turkish rule many Cretan families converted to Islam, especially during the 18th century, on a scale unknown elsewhere in the Aegean. But these converts continued to speak Greek, drink alcohol and had names such as Effendakis and Mehmedakis, which were a bizarre jumble of Greek and Turkish elements. Villages continued to be called by their Greek names even after all their inhabitants had converted.

From 1770 onwards, a series of revolts broke out against Ottoman rule. It took more than a century before they succeeded in their aim of independence in a Greek state; nevertheless these insurrections altered the bal-

ance of power on the island as many Moslem farmers sold out to Christians before moving, first to the coastal towns, and then, at the turn of the century, off the island altogether.

But the revolts also had a catastrophic effect on the island's economy. Passing through the interior shortly after the 1866-69 insurrection, Tozer noted: "every village that we passed through, and all that we could see along the hillsides, had been plundered, gutted and burnt." Even today, abandoned villages are not an uncommon sight inland.

In 1896, when the next major revolt broke out, the inadequacies of Ottoman rule were so evident that the European powers stepped in. On the whole island there was just one short stretch of carriage road—from Hania to Suda Bay; and as William Miller reported in 1897, in Iraklion, the largest town on the island, there were no carriages, "for the two that used to exist were last employed for the conveyance of the admirals on the Queen's Jubilee last year, on which occasion the bottom of both vehicles fell out, and the distinguished officers had to walk inside the bottomless machines."

Troubles in Ottoman Crete in 1897 provoked a wave of sympathy on the mainland. Greek naval forces were sent to the island while the army marched northwards—only to be checked by the Turkish forces who pushed back down into Greece. This defeat was humiliating for the Greeks, but it proved only to delay the future enlargement of the kingdom.

The next year the island was made an independent principality under Turkish sovereignty. The new prince was, significantly, a member of the Greek royal house. The writing was on the wall and within a few years union with Greece had been achieved.

In 1909, junior army officers staged a revolt against the political establishment in Athens. At their invitation a new politician with a radical reputation, Eleftherios Venizelos, came to Athens from Crete to form a new government. A consummate diplomat and a man of great personal charm, Venizelos channeled the untapped energies of the Greek middle-class into his own Liberal Party, which dominated Greek politics for the next 25 years.

Left, watercolour of urban Cretan costume. Right, a naïve painting of Eleftherios Venizelos.

THE ISLANDS TODAY

The islands did not all become part of independent Greece at the same time. Only the Cyclades and their neighbours formed part of the original state in 1830. The Ionian islands were added in 1864, Crete and the Northeast Aegean islands in 1913, the Dodecanese only in 1947. Since several of the islands were wealthy ports at a time when Athens was still a village, it is scarcely surprising that their influence on developments in the new state was enormous.

In politics, the Hydriot families of Voulgaris and Koundouriotis, the Metaxas dynasty on Corfu, not to mention the Cretan Eleftherios Venizelos—in many ways the founder of the modern Greek state—all typified the vigour which the islanders brought to the political scene. Nor did their influence stop here: Greek literature was marked by the Ionian islands' close links with Italy, while Lesvos has produced both the Nobel Prize-winning poet Odysseus Elytis and the naïf painter Theophilos.

The islands' economic influence has also been profound, especially before the Balkan Wars of 1912-13 added the fertile regions of northern Greece to the impoverished state. The shipping fleets of the Aegean islands, currant and oil exports from Zakinthos and Kefalonia, emigrant remittances from islanders scattered across the globe—from Romania to Australia to Florida—have all helped to bolster the feeble economy of the mainland.

But islands had other uses, too. Limnos, under Turkish rule, was used as a place of exile for political offenders. Henry Tozer, who visited the island in 1884, learned that a former Grand Vizier had been living on the island for eight years and was "almost forgotten at the capital."

This policy did not cease when the islands became Greek. The dictator Metaxas in the 1930s sent his opponents to forbidding islands, and during the civil war (1947-49) several barren islands off the Attica coast held prison camps for political detainees.

Left, Cretan peasant, about 1950. Above, a pelican once started an inter-island feud between Mykonos and Tinos.

Fortunately, this was less the case when the Colonels came to power in Greece on the morning of 21 April, 1967. The junta was motivated by a mixture of self-interest and hazy nationalism. In their policies and attitudes the Colonels drew on earlier traditions—with peasant or lower middle-class backgrounds, they symbolised a provincial reaction to a new world of urban consumers. Thus they laid great stress on the need for a return to traditional morality and religion. They closed the frontiers to bearded, long-

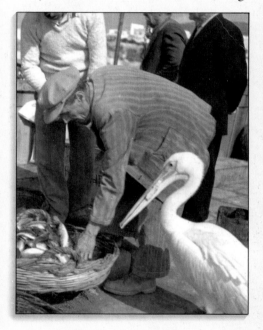

haired or mini-skirted foreigners—at least until they realised the implications for Greece's tourist trade.

Islands for outcasts: But other outsiders *were* confined to islands: one of the more magnificent relics of Aegina's moment as capital of Greece is the now disused prison, still more or less intact. And the fortress islet of Spinalonga, off the northeast coast of Crete, after a long career as Venetian outpost and Turkish village, was used as a leper colony until the late 1950s.

Today tourists can visit the ruined fortifications of Spinalonga on day trips from Crete, signalling perhaps a sort of economic progress, as tourists bring in money the islanders once only dreamed about.

These new arrivals indicate the most recent transformation of the islands—into places of pleasure. Mass tourism is one aspect of this, but the trend was seen most clearly in the vogue which began 30 years ago among shipowners to acquire islands for their private use. When Niarchos bought Spetsopoula in the Saronic Gulf in 1958, he was swiftly imitated by his rivals, and real estate prices for barren islets off the Peloponnesian coast soared. With extensive investment in consumer goods, radar and police personnel, these rocky outcrops were to become mid-20th century equivalents of

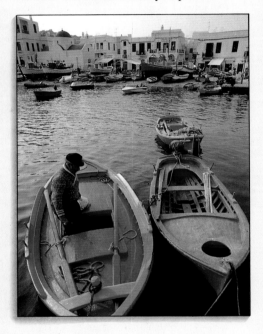

Circe's island. How ironic that this vogue should have coincided with an unprecedented wave of emigration from the larger islands. Of course, there had always been island emigration, especially over the past two centuries—but in the 1960s it accelerated rapidly.

Several reasons lie behind this failure to emigrate until the latter half of the 20th century. In the first place, would-be emigrants were constrained by the availability of transport. An extreme case of such isolation was to be found in Gavdos, an islet off Crete. According to Spratt, who visited there in 1865, the inhabitants did not see a boat

approach for months on end, and he himself disembarked among naked swimmers who he found were "primitive in their habits and ideas...a mixed and degenerate race." Thus, to some extent, the opportunities for emigration depended upon improvements in transport and communications.

In the second place, several islands initially prospered upon incorporation into the Greek state. Syros, for example, became the most important port and manufacturing centre in Greece in the first few decades after 1830. Even after the rise of Piraeus it remained an important centre where the standing may be gauged by the fine 19th century villas and warehouses of its capital Ermoupolis. On other islands, such as Andros and Naxos, the late 19th century was a period of rapid exploitation of mineral resources.

By World War One, however, much of this activity had slowed down, and emigration both to Athens and abroad was increasing. With the collapse of international trade between the wars this trend was interrupted for several decades, but it gathered pace once more with the European economic "miracle" of the postwar years.

Improved communications: By now, the road and rail links between Greece and western Europe had been modernised. So, too, had links between the islands and the mainland: the first air connection with Athens had been established as far back as 1927 by the Italians, but it was only in the 1960s that aerial links with the Aegean were extended. In the same period, car ferries were introduced. These developments opened up the closed societies which had survived on the islands well into the 1950s.

Improved communications also opened up the closed island economies—which had come close to starvation during World War Two—to a new world of consumer delights. In Athens newcomers from the islands formed closely-knit communities, each with its own clubs and cafés—islands of familiarity in an ugly urban sprawl. Many moved further afield—to Italy and West Germany.

Thus, even as the era of mass tourism brought western Europe to the Greek islands, the islanders themselves had gone off to find western Europe.

Left, fishing boats are hired by tourists in the summer. Right, an island washing line.

PORTRAIT OF AN ISLAND FAMILY

Early evening on Halki in the Dodecanese and the sun sets behind the crusader castle, high above the village, turning the sands of Pondamos Beach a deep rose colour.

Michaelis Perakis, 18, leads his donkeys down to drink from the trough in the rocks and fills his plastic containers from the watering hole. Halki has no fresh water, rivers or springs, and relies on the water boat to bring supplies. Daily life revolves around stocking up cans, filling wells (known as *sterna*) and making sure the animals—for many families the only form of transport or wealth—get properly watered.

It's summer and Michaelis, studying to be an electrician in college in Rhodes, is home for the holidays. His mother, Lefkosia, aged 40, one of the island's best cooks, has just opened a small taverna down on the harbour. Once a week during the tourist season she carts her pots and pans, slabs of ice and ingredients by donkey or three-wheel dumper truck up to Horio, Halki's deserted village, where she caters to a small group of British visitors who make an evening trek up to the castle.

There's no electricity so Lefkosia cooks by gas by the light of oil lamps in the old school room where she used to attend lessons. It's a real family affair. Michaelis waits on tables, sometimes helped by his 20-year-old sister Katholiki. Their father, Stavros, prepares the charcoal grill for the *souvlakia* and roast lamb, gathering sticks and handfuls of aromatic herbs, while young Metaxas, 12, dragged away from his BMX bike, gets under his mother's feet. He's usually first to sample the food—homemade *taramasalata*, meatballs, stews, *dolmades* and fresh fish. Bread is baked to Lefkosia's own recipe in the village bakery.

Stavros, 54, known to everyone as Fanos, has his own fishing-boat. When he's not out laying his nets with Metaxas or bringing in the catch he prepares food and helps his wife in the harbourside taverna.

The Perakis family is well-off by Halki

standards. As well as the new taverna and the fishing boat they keep flocks of sheep in the mountains and make a living selling the wool and meat on Rhodes. Once fertile, the island became barren when seawater seeped into the boreholes. Now the islanders grow nothing except olives, and goats nibble where a dairy herd once grazed.

The soil is rich and if plans to lay water pipes under the sea from Rhodes ever materialise the island could flourish again. Meanwhile, Halkians rely on all their food and produce coming in by boat, or go on shopping trips to Rhodes.

From riches to rags: Once rich with copper (hence its name) and a major sponge-fishing centre the island has dwindled from a population of around 3,000 in its heyday to 300. As the sponge industry declined, Halkians went to Tarpon Springs in Florida to seek their fortunes. Horio became deserted as people moved down to Emborio, the harbour, when the grand old sea captains' houses crumbled.

In 1987 the Greek government stepped in to bring work to Halki and under a UNESCO scheme declared it the Island of Peace and Friendship. A hotel was built for foreign tourists in the derelict olive oil factory and local people were given jobs restoring the houses. For the first time package tourism came to Halki.

"Tourism has brought new life to the islands," said Lefkosia, smashing huge slabs of ice with a meat cleaver to keep her retsina cool. "Before, we were very poor; there wasn't work. But now there are new jobs and new opportunities."

Life on Halki is unavoidably bound to Rhodes. There's no senior school on the island so for further education children have to go to Rhodes which means, especially in the case of the girls, mother goes too.

Many women have second homes or stay with relatives on Rhodes during term time, returning to husbands and younger children at weekends. Grannies and aunts all help raise the children. While Katholiki was at school Lefkosia lived in Rhodes with Metaxas for four years, working in a taverna and returning home to Halki in summer.

Halkians are used to this split way of life. But it's expensive and physically wearing. "It's very hard but there's nothing else we can do," said Lefkosia, in between boiling up a feast of snails (and chips) for the local shepherd community.

This morning she rose at 4 a.m. and did housework. She fed the sheep near the house, a traditional neo-classical villa at the back of the village. She gave milk to the lambs, fed the chickens, ducks and rabbits, then nipped onto the mountainside to pick *horta* (wild greens) before going to the taverna.

"I cook all day for lunch and dinner. We usually close about 2 a.m. so I might get two hours sleep if I'm lucky. When I have this

outside lavatory and shower. Like many islanders, the Perakis family works night and day in summer and spend little time at home.

In autumn and winter it's different. With tourists around, it's time to pick olives and make the oil, or go fishing for the local equivalent of whitebait. Fanos catches fish for the family and is part of the island's co-operative, but other fishermen sell their wares from loudspeaker vans around the Rhodes suburbs. This affords them the opportunity to visit wives and school-age children based on Rhodes.

Lefkosia pours more coffee into the smart gold and white cups bearing her name. She plunges her hands into the *tsatsiki*, mixing

group to cater for up here I don't have any sleep at all. Tomorrow I'll be exhausted."

Some people manage to grab a *mesimeri* or nap, in the afternoons, but it's often impossible for those islanders involved in the busy tourist trade.

Home is basic by western European standards, quite comfortable by theirs. The kitchen has fitted units and a modern stove—Lefkosia's pride and joy—and there is a simple living room. Up the wooden stairs a vast bedroom houses three beds in a row for the children, a cubicle with a huge double bed at one end for Mum and Dad, and a giant colour TV. There's no bathroom, just an

the oil into the yogurt.

"It is difficult in the winter," she adds. "Especially if you are taken ill and have to go to Rhodes. If the weather's bad the boat can't sail. One girl had a miscarriage because she couldn't get to hospital on time". In winter she bakes the family's bread outside in the wood-fuelled oven. Lambs, too are spit-roasted outdoors. It's all very medieval. "It takes an hour to get the oven hot and an hour to cook the bread, and I also have to gather the sticks and make food for the animals."

Although Halki has a doctor, emergencies and maternity cases have to be dealt with across the water—a two-hour trip in rough seas. Sometimes the storms are so bad the sea fills the tavernas, so boats are anchored out of the harbour in case they get smashed up.

Winter's hard for the young people who don't escape to Rhodes. Michaelis says he's lucky. While at college he can enjoy city life, like a trip to the cinema. But he's not a *kamaki* or playboy. He doesn't enjoy discos and prefers traditional Greek music and dance, particularly Halki's own fast and furious *sousta*. He's the island's champion young dancer, and often leads the circles at any village festivals.

Kafeneion society: When he comes home in winter, he tends the sheep brought down from the mountain for shelter. He might read at home, play football or go to the *kafeneion* with his *paréa* (friends) to play cards or to have a go on the Space Invaders machine. The *kafeneion* tends to be a men-only domain in winter where fishermen, shepherds and soldiers spin out the hours with blue videos and card schools.

In summer you'll see the more liberated Halki girls in the cafeteria, especially when Greek teenagers from Athens, Rhodes or even America turn up for the holidays. But parents keep a watchful eye on them and you'll often see father whisking a protesting daughter home like Cinderella. In winter girls remain indoors and do embroidery or lace-making and learn to run the home. Some of them fraternise with the soldiers, much to the horror of the villagers.

The girls often see the soldiers as escape routes from a hum-drum island life, especially with few Halki suitors around. The island barracks has national service conscripts from all over Greece and village girls often think if they can land a husband from Thessaloniki, Athens or another big city, life will be rosy.

Dressed in army uniform one girl stole off with a soldier on the early morning ferry. The boatman's son noticed the "soldier" was wearing women's shoes, but didn't give them away. They telephoned her parents from Rhodes who insisted the couple should be married immediately because of the family shame. She was 14. And pregnant. Now the husband wants a divorce and she's back on the island, trapped.

Left, many island villages do not have electricity for baking.

"Girls like her are crazy," says Katholiki, who is training to be a hairdresser on Rhodes. "We all have the same opportunities but they ruin their lives."

Tourism may bring work to the island, but the influx of foreigners with Western ideas can lead to problems, she feels. The old ways and the new clash head on and young Greeks are the victims in the middle. It may be accepted that boys chase after tourist girls but if they have more serious intentions family and neighbourhood close ranks. Parents want their young to marry other Greeks. Not just because of religion: they know the rules and traditions.

"Life is still difficult for women in Greece," says Katholiki. "My generation wants modern things like bikes and personal stereos, and we want to mix with other people. But our parents and grandparents are years behind and don't understand. I think the gulf will narrow in time and the next generation will be free."

Spring is a favourite season for several members of the family. Lefkosia, a keen singer and dancer, enjoys stepping out at the festivals, particularly Easter when all island women begin their rituals.

The house is cleaned inside out on Clean Monday, *Kathari Deftera*, when blankets and clothes are washed and the house is painted and whitewashed. The family goes on a Lenten fast (no meat or olive oil) and Lefkosia has to prepare pickled vegetables, lentils and special split pea soup.

As Easter approaches, she makes biscuits and dyes hard-boiled eggs red. On Easter Saturday the family's Paschal lamb is killed and she makes *patsas*, a special meal, with the innards, head and feet. On Sunday the lamb is roasted and it's party time.

But, at the moment, it is summer and the height of the tourist season. Down in the harbour at 3 a.m. Metaxas and Michaelis are fast asleep in the taverna, stretched out on chairs. Fanos is going fishing, and Lefkosia is washing up.

She isn't going to bed. Tomorrow will be another long day. "If only we had water here," she sighs. "My biggest hope for the future is our own fresh water so we could grow our own vegetables and fruit and have a proper tourist industry and real work for everyone. Yes, life here is very hard. But what can we do?"

COPING WITH TOMORROW'S TOURISM

Greece is a small place—just a jagged hump of rock, sand and grey-green vegetation that supports an indigenous population of 10 million. Yet every summer, that population nearly doubles with the influx of tourists. By the late 1980s, more than eight million tourists were descending on Greece and pumping more than $3 billion a year into the economy.

Apart from direct exports, tourism was the country's biggest foreign exchange earner during a period of severe balance of payments problems. Tourism had become, by all accounts, *the* national industry and in its honour Greece's first Ministry of Tourism was founded with Nikos Skoulas, a knowledgeable Greek-Canadian businessman, as Minister. Under his tutelage, a national consensus on tourism policy took shape. And none too soon: the future of Greek tourism into the 21st century depended on it.

Greece's limited resources and facilities had begun to be stretched to their limit. Every summer, the most popular island destinations—Corfu, Mykonos, Rhodes, parts of Crete, Hydra, Aegina, Santorini, Skiathos—teemed with hundreds of thousands of visitors. From June until September, when tourist numbers swelled exponentially, streets that had been constructed for a donkey and one or two passers-by became a sea of slow-moving gawkers.

Natives with other business to conduct often lost their tempers, privately. Hotels were booked up much ahead of time and some turned away foolhardy travellers who arrived without a reservation. Arid islands, to which water is supplied by tanker, had to ration water at certain hours of the day.

Beaches were often crowded with cheek-by-jowl sun-worshippers lying only inches from one another. Nude sunbathers, in search of the ultimate sybaritic experience, appeared more and more on family beaches. Native Greek islanders, whose pleasures and priorities centred on church and community, were not amused.

Preceding pages: passage to paradise; sleeping rough. Left, gearing up for a good time.

ISLAND-HOPPING

Island-hopping may be the choice of the tourist, but ferryboats are for the convenience of the Greeks. This fact—conflicting, frustrating and woefully under-publicised—has been the undoing of many a holiday.

The pleasures of travelling from one island to another using the country's series of inter-linking routes are numerous. There is the never ceasing view—a bas relief pattern in blue of low, mysterious mountains. A chance to mingle with the Greeks themselves who pile on board with food, children, and as often as not, a *bouzouki* or two. Plus, a unique opportunity to visit other islands not on the itinerary—15 minutes in a port closely observed from the top deck can reveal much about a place and its people. A bustle of activity takes place within view—reunions, farewells, and the redistribution of a virtual warehouse of goods. Is that a piano being loaded on board? Is that crate of chickens really being exchanged for blankets?

Without advanced research, however, it's all too easy to fall prey to the worst aspects of island-hopping in the form of missed connections, being stranded, or—a particularly Greek pastime—sailing straight past a chosen island, requiring a two-day journey to reach it again. In order to travel wisely, it helps to be in possession of a few basic facts.

First, ferry journeys can be long. The trip from Piraeus to Crete can take anywhere up to 22 hours, an unenthusiastic prospect for anyone on a two-week holiday. Ferry journeys can be frustrating. Should a trip to one of the smaller islands terminate in the middle of the night, no one will bother to wake you even if you've paid for sleeping accommodation. Seasoned travellers always pack an alarm clock, just in case. This haste to disembark in darkness has resulted in more than one independent traveller finding himself on the wrong island altogether.

Less frequently, and with a commendable disregard for time, purpose, or duty, ferries have been known to lie banked on the water for hours on end, oblivious to the needs of fee-paying passengers. "The Captain wants to fish," was a first-mate's response to one agonised plea.

There are ways to circumvent these problems. One is to travel in the high season, when Greek transport is relatively organised and hydrofoils, caiques and the little known inter-island subroutes are fully operative. A trip from Paros to Sifnos in the Cyclades, for example, will take about four hours in August (when ferries sail direct); and up to 20 hours in late September, when the only way to travel the minor distance between them is to return to Piraeus and head out again. Unfortunately, the high season is also the time when island accommodation is at a premium and the beaches are packed.

Fortunately, there are a number of established ferry routes which provide satisfying island-hopping with a minimum of fuss several months of the year. The best known are the central Cyclades route (Santorini, Ios, Naxos, Paros and Mykonos) and the Saronic Gulf route (Aegina, Hydra and Poros). Another is by cruising the major Dodecanese; travelling between Rhodes, Kos, Kalimnos, Leros and Patmos should pose few problems.

Less well known, and therefore more satisfying, are the western Cyclades (Kithnos, Serifos, Sifnos and Milos) and three of the four Sporades islands (Skiathos, Skopelos and Alonissos). These chains depend on domestic—rather than tourist—travel and operate all year, albeit at a reduced level. Both Rhodes and Kos in the Dodecanese act as hubs for a number of satellite islands which are easily reached in summer by tourist caiques and hydrofoils, and out of season by keeping a close eye on the long-haul cargo and passenger boats used by the locals.

Bookshops in Athens sell a guide called the *Greek Travel Pages* which gives details of most sailings. A map is useful when studying it, for some islands are listed under the name of the island; some under the name of the port.

There is one final, vital rule: always leave plenty of time at the end of your holiday to travel back to Piraeus. Greek ferries may be cheap and cheerful, but international flights rarely linger.

One for the alarm clock, perhaps.

Sleeping under the stars: Still less popular were the thousands of young backpackers who arrived on the most crowded islands without a place to stay. They often had barely a drachma to their names, pushed up the island crime rate, and drove out quieter tourists. Many shelterless visitors were forced to sleep on rooftops or beaches with nothing but the stars for cover.

Ferry boats to several islands, acrid with the smell of churning humanity and petroleum fumes, were spilling over with Greek families, replete with bawling children and awkward bundles, and small cliques of impecunious tourists huddled against backpacks. Seats on island-hopping airplanes

Many boats were turned away for lack of a berth, and facilities were often minimal: marinas were little more than boat-garages, and neighbouring countries such as Turkey were attracting potential marina users away from Greece. It was an ironic twist—Greece's greatest tourist-related asset was its phenomenal 9,300 miles (15,000 km) of seashore—almost double that of Turkey—and it was barely being exploited.

Something had to give. Tourist arrivals and income were escalating annually. But international studies predicted an onslaught in the future of young, lower-income tourists as leisure time increased. In the 1990s, travel could become the largest industry in the

were so hard to get they had to be booked as much as two months in advance, and Athenians with island homes often reserved seats in the spring for the entire summer.

For a time, cruiseships berthed in foreign—rather than native—ports as a result of a series of terrorist attacks in the 1980s. Marinas were congested with the huge yachts of moneyed Greeks and foreigners, the chartered yachts of temporary high-fliers, and the small pleasure craft of devoted boatmen and fishermen.

Above, island arrival.

world. By the year 2000, an estimated two billion travellers will tramp the globe in search of individualistic holidays.

Government tourism officials decided to gear Greek tourism away from the mass market that brought in so many penniless backpackers, and to concentrate instead on specialised packages for the upmarket traveller. A programme had to be devised to put things right. It was, but with great difficulty.

The job fell to Mr Skoulas, first as General Secretary of the Greek National Tourist Organisation and later as Minister of Tourism, who used his managerial skills to coalesce disparate elements of the highly opinionated Greek tourism industry. Hoteliers, cruiseship owners, tourist agents and government officials eventually hammered out a national consensus: to develop selective (i.e. upper-income and specialised) tourism, and to build projects to back that up.

Classical goals: The most immediate goals were to turn Greece into the first marine tourism country in the world by 1992, to build special programmes around Greece's Classical and Byzantine monuments and to develop a high level of professional services.

All this was in the name of building up quality tourism for the quality tourist. The emphasis would not be on quantity—in fact, controlling the number of incoming tourists

would be a prime consideration. The idea was to avoid straining Greece's limited resources and to increase tourism income by increasing *per capita* spending, i.e. by attracting the well-heeled.

One of the first measures taken was to forbid charter passengers to stay without an accompanying room reservation. This affected mainly the English, who numbered one in four arrivals. These roomless young travellers congregated on islands such as Corfu, sleeping in the open and spreading minor crime waves. The new measure put a stop to what Greek officials called "hooliganism" among young tourists.

National aims: The Greek government also put a halt to licensing accommodation categories on islands where there was an oversupply, in an effort to let supply shape tourist demand. Officials decided when permits would be granted based on available space, and prior availability of basics such as roads, water and sewers. At the same time, more permits were granted for construction of four-star and five-star hotels.

"But beds alone cannot do it," as Mr Skoulas said. Officials pushed through a law giving up to 50 percent grants to build supplementary and entertainment facilities, especially in areas where no new beds were allowed. Such facilities included golf courses, marinas and tennis courts.

To corner the marine tourism market, at least 21 new full-service marinas are to be built and the 12 existing ones scheduled for improvements and extensions—all with financing from the European Community's Integrated Mediterranean Programmes.

Three schools of tourism management are to be established for the first time in Greece with the help of a French government agency, and a Tourism Research Institute will soon begin operation.

Advertising in the late 1980s became a national affair, directed by the Ministry of Tourism and funded by both government and private tourist-sector money. The first campaign attempted was a huge $100 million three-year marketing programme—the largest ever attempted in Greece—which appealed to the upper-income tourist.

With the advent of airline deregulation, Olympic Airways, better late than never, realised it would have to go modern or perish. To the existing stock of 37 airports, most on islands, they will add 20, 30, and 50-seater helicopters for "the people who can afford them." To preserve local cultures, few new airports will be added; but as short takeoff and landing aircraft come onstream, new facilities are to be constructed.

Finally, the impact of terrorism on tourism— a recent and worrying phenomenon —is expected to fade. The future of Greek tourism may not be all wine and roses, but, as one tour operator put it, "It'll be a heck of a lot better than it's ever been."

Left, young visitors contemplate Knossos. Right, tranquillity returns to the islands.

ΑΓ. ΑΘΑΝΑΣΙΟΣ Λ.Μ. 49

105

·ΗΛΙΑΣ·Λ.Μ

JUGOSLAVIJA

BĂLGARIJA

Kičevo

TIRANA

Prilep

Strumica

SHQIPËRIA

(YUGOSLAVIA)

Drama

Ohriosko jez.

Bitola

Kilkis

Serres

Kavala

Xa

(ALBANIA)

Prespansko jez.

Edessa

Berati

Giannitsa

Thessaloniki

Stratoni

THASSOS

Vlora

Korça

Kalamaria

Th

Kastoria

Katerini

HALKIDIKI

Gerakini

AG. OF

Kozani

Olymp

SITHONIA

Ktismata

Kalpaki

2917

KASSANDRA

Elassona

AG. E

CORFU
(KERKIRA)

Corfu

Ioannina

ELLAS

Larisa

AG. E

Trikkala

SP

PAXOS

Volos

GIOURA

PIPERI

Karditsa

SKIATHOS

ALONISSOS

ANDIPAXI

Arta

(GREECE)

SKOPELOS

SKANDZOUF

Preveza

Lamia

Loutra Edipsou

SKIROPOULA

LEFKAS

Vonitsa

Lefkada

Karbenisi

SKIROPOULA

Agrinio

Paralia Kimis

Astakos

Mesolongi

Parnassos
2459

EUBOEA

CEPHALONIA

ITHAKI

Delphi

Livadia

Thiva
(Theben)

Halkida

Sami

Patra

Kalamos

Egio

Korinthiakos
Kolpos

Megara

ATHINA
(ATHENS)

Karistos

Lechano

PELO-

Corinth

Piraeus

Zakinthos

PONNESE

Argos

Ireon

AEGINA

Vouliagmeni

ANDROS

ZAKYNTHOS

Pirgos

Olympia

Tripoli

Saronikos
Kolpos

KEA

Sounio

GIAR

Nafplio

Epidavros

Kalo Nero

Megalo
-poli

Portoheli

HYDRA

SIF

KIKLAD

KITHNOS

Kalamata

Sparti

SPETSAI

SERIFOS

Pilos

Kiparissi

SIFNOS

Githio

KIMOLOS

(CYCLA

Monemvasia

MILOS

F

GAND

Kithira

KITHIRA

ANDIKITHIRA

Sea

Platanos

Hania

Paleohora

Ret

Ag. Galini

Mi

Mediterranean Sea

Ionian Sea

Korinthiakos Kolpos

Messiniakos Kolpos

Lakonikos Kolpos

Argolikos Kolpos

Thermaikos Kolpos

Greece

100 km

PLACES

"Greece rests on the sea," said the poet Odysseas Elytis, an observation few countries could claim with such authority. Some 10,000 sq miles (25,000 sq km) of the Aegean and the Ionian seas are covered by islands, the exact number of which has, in characteristic Greek fashion, been the topic of discussion and dispute. There may be 3,000 islands and islets, of which 167 are inhabited; there may be only 1,000, of which under 60 are inhabited. The frame of reference, too, which defines a populated place is open to interpretation. Does a tiny outcrop, bare save for one shepherd and six goats, constitute an inhabited island? Can an island totally deserted except for pilgrimages made annually to a small chapel at its summit claim to be inhabited?

The reality matters much more to foreigners than to Greeks, who are interested in sea and sky rather than in facts and figures. What is indisputable, however, is the sheer variety of landscape and experience to be found lurking behind the obvious clichés.

It is this we attempt to show here, islands with an ancient past and a modern outlook, the complex choice and the pure simple pleasures.

In order to accommodate much of what is implied in the phrase "a Greek island" almost as much space has been devoted to little-known Ayios Efstratios as to over-exposed Corfu, to the attractive islet Telendos at, perhaps, the expense of Mykonos.

Those clichés you can read in other guidebooks. For now, welcome aboard the ferry.

Preceding pages: knapsacks at the ready; a man works on his boat; a classic view of a classy island; a festive occasion in Olympos, Karpathos.

71

ATHENS STOPOVER

The columns of the classical temples on the **Acropolis** used to be so clearly etched against the blue Attica sky that literary-minded tourists compared them to the strings of a harp. Now they are often blotted out by the haze of pollution that Athenians call the *nefos*—Greek for cloud.

But they remain as impressive as ever, looming into close-up as you clamber up the rocky hill. Stop for a moment while crossing the wooden walkway through the **Propylaea,** the monumental gateway that was designed to frame the Parthenon Temple from exactly the right three-quarter angle. Looking up to the left, you can see part of the coffered marble ceiling of a top-quality fifth century B.C. building: they hardly ever survive.

To the right is the **Temple of Athena Nike**, completed around 420 B.C., roped off on a bastion that recalls the hill's original use as a fortified citadel, long before Pericles decided to spend a fortune in taxpayers' money to make Athens the marvel of the age.

Soon after Greece won independence from Turkey, the archaeologists moved in to pull down a maze of ramshackle buildings around the temples and start excavating—a generation after Lord Elgin stripped most of the sculptures from the Parthenon. He was keeping up with a tradition of looting ancient Greek treasures that started when the 39-ft (12-metre) high gold-and-ivory statue of the Goddess Athena that stood inside the temple was taken off to Constantinople in late antiquity.

Parts of the **Parthenon**, completed in 432 B.C. in honour of the virgin goddess and patron of ancient Athens, are being dismantled in an ambitious restoration programme that may take 25 years to complete—seven years longer than it took to erect the structure originally. To avoid masking Athena's temple with scaffolding, a folding crane was placed inside on a specially laid floor. It lifted down the blocks in turn so that non-rusting titanium clamps could be inserted in place of the iron fixtures used by restorers in the early 1900s. The iron had corroded and expanded, threatening to split the marble.

The last remaining sculptures have been removed, their delicately carved details blackened and pockmarked by air pollution—sulphur fumes combine with rainwater to form a dilute acid that turns the marble surface into gypsum.

The **Erechtheum Temple**, built over the tomb of a legendary Athenian king, has already been restored so successfully that some experts complain too much was done by way of filling in the gaps with freshly-cut marble from the ancient quarries on Mount Pendeli, north of Athens, even though no attempt was made to pick out architectural details in bright red, blue and green as the ancient Greeks did.

Four of the original Caryatid Maidens can be seen in the **Acropolis Museum,** looking battered but still dignified inside a nitrogen-filled case. And even the **Acropolis Hill** itself has been

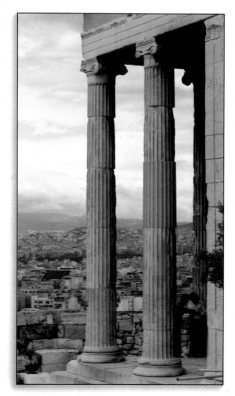

Left, the
Parthenon
encased in
scaffolding.
Right,
Athens as
seen from
the
Acropolis.

COPING WITH PIRAEUS

There's no point in pretending that Piraeus is the kind of place anyone wants to spend much time in—unless that person happens to work in one of the air-conditioned shipping offices overlooking the harbour. But it is possible to idle away a few hours while waiting to catch a ferry, even if there are few echoes of *Never on Sunday* these days. (Low life moved to Athens during the puritanical colonels' dictatorship. After democracy was restored successive mayors have been elected on a "smarten up Piraeus" ticket).

The basic rule about Piraeus ferries is to get there one hour before sailing time so that there is half an hour to find the right quay before the boarding deadline: unlike other kinds of transport in Greece, ships really do leave on time. But, unless it's high summer or a berth is required, don't worry about getting tickets in advance: these can be picked up from one of the dockside agencies.

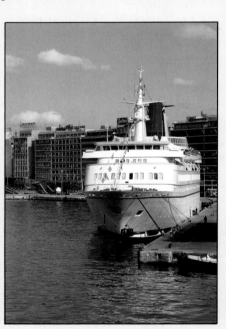

An express bus now runs direct to Piraeus from both terminals at Athens airport and stops outside the Port Authority (OLP) passenger building on Akti Mirouli Street—a useful place to know since bags can be left in the café upstairs free of charge between 6 a.m. and 7.30 p.m. (the other passenger terminal on Provlis Tselepis Quay where the Mykonos boat comes in is more crowded and the staff are less accommodating). Unencumbered, it's now easy to get equipped for the islands and take a look at Piraeus and its environs.

Drakopoulos' bookstore on Second Merarchia Street has a good selection of English paperbacks, maps, and island guides as well as useful items like toothpaste and stationery. For a quick meal, the Do-Nut shop nearby offers something for every stage of the day, from orange juice and breakfast to *patsas* (tripe soup)—a traditional late-night dish when arriving back in Piraeus in the early morning hours and unable to find a taxi on the deserted streets.

Nuts and fresh fruit for the voyage are on sale at the stall next door. For something lighter, try the *ouzerie* round the corner on Filonos Street.

To enjoy the view over Piraeus or catch a breeze, take a taxi up to the Veiakeion open-air theatre at the top of Kastella hill. Further along at Neo Faliro is the Palais des Sports (the Stadium of Peace and Friendship), the venue of rock concerts and political gatherings as well as sports events. If totally lethargic, one of the few patches of green grass to stretch out on is the park opposite the Town Hall on Akti Miaouli.

The radical cosmopolitan atmosphere for which Piraeus was famous in classical times still flourishes 2,500 years on—both the port and its industrial suburbs are left-wing strongholds—but few visible remains survive. A stretch of elegant fourth century B.C. wall runs beside the coast road beyond the Pasalimani yacht harbour and an amphitheatre backs on to the Archaeological Museum on Philhellinon Street, which is well worth visiting if there's time before the ferry.

Its prize exhibits are two bronze statues found by workmen digging a drain in Piraeus: a magnificent *kouros*, (sixth-century B.C. figure) of a young man, and a fourth-century helmeted Athena, looking oddly soulful for a warrior goddess. Both are thought to come from a shipment of loot overlooked by Greece's Roman conquerors in the first century B.C.

Pasalinani is crowded with medium-sized yachts—a floating campsite in summer—but towards the Flying Dolphin hydrofoil terminal huge, old-fashioned two and three-masters and sleek motor-yachts can be admired. Further round the headland are fishing dinghies moored in the rocky inlets beneath the ancient wall and the cafés and fish restaurants frequented by Piraeots which overlook the Saronic Gulf. The gulf is badly polluted but brilliantly blue from a short distance.

Back toward Athens—it's easier to take the yellow trolley or green bus—lies Tourkolimani (sometimes called Mikrolimani), a small yacht basin surrounded by fish restaurants. This is the place for a leisurely lunch to bring on the island mood. Although tourism has given most establishments a glossy look, the Black Goat, close to the boatsheds beneath the Yacht Club, still has the atmosphere and rowdy ambience that old-time Aegean sailors remember.

restored, strengthened, like a broken hip, with metal pins to hold the crumbling limestone together.

You could be forgiven for not bothering to hunt down the lesser monuments of Athens (in fact, to avoid the high season crush on the hilltop, it's perfectly possible to sit on the terrace of the Dionyssos Café opposite and enjoy a striking view of the Parthenon). But some are worth looking out for.

The grandiose **Herod Atticus Theatre** beneath the Acropolis, built by a Roman millionaire in the second century is best seen from a seat in the front rows during the Athens Festival as the moon rises above the towering arches. Whether the show is classical drama or imported opera or ballet, the spectacle is what counts. (Performers also say it's unforgettable looking up at the steep tiers packed with people).

While shopping in the **Plaka district** on the other side of the Acropolis, keep an eye out for the **Tower of the Winds**, a tall marble octagon dating from the first century B.C. The winds are shown

as relief figures flying amid swirling draperies. In Ottoman times, the building was the centre for a sect of whirling dervishes. Look out, too, for the 13th-century Byzantine **Church of St Caterina Sinai**, a few feet below street level in a palm-fringed courtyard near Hadrian's Arch.

For a restful hour or so, try the **Kerameikos Cemetery** in the ancient potters' district of Athens. The funerary monuments—sphinxes, a prancing bull, scenes of farewell—were erected by wealthy Athenian families of the fifth and fourth centuries B.C. A stream trickles through the ruins and there are turtles in the undergrowth. The museum boasts a remarkable collection of pottery that illustrates Greek vase-painting over 500 years.

Further afield—a 20-minute taxi ride from the centre of town—is **Kaisariani**, a Byzantine monastery at the foot of Mount Hymettus, once famous for its honey. The domed church goes back to the year 1000 but the frescoes are much later, dating from the 17th century, with

A view fit or the ods.

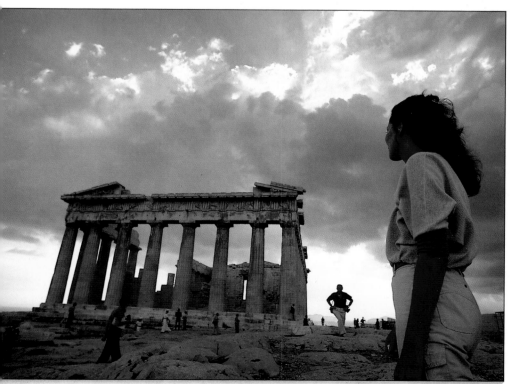

pale faces gazing out from a blue-black ground. Next to a shady plane tree outside the gate, spring water from a fountain with a ram's head is still supposed to encourage pregnancy.

From the slopes above the monastery—a 10-minute walk up the road takes you to a ruined medieval watchtower—there is a panoramic view of Athens spreading down the shores of the Saronic Gulf.

On the other side of Athens—40 minutes by car from the centre—next to the site of the summer wine festival stands **Daphni Monastery**, built in the 11th century. A Gothic porch was added later when it was taken over by French Cistercian Monks and it also became the burial place of the Frankish Dukes of Athens. Its 11th-century mosaics glisten high up in the dark interior, and a gloomy Christ Pantocrator looks down from the dome.

If you have an afternoon to spare, take a trip to **Cape Sounion** and **Poseidon's Temple**, still a landmark for sailors rounding the tip of the Attica Peninsula.

The organised tour is easiest, routed either down the coast road (its construction triggered the first Greek seaside property boom), or through the Mesogeion, the olive-and wine-growing heartland of ancient Attica.

The temple dates from the mid-fifth century B.C. and among the travellers' graffiti carved on the columns, you can find Byron's name. Sunset is the traditional time to be there.

Naturally, Athens is rich in museums: the **National Archaeological Museum** holds the world's largest collection of Greek art, much of it badly displayed and labelled. But it's still worth fighting your way past the crowds for a glimpse of some superb objects.

In the Mycenean room, head for the sheet-gold deathmask of a bearded man from one of the shaft graves. (The excavator, Heinrich Schliemann mistakenly thought he was King Agamemnon, leader of the Greek expedition against Troy). Then seek out the two gold cups found at Vafeio near Sparta but probably made by a craftsman from Crete.

An Athenian pleasure: eating outdoors in Plaka.

Stride through the sculpture galleries until you stop short at the bronze figure of Zeus, tensed and ready to throw a thunderbolt. It dates from around 470 B.C. In the same room is a remarkable marble relief of the fertility goddess Demeter handing an ear of corn to a boy called Triptolemos.

Further on comes the heavily restored bronze racehorse from the Hellenistic period, with an anxious-looking boy jockey perched on its back. And don't miss the frescoes from Santorini (also known as Thira and soon to be returned to the island), found in a prehistoric Pompeii beneath layers of volcanic lava that engulfed the city in the late Bronze Age. (The swallows-in-spring painting caught the imagination of film-set designers and features in more than one exotic epic set in the Himalayas).

Athens is a complex and multi-faceted city.

If you have time and inclination for just one museum, the **Benaki** is crammed with treasures from every period of Greek history (as well as some Asiatic collections). Between the basement filled with silk and gold embroi-dered folk costumes and the terrace café on the rooftop, the neo-classical mansion is filled with delights.

The museum was the lifelong hobby of Emmanuel Benakis, a wealthy Greek from Egypt and it reflects his eclectic taste for all things Greek and often Turkish, Persian and Arabic—not to speak of Coptic. There is a stunning roomful of jewellery from Mycenean times onward, two early works in the icon room by El Greco, who was born on Crete, and a vast collection of pictures, weapons and other memorabilia from the War of Independence period, including crockery used by Lord Byron.

Near the Benaki is another museum with a world-renowned private collection on display. The **Museum of Cycladic and Ancient Greek Art** features the prehistoric white marble figurines which were dismissed as barbaric by turn-of-the-century art critics but rated Picasso and Modigliani among their admirers. They come from graves in the Cycladic islands but scholars are still uncertain of their purpose.

THE IONIAN ISLANDS

The islands of the west coast are known in Greek as the *Eftan-isa*—the seven isles—which refers to the principal islands Corfu, Paxos, Lekfas, Ithaki, Cephalonia and Zakynthos. The seventh island, Kythera, lies off the southern tip of the Peloponnese, and as it is isolated from the others, is not linked by history, culture or architecture.

During the eighth and seventh centuries B.C. wanderers from Corinth settled on the most northern of these islands, bringing with them a distinct culture. Two centuries later the secession of Corfu from Corinth brought about the beginning of the Peloponnesian War. Over the years the Ionians have had many warrior landlords, but it is the long period of Venetian rule that has left the most indelible mark.

Artists, craftsmen and poets were often sent to Venice for their education, bringing back to the islands a cosmopolitan and international perspective. Even today, thanks to good air and sea links with Italy, the islands have a distinctly Italian flavour; pizzerias vie with tavernas on many a harbour promenade.

It is the heavy rainfall which makes the Ionians among the greenest of Greek island chains. Olive groves and vineyards are reminders that agriculture, rather than the dubious riches of tourism, still claim a part in the economy. But it is this same unsettled weather that has ruined many a traveller's holiday; from mid-September until mid-May, rains can wash out any beach outing suddenly and without warning. Fortunately, escape is never far away. The Ionians' links with the mainland are very good, and several coaches daily at the height of the season make the journey from Athens to Corfu (allow at least 10 hours), via a connecting ferry service. It's also possible to reach Cephalonia or Zakynthos by bus from Athens.

Today the Ionians are threatened, not by invaders (other than tour companies), but by earthquakes. A series of quakes has at various times beset the islands, the most recent and serious in 1953. Casualties were great and the beautiful Venetian-built capitals of Cephalonia and Zakynthos were flattened.

Reconstruction began almost immediately. The residents of Argostóli in Cephalonia put up makeshift buildings which still remain, in order to resume busy, industrious lives. Zakynthians, however, elected to recreate their Venetian city on a grand scale, using original plans and grids. These contrasting attitudes to tragedy tell an island tale.

Preceding pages: a trio of beach bums. Left, a Corfiot mask for sale.

CORFU

A torturous catalogue of bloody invasions and changing foreign rule chequers the history of Corfu (Kérkyra). Today, the Corfiots reap the benefits of all those battles. Left a rich inheritance of olive trees dating from Venetian rule, they prosper from agricultural wealth and a thriving tourist trade.

Tourist dodging can become a game in itself for the more adventurous visitor; there is a real thrill in finding an unspoiled spot. Alternatively, mixing with the masses can be fun. Sadly, package tourism has brought a sprinkling of modern-day Vandals with it, intent on thoughtlessly trampling on the culture, customs and kindness of the islanders.

Corfiot hospitality to strangers remains remarkably unscathed. The legendary friendliness of the islanders dates back to a tale told of Odysseus, who, shipwrecked and exhausted, was washed ashore and rescued by the beautiful Princess Nafsicaä, whose family offered him a fabulous welcome. The traveller today who is not running with the tourist pack will be showered with generosity, as if another naked Odysseus, washed ashore by the waves.

Corfu Town: The pretty, bustling town of Corfu is an unmissable starting point for a visit to the island. The people and the places are extravagantly cosmopolitan. Each turned corner reveals a new architectural delight, with a mass of different historical influences evoked.

It takes time to find ways round the different parts of the town and lap up its medley of moods. Directionless wandering is best enjoyed while dodging a colourful *monippo* (horse-drawn carriage) in the narrow streets of the **Old Town**, squeezed between two ancient forts. The sounds of a brass band rehearsing in the upstairs rooms of dilapidated Venetian houses competes absurdly with Greek piped music blaring from the tourist shops below. High up in the quieter alleyways, the week's washing flutters on lines strung across the streets, looking like bunting strung up for an impending carnival.

In the heart of this charming chaos looms the darkly tranquil church of **Ayios Spirídon**, the island's most dearly loved Saint. In a glittering chapel his mummified remains rest resplendent in a silver casket, ready to hear a hundred whispered prayers.

The ancient landmarks of the town's brave past are the two forts, the **Néo Froúrio** (New Fort) and the Old Fort, the **Palió Froúrio**. The Old Fort is now a crumbling monument to the centuries of Corfiot heroism in guarding their citadel. Ambling through the overgrown buildings, its history comes alive, as one happens upon a Byzantine inscription or the bizarre British-built church of **Ayio Yiórgios**.

Flanking the eastern side of the Old Town, the pavement cafés suddenly have a Parisian air, and it's not surprising to discover that the **Listón** façade, modelled on the Rue de Rivoli, was erected during the French occupation. *Tstinsi birra* (ginger beer), a remnant of the British influence, is the drink to sip

eft, an legant assage in orfu Town.

Corfu
Kerkira

Map/ Text
Ag. Matteos/ Ayiós Matthaéos
Argirades/ Aryirádes
Lefkimmi/ Lifkimmio
Mesongi/ Messongi
Strongili/ Strongylí

in these culturally-confused cafés, where you can watch cricket being played on the **Spianáda** (esplanade).

The regency style **Palace of St Michael and St George** dominates the north side of the esplanade. It houses the splendid **Museum of Asian Art**, to add yet another dimension to the town's cultural diversity. At the southern end of the esplanade, the **Archaeological Museum** boasts the locally-discovered Corinthian sculpture of Medusa and a stroll along the sweeping bay leads towards the chic and expensive area around **Mon Repos**.

North Coast: Taking the coast road north from Corfu Town, there are a series of naturally beautiful but very busy bays, monopolised by the package tour operators. By **Nisáki**, the scenery becomes more dramatic, the tourists more sedate and the sea a deep sapphire. Beyond this lies the magical stretch of coast made famous by Lawrence Durrell's *Prospero's Cell*. Dropping down to **Kalámi**, there's a tranquil taverna in the White House, where Durrell stayed.

Little bays offer enticing views across the crystal water to Albania.

Seeking solitude is a question of timing in such places. The unlucky traveller's visit may coincide with an invasion of the holiday-making hordes on a pleasure-boat cruise, stopping to noisily spew onto the shores of your chosen spot to eat, drink and disrupt your tranquillity. The thronging masses are to be found making merry in the ancient harbour town of **Kassiópi**, which has gorged itself on tourism. One wonders what past visitors such as Nero, Cicero and Cato would make of the town today. Perhaps the amorous Casanova, another early tourist, would enjoy endless conquests at the swinging discos.

On the north coast, the scenery becomes standardised, the coastal resorts uniform. Tourism at **Róda**, **Astrákeri** and **Sidári** conspires to ruin what must have been a luscious stretch of sandy beaches. Throughout Corfu, the most interesting places are consistently off the main roads and often inland. Looking for unspoiled villages hugging the

Cricket is a popular sport, usually played on the Esplanade.

languid northern beaches is pretty fruit-less, with the exception of tumbled-down **Perouládes**, which secretly hides a little cove where the local children play in the waves, surrounded by majestic cliff formations which mock their poor relations.

With such a history of invasion, the vulnerable islanders tended to live away from the coast so that much of the real Corfu lies quietly hidden in the hills. Treading carefully, the traveller can still find these timeless villages amongst the lush vegetation and spectacular scenery in the northwest part of the island. After the northern coastal resorts, travelling inland is to find a corner of heaven in a nightmare of tourism.

West Coast: Going down the west coast, it's easy to appreciate why **Paleokastrítsa** has become such a popular resort, comprising a series of beautiful bays embraced by ancient jagged rocks and a backdrop of dramatic greenness. Away from the maddening masses, the enterprising can discover a cluster of secluded coves where the only sound is of the silky sea water licking the shores. At Paleokastrítsa's gleaming hillside monastery, the bizarre mixes with the Byzantine. Coachloads of tattooed tourists noisily dodge priests and goats on a two-minute tour of the church. Easily distracted by the beer-drinking pet goat in the taverna opposite, the sacrilegious soon depart from the house of God and the monastery can be visited in temporary tranquillity, before the next air-conditioned onslaught appears.

Although the mid-west coast is now being hit by property developers it still feels less frenetic compared to the east and northern shores. By **Pélekas**, the tourist combination is a strange mix of the package variety and summer hippies, who sleep out on the quieter beaches round **Myrtiótissa**.

The South: The southern part of Corfu is often neglected by visitors. The landscape becomes flatter and less interesting, but there is ample opportunity for discovering the undiscovered. A venture down the eastern coast road through the tourist tat of **Benítses** and **Messongi** would lead most discerning travellers begging to differ, but as with the north, the inland road opens up another country. A visit to the **Achillion** invites you inland. Loved and hated, this strange folly was created by Empress Elisabeth of Austria in a kitsch attempt at neo-classical style. Taking the road high up to Ayios Déka, the journey south is best enjoyed meandering down along the road through **Strongylí**. The east coast then begs for reconsideration by the time **Aryirádes** is reached. Coastal villages such as **Boukarí** and **Petríti** feel a refreshing million miles away from the dismally over-subscribed resorts up the coast.

With a river cutting into its heart, the visitor will note the deep south feel of the heated, dusty town of **Lifkimmío**. The southerners seem to have a healthy contempt for the *en masse* holidaymakers, keeping them carefully herded in at the fish and chip resort of **Kavos**, a ghastly enclosure at the southern end of the island. Continuing on the road south of Kavos, the polite conspiracy to keep tourists at bay seems to reach its epitome. The signposts are strangely concealed by overgrowth and the road becomes sufficiently rough to deter giggling girls from hobbling far in their holiday high heels. However, the conspiracy theory can be left behind on reaching the unspoiled villages of **Spatera**, **Bastatika** and **Kritika**, as explorers are congratulated for their effort with warm welcomes.

Pretty villages: The western coastal section going north towards **Ayios Yeórgios** boasts long stretches of sandy beaches, which have a windswept, barren appeal. The marshland surrounding **Lake Korission** indicates that it is not going to be as exotic as its name, but the long, flat stretches of land and still water are fairly atmospheric. North of the charming town of **Ayios Matthaéos**, the scenery again returns to hilly splendour and the beaches get busier. Picturesque roads wind through pretty villages across the slim waist of the island, back to the centre of Corfu Town.

Swimming near Pondikonisi (Mouse Island).

TRADITIONAL AGRICULTURE

The silver olive trees which grace the Ionian landscape play more than just a picturesque part in island life. For thousands of years the olive and the rich, distinctive oil it produces have formed a staple part of not only the Greek diet, but the Ionian economy as well.

For most island farmers, however, agricultural produce is for domestic use only and traditional non-mechanised farming methods, due to Greece's hilly terrain, are in some respects preserving an agricultural system which is well on its way to extinction.

A typical farming community is a disorganised scatter of between 20 and 100 houses, closely packed together with small yards where chickens and the occasional pig (being fattened for Christmas) might be found. Most of these remote villages now have road communications and at least one telephone, but running water can often be a problem, especially at the height of a busy summer.

A village on any Greek island which is farmed in the traditional way can usually be spotted by the irregular fields which form its territory. It is the system of splitting up the land to form inheritances and marriage dowries which has resulted in this unusual visual aspect of the rural landscape.

A remote village has probably three types of farmers. First, there's the large-scale goat-herder with 100 to 500 head of animals, who purchases food such as maize and prepared cake. He concentrates on producing kids or lambs for the peak periods of Easter and the New Year. The second type is the small-scale farmer, often a man who, in his retirement, wants to keep his household supplied with bread, pulses (lentils, broad beans and chick peas—the staple diet of winter) and vegetables. Finally, the list includes single, elderly women working on their own.

An example of the latter is Voula, a 50-year-old spinster who farms on the mainland island of Euboea, but whose aged, bent figure can be seen throughout Greece. Voula's father was deaf and mute. Fearing that any children would suffer the same disability, no villager would marry her. She has two acres split into about 10 fields, on which she keeps four goats, all female. After the first gentle rains of autumn, most of Voula's fields are sown with crops.

Ploughing is done by donkey or mule. The plough is bladed and controlled by means of a handle at the rear. Crops for Voula's goats include barley and oats; crops for herself might be wheat, lentils and broad beans.

Once the bitter winds of winter arrive, most small-scale farmers collect branches from wild bushes like the Greek strawberry tree which they bring down from the hills by donkey for feed. In some remote villages the proportion of elderly people is quite high, and it is not unusual to see 80-year-olds scaling mulberry trees.

In spring, people like Voula take their animals to graze in fields away from the village, once the height of the crop reaches four or five inches. As the season progresses the ubiquitous vegetable gardens begin producing tomatoes, potatoes, beans, and aubergines. These crops supplement the diet well into the summer but involve the investment of much time, labour, and effort.

In June the work in the fields is back-breaking, for the harvest is reaped by hand with a sickle or scythe. The cut crop is laid out in the fields to dry, then (if grain) carried back to be threshed.

Threshing is now usually done by machine but in some islands, such as Kárpathos and Amorgos, it is still done by walking a team of hired mules or donkeys over the strewn crop to smash the husks with the animal's hooves. The crop is then winnowed, thrown into the breeze to free the straw and chaff, then sieved.

These traditional farming methods are quickly disappearing. The exodus of the youth from the villages to the towns or mainland to find work, plus the introduction of Greek farming into competition with other European Community countries have meant that methods must change. The large proportion of elderly people within many villages, plus the number of fields overgrown with scrub, bear witness to this fact. This difficult but picturesque way of life does still exist, however; it just needs a sharp eye to detect and the willingness to climb a few hills to witness.

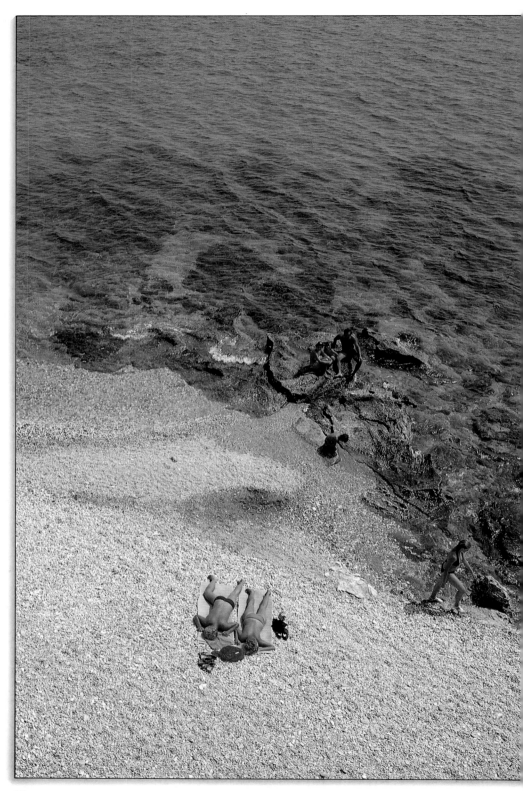

THE IONIAN ISLANDS

PAXOS: Modest Paxos (Paxi, Paxoi), a three-hour sail from Corfu, is often written up in glossy magazines as the ideal Greek island. Natural beauty consists of rugged cliffs, a number of littoral caves, and several fine beaches, all interspersed with groves of olive trees. The gnarled, twisted trunks of these trees and the leaves like handfuls of silver coins tossed to the breeze are landmarks of the island, one of only several reasons why some people return to Paxos season after season.

The pleasures of a stay on Paxos are simple. There is little in the way of organised entertainment, and although each year the island becomes more popular, the unpredictable Ionian weather means that ferries and smaller craft occasionally cannot land at all, unintentionally preserving a tranquil and low-key atmosphere.

Most accommodation is located in the main port of **Gaios**, where island life is played out around one square consisting of *kafeneia* and shops. Gaios is sheltered from the winds by the islet Ayios Nikolaos. Its 14th-century fortress has earned this rocky outcrop the predictable nickname "**Kastro**". Paxos's main road begins and ends at the bus station, although tracks do criss-cross the olive groves to service the farming communities. The road leads to the northern village of **Lakka**, a picturesque second port containing a Byzantine church.

Best beaches, however, are to be found in the south, on the lovely and insular islet **Antipaxos** (Andipaxoi), reached by caique from Gaios. Home to just 126 people, the eastern coast of Antipaxos is gentle and rolling; the west coast wilder and more dramatic. Uncluttered sandy beaches are to be found on either side of Ormos Agrapidias, the harbour. A day spent in Antipaxos is made all the tolerable by sampling the red or white wine, locally produced.

LEFKAS: Connected to the coast of Acarnania by a long causeway, Lefkas (Lefkada) feels much like a mainland appendage. Several buses daily from Athens make the trip over the 75-ft (23-metre) canal which separates the two, depositing visitors in the rather disappointing capital **Lefkas.** The town was rebuilt after an earthquake in haphazard style, and its proximity to the mainland has resulted in commercialisation.

The island itself fares better. A good network of local buses plies the road which follows each coast, linking several small villages which specialise in handicrafts. The east coast contains Lefkas's most attractive resorts. The first, **Nidri**, is a fashionable spot popular with yachtsmen. The beach is fair, the ambience relaxed and the tavernas offer decent but pricey food. Nidri looks out over a lovely bay containing the wooded islets of **Sparti**, **Meganissi**, **Mandouri**, and **Skorpios**. In the high season caiques make frequent runs from Nidri to the first three islets; Skorpios is owned by the Onassis family and was once a private playground for Jackie Kennedy and her children.

Three miles (five km) beyond is

Vliho, less crowded and similarly pleasing. Perhaps the most attractive of all is **Vassiliki**, 25 miles (40 km) south of Lefkas and situated at the mouth of a deep blue bay. A long pebble beach lined with trees provides refuge from the heat and rooms are quite plentiful.

An athletic walk (or, more popularly, frequent caiques from Vassiliki) leads to the island's best-known landmark, the bare, rocky headland known as **Sappho's Leap** 235 ft (72 metres) above an angry sea. It was from these white cliffs that Sappho and others allegedly followed a local tradition. An ancient legend (immortalised by Byron) held that a cure for unrequited love might be sought by flinging oneself from these cliffs into the Ionian Sea far below. Death was the usual outcome, which is certainly one way to end a heartache.

ITHAKI: This island, also known as Ithaca, is commonly thought to be the home of Odysseus, the voyager in Homer's *The Odyssey*. In chapter nine the hero of the Trojan War reveals himself to King Alcinous: "I am Odysseus, Laertes' son. The whole world talks of my stratagems, and my fame has reached the heavens. My home is under the clear skies of Ithaca. Our landmark is the wooded peak of windswept Neriton. For neighbours we have many peopled isles with no great space between them, Dulichium and Same and wooded Zacynthus. But Ithaca, the farthest out to sea, lies slanting to the west, whereas the others face the dawn and rising sun. It is a rough land, but a fit nurse of men. And I, for one, know of no sweeter sight for man's eyes than his own country."

Some scholars have disputed Ithaki's claim to be the "precipitous isle" of the fable, but few visitors who make the one-mile journey from Cephalonia, or disembark by ferry at the pretty wooded capital of Vathí would agree. The island is indeed a "rough land", heavily indented with navy-blue bays and flower-studded mountains.

It is a peaceful, low-key place, and the people who visit either linger only a short time to savour the Homeric associations or keep to themselves. There is

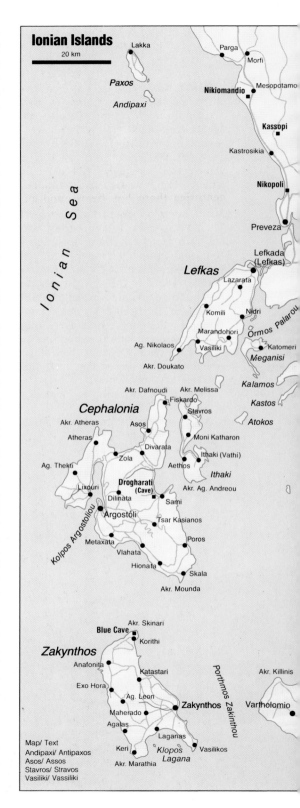

90

little to do on the island save to walk and talk and enjoy the tranquillity of this "island of goat-pastures", but the locals are exceedingly friendly and eager to converse. Many of the men speak a curious *patois* of Greek and English, having sailed the seas on merchant ships, and then like the local hero, returned home again.

Ithaki is actually two peninsulas joined by an isthmus barely wide enough for the island's main road. For centuries there has been good-humoured rivalry between the inhabitants of each peninsula as to which can claim to be Odysseus's true home. Best contender would seem to be the prehistoric acropolis in the south of the island where archaeologists have unearthed significant finds of both the Classical and the Hellenistic eras.

Many of these relics are now in the British Museum in London. Although all that remains of the acropolis today is one ruined tower and some ancient walls, the structure has been optimistically named the **Castle of Odysseus.**

The town of Vathí is located at the end of a fjord-like finger of water off the Molos Gulf. The gulf, backed by silent green hills, is plunged into shadow much of the time so after a rather brooding ferry ride rounding the corner to sparkling white **Vathí** is a dazzling surprise. The houses ring a horse-shoe shaped bay, in the middle of which is an islet of pine trees off which Lord Byron is said to have gone swimming.

Buses leave from Vathí to the island's handful of villages. There is also a small **Archaeological Museum** containing vases from the 8th century B.C. A short but energetic and hot two-mile (three-km) walk leads to the **Cave of the Nymphs** where Odysseus is believed to have hidden the treasures bestowed on him by the Phaiakes.

Three miles south of Vathí is the spring of Perapigadi, identified as Homer's **Fountain of Arethusa.** The springs are said to have been named after a nymph of Artemis, who on hearing of her son's death wept so copiously she turned into a fountain.

An interesting specimen in the Ionian sea.

To appreciate fully the beautiful northern peninsula it is necessary to have transport (scooters and bicycles can be hired in Vathí). However, the three principal villages can be reached by bus. These are the coastal resorts of **Frikés** and **Kióni** and the attractive town of **Stavros**, 10 miles (16 km) northwest of Vathí. Stravros has only one main street and a beautifully-proportioned church. Within striking distance is **Polis**, the north's contender as the home of Odysseus's palace.

CEPHALONIA: The largest and most mountainous of the Ionians, Cephalonia (Kefalonia) has long been popular with Greeks interested in rambling and exploring. Only in the past few years have foreign operators begun to exploit Cephalonia's potential and even now it isn't an island for everyone.

Distances are long, and public transport not only minimal but death-defying; the bus from the port of Sami to the capital, Argostóli, ricochets along a mountain road which is level with the tree tops in the ravine below. Mopeds and car hire can be expensive, even by Greek standards, but some form of transport is necessary to enjoy the island, for its appeal lies in the landscape—lush, green and rugged. **Mount Enos** rises to a towering 5,340 ft (1,628 metres); its slopes are covered with a rare tree known as the "Cephalonia fir".

For some time the island has been of interest to geologists and students of animal behaviour. As well as providing a "bottomless" lake and a "rocking" stone, until 1963 no one was able to provide an explanation for the sea-water at Katavothres, just outside Argostóli, which flows into two rifts by the shore. The mystery was solved by a team of Austrians and now the buildings around these "sea mills" (also known as swallow holes) with their big, gently rocking wheels, have been turned into a nightclub where plate smashing takes place on many a summer's evening.

Snakes and goats provide stories which have as much basis in science as in myth. The first story, to which locals swear, concerns the snakes at a small village in the southeast, **Markopoulo**. Apparently, during the hot summer month of August, small, harmless snakes appear and, wiggling in a convoy, set out for the church, heading for a silver icon of Our Lady.

Although some scientists believe the phenomenon has more to do with migratory patterns than religion, villagers regard "Our Lady's snakes" as a good omen and now catch the escaping reptiles in bottles to return them to the church. The "goats with silver teeth" to be found in the region of **Mount Ayia Dinati** can also be explained by science; the soil on which the animals graze contains minerals which discolour the animals' teeth.

The village of **Fiskardo**, 34 miles (54 km) northeast of Argostóli, is the only town on the island not to have been devastated by the earthquake of 1953. Pretty and quaint, its Venetian houses are clustered around an attractive harbour. Fiskardo is popular with yachtsmen, and increasingly, foreign tourists especially Italians.

An elegant overview of Cephalonia.

Assos, well-known for panoramic views, a Venetian castle and a good, sandy beach, has the island's best night-life, while the rather dreary port of **Sami** is best used for catching a ferry to Ithaki or as a base for exploring two of the island's many caves. **Melissani Cave**, one mile north, contains an indoor lake which catches the sun's rays in breath-taking configurations. **Drongorati Cave** lies just west of Sami. Its main attraction is an enormous chamber filled with multi-coloured stalactites and stalagmites. In the summer months concerts are occasionally held here under the illuminated ceiling.

The capital town of **Argostóli** has been rebuilt in a utilitarian, rather than a graceful style. Buildings are squat, square and unlovely, giving a vague impression of the frontier towns seen in a hundred cowboy films. Nevertheless, the town has a rough and ready charm centred around the main *plateía*. On Saturday night locals eat spaghetti outside one of the many tavernas and call out warnings to their teenaged children who insist on revving the motors of their souped-up cars.

Sights to see include an **Archaeological Museum** and the **Korgialeneian Library** which contains a collection of Byzantine icons. **Platisyalos** beach lies just outside town. Other sandy beaches on the island include **Mirtos, Makri Yalos, Plati Yalos**, and the shores around the resort of **Poros**.

ZAKYNTHOS: Both Pliny and Homer found Zakynthos (Zante) appealing and there are understandable reasons why the island has been one of the more recent choices for international development. Its beaches are broad and sandy. An abundance of natural springs once earned the island the sobriquet "the Flower of the Levant" from the Venetians, and even now the twisting lanes and banks of wild flowers keep the land fragrant and fresh. For many years perfume has been made and sold locally from these flowers. The wine, a full bodied white or rosé, is perfectly palatable and very popular.

Zakynthians had, in the past, a rich

Panorama of the port of Zakynthos from Pohali.

store of ethnic customs and a high cultural standing in the arts. Among a distinguished list of writers, artists and musicians two are outstanding: Dionysios Solomós and Panayiótis Doxarás. Dionysios Solomós was born in Zakynthos in 1798. At the age of 25 he wrote the poem *Hymn to Liberty*, which, when set to music, became the Greek national anthem. Panayiótis Doxarás and later, his son, became leading lights of the Zakinthos School of Painting. Fuelled with enthusiasm by a trip to Venice, Doxarás returned to revolutionise the existing concepts of Byzantine art; his influential icons can be seen in the church **Kyrias Ton Angéllon** (Our Lady of the Angels).

Once the island airport began to accept international bookings, hotel complexes and tour companies could not be far behind. Most of this development has taken place on the south coast, along the soft sands and clear shallow waters of **Laganás**. Here is the usual proliferation of tavernas, rooms, cafés and hire companies, but the beach is large enough to accommodate the crowds. So far—but the unprecedented rise in tourism has in fact brought about a serious threat to the ecology which is dividing the opinion of the islanders.

Other beach resorts popular with tourists are **Kerí** on the southwest coast, and **Alikes** on the bay of the same name. Beaches at **Vassilikos, Gerakas** and tiny **Pórto Róma** attract fewer people, especially out of season. Inland villages have up till now been spared the developer's axe, and Zakynthos's sweet smelling terrain makes cycling to the beach a genuine pleasure. Try the village of **Lithakia**, eight miles (13 km) south of Zakynthos Town, or in the north **Maries, Othonies,** or **Volimes**; each claim important churches. From Volimes it is possible to take a boat to a well-known and interesting attraction, the **Blue Grotto**.

It was on the hill known as **Strandi**, just above Zakynthos Town, that Solomós was inspired to write the song which inspires a nation. His tomb occupies the ground floor of the **Dionysios Solomós Museum** in the centre of town. Zakynthos Town itself is an admirable attempt to recreate the architectural splendour the town enjoyed before the earthquake of 1953.

When approached by sea at night, it does indeed rise up in magnificent splendour, its towers and tall elegant buildings illuminated by shafts of light. In the day-time the effect diminishes, as it becomes obvious that this is a "new" town. Still, amenities are good, restaurants are above-average and the boulevards remain pleasant and broad.

Examples from the Zakynthos School of Painting can be seen in the **Byzantine Museum** and in the previously mentioned Our Lady of the Angels church.

Other churches worth visiting are **St Nicholas of Molos**, **St Dionysios**, with its relic of the island saint, and the **church of the Virgin Chrysopigi**, two miles (three km) west in the garden suburb of **Bochali**. Wonderful views of the sea and the town are best enjoyed from the medieval walls of the ancient **Acropolis**.

The Venetians called Zakynthos "the Flower of the Levant".

94

TURTLES UNDER THREAT

The loggerhead turtle (*Caretta caretta*) crawls out of the sea onto the moonlit beach of her birthplace, the island of Zakynthos. She has crossed the length of the Mediterranean to return, at last, to this spot.

Summoning all her strength, the 200-lb (90-kg) reptile carefully selects a place in the sand where she digs a nest with her rear flippers. Satisfied with her cocoon, she lays 100 soft eggs, each the size of a ping-pong ball, covers them with soft sand and returns to the sea to rest, exhausted in the shallows. Then she swims away, unaware that her maternal labouring may have been in vain. For here on Zakynthos, tourism threatens these ancient creatures with extinction.

The survival of the loggerhead is endangered before she even reaches the beach. In the early evening, the shallow coastal waters are filled with female turtles resting after their long journey to the island. It has been estimated that nearly half these turtles are maimed or killed by the propellers of pedalos or speedboats taking out waterskiers and para-gliders. Carelessly discarded litter from the 30,000 tourists creates another hazard, as turtles suffocate trying to swallow plastic bags which they mistake for jellyfish, a favourite food.

For the female turtle, the hazards increase when she slips ashore. Disorientated by the glittering lights of hotels and the strange noises emitting from the tourists and tavernas, she may scurry back to the seas, uncertain where to deposit her efforts to continue a species that has lived on the earth for 90 million years.

Those mothers who bravely attempt to continue their labours, ignoring this strange new world, will suffer the indignity of ignorant spectators brandishing torches and flashing camera lights at their maternal activities, frightening the turtles back into the sea where the eggs may be released never to hatch.

The eggs successfully laid in nests are often doomed by motorcyclists, horse riders and car drivers who speed across the sand, packing it down so that it is impossible for the hatchlings to emerge. Beach umbrellas are unwittingly driven into nests, piercing the eggs. Tamarisk trees, planted in haste to shade the sunbathers, pose other problems as hatchlings become tangled up in the tree roots. Even the innocent sandcastle-maker may create holes which become shallow graves for the hatchlings.

Hatching takes place from early August to late September—the same time of year as most of the tourists arrive. Only one egg in 1,000 will reach puberty, even in normal circumstances. The two-and-a-half-inch (six-cm) hatchlings may emerge from their hazardous 50-day incubation and, instead of heading instinctively to the light on the horizon line at sea, frequently wander confused up the beach to the dazzling lights of the hotels and restaurants. This error brings death from exhaustion or dehydration.

The natural struggle from nest to sea is of no small biological significance. The beach's sand etches marks on the young turtle's shell, which guides the female back to the same place, perhaps 20 years later, to lay her eggs in her own birthplace. For thousands of years Zakynthos has boasted the greatest concentration of nesting turtles in the Mediterranean. The Langanás bay coastline was once a favourite spot for the nesting mothers. Confused by the combination of boats, buildings and noise the past few years of tourism have brought, the turtles have abandoned the busy sands. The majority now nest in the more secluded beaches of Sekania and Daphni, where there is barely room for the activities of the bewildered reptiles. Only 800 turtles now reproduce on Zakynthos, almost half the number to be found 15 years ago.

Conservation efforts have led to the prohibition of building construction near the nesting sites. However, the islanders are divided on the ecology issue and the debate rages in many a taverna or *ouzerie*. The income available from tourism glitters with a profitability that outweighs very much interest in protecting the turtles. While this war continues, visitors to the island can all make a contribution to the survival of the turtles, with a little understanding of the loggerheads and their battle against extinction.

THE SARONIC GULF ISLANDS

The five islands of the Saronic Gulf might best be described as "commuter" islands. Lying only half an hour by ferry or hydrofoil from Piraeus, the temptation is to treat the islands as an extension of the mainland, or specifically, suburbs of Athens. This is partially true: Athenians build summer homes on the islands; islanders farm the mainland on the other side of a strait which may be only several hundred feet wide.

Merchants, too, have been quick to exploit the proximity. The short cruise from Piraeus which calls at three Saronic islands is a very popular attraction for tourists visiting Athens, rivalled, perhaps, only by Delphi as the most enjoyable day spent out of town. When the cruise ships mingle with the hydrofoils, the ferry boats, and the regularly-scheduled caiques, there is often a virtual traffic jam on the waves, and foreigners greatly outnumber Greeks at most Saronic ports.

In spite of all this, the islands are distinctive, rich in history and—behind the crowds and chi-chi boutiques—remarkably attractive. Salamis is renowned for the epoch-making naval battle in 480 B.C. which decided the outcome of the Persian Wars. Aegina is the site of the Temple to Aphaía, one of the most important antiquities located on any Greek island.

Poros has been immortalised by Henry Miller in one of his books and Spetsai by John Fowles in one of his novels. Not to be outdone, Hydra is the part-time home of the singer Leonard Cohen, who can occasionally be seen in the local cafés and bars.

Preceding pages and left, lunchtime on Hydra and Spetsai.

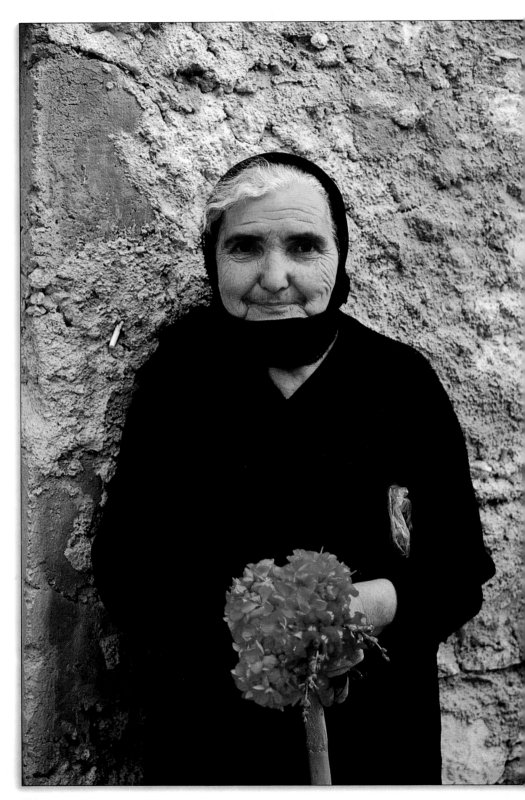

THE SARONIC GULF ISLANDS

SALAMIS: This low, flat island (also called Salamína) is popular with Athenians but offers little interest to visitors. The most fun to be had might well be the half-hour journey from Piraeus; the tiny caique laden with commuters reading tabloid newspapers, threads its way between huge liners destined for more exotic locations.

Boats dock at **Selinia** on the east coast, an unimpressive port with a muddy beach and a few *pensions*. Most passengers take one of the larger ferries from **Perama** on the mainland to the main harbour **Paloukia**, a town with a strong naval presence and a couple of waterside tavernas.

The island's capital, **Salamis,** lies two miles (three km) northwest, and hugs an expansive bay. The quayside teams with activity as much gossiping as well as shopping takes place at the open-air fish stalls directly in front of the harbour. At night, when the bay is lit by lights hung in the trees which separate the beach from the street, a much-needed touch of style is introduced.

Relics from the island's distinguished past can be found in the **Archaeological Museum**. Ancient sources have shown that not only did Salamis participate in the Trojan War, but it was also the site of a famous naval battle in 480 B.C. between the Greeks and the Persians. This skirmish was decisive for the outcome of the Persian Wars and Greek independence.

Eántio (also known as Mouliki) lies four miles (seven km) southwest of the capital. Eántio throbs to the sound of a disco beat and offers a sweeping view of the southern peninsula. It is the best place to eat seafood, preferably at sunset when the bay turns golden red. The only site worth visiting by the surprisingly good bus network is the **Panayia Convent**, five miles (eight km) northwest of Salamis. Situated among pine trees, the chapel dates from the 11th century. Walls are decorated with handsome frescos and more than 3,000 figures are painted in detail.

AEGINA: The island's close proximity to Athens and a strategic position in the Mediterranean trading waters has meant that, since ancient times, this sophisticated community has enjoyed an outlook more urban than Greek island. The first settlements on the island date from around 3000 B.C. In 650 B.C. European coinage was minted here, and in 1828, the year Aegina became the capital of free Greece, drachmas were made in a local foundry. John Capodistrias, the first governor, ordered the building of fine mansions, many of which still line the streets of the modern capital today.

Unfortunately, the same qualities which produced this worldly aspect are responsible for Aegina's present-day disadvantages. Passengers from the 30-minute hydrofoil journey and the one-day cruises from Athens flood in by the thousands and the merchants are quick to cash in. Souvenir shops and tacky stalls selling (admittedly very fresh) pistachio nuts clutter the landscape and

Left, the Saronic Gulf islands are rich in pistachios and flowers.

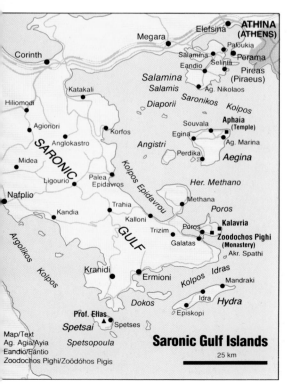

Map/Text
Ag. Agia/Ayia
Eandio/Eántio
Zoodochos Pighi/Zoödóhos Pigis

Saronic Gulf Islands

25 km

the island's masterpiece, the magnificent Temple to Aphaía, can barely be appreciated above the babble of multilingual tour guides.

There are a few compensations. Roads are good, beaches are maintained and easily reached by bus, and most people speak English. Fortunately, the trippers tend to congregate in only two towns, **Ayia Marína**, a resort on the east coast, boasting a sandy beach backed by pine trees, and the island capital nine miles (14 km) west, which is also called Aegina.

Aegina is a handsome town, its wide marina dominating the seafront and its well-proportioned 19th-century buildings providing a dignified aspect. The cathedral, where Capodistrias was sworn into power, dates from 1806. High above the crescent-shaped harbour lies the most ancient part of town, the **Hill of Korona,** where one column of a **Temple to Apollo** can still be seen.

This is a place to seek out relative tranquillity until the daily boats depart and life resumes at a more pleasing pace. Twilight in the capital is played out against a backdrop of strolling tourists, seafood restaurants and the clip-clop of hooves from the horses which pull brightly decorated carriages.

The **Temple to Aphaía** (Aféa) was constructed on the highest point of the island, seven miles (12 km) northeast of Aegina. From time to time its marble columns can be glimpsed from the road, which weaves through pine forests (the resin is used in the production of retsina) and pistachio groves.

The temple is one of the most important in antiquity and, outside the holy island Delos, one of the finest ruins to be found on any Greek island. Dedicated to the goddess of wisdom and light, Aphaía is thought to have been built between 510 and 480 B.C. and commands a stunning view of the sea and the island—try to go at sunset.

Of the original 32 columns, 24 have been preserved, as well as the foundation of an altar and the remains of a priests' chamber. The magnificent sculptured pediments depicting scenes

The Temple to Aphaía, one of the finest ancient ruins to be found on the islands.

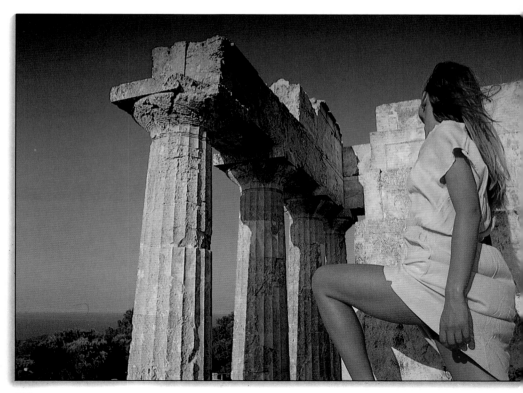

from the Trojan War were, sadly, removed by Prince Ludwig of Bavaria in 1813 and are now housed in Munich, although lesser finds from Aphaía are on display in the **Archaeological Museum** in Aegina.

Palaiochora is a spooky Byzantine hill town riddled with churches and ruins, worth a dedicated ramble if stout walking shoes are to hand. Islanders sought refuge here from pirates in the ninth and 10th centuries and the site was a flourishing community right up until 1800, when the population drifted slowly back to the sea ports.

Perdika, six miles (nine km) southeast of Aegina, is a popular resort with Athenians. Excursions from Perdika can be made to the neighbouring islet **Moni**, although both are to be avoided at weekends due to crowds.

POROS: Sailing through the straits of Poros is so impressive ferry captains often call out for passengers to hasten deck-side so as not to miss the view. Henry Miller, writing in *The Colossus of Maroussi,* describes it this way: "To

sail slowly through the streets of Poros is to recapture the joy of passing through the neck of the womb. It is a joy almost too deep to be remembered."

Miller's "streets" are actually 1,300 ft (400 metres) of water which separate Poros from the mainland and from which the island takes its name. (The word *poros* means passage.) Sailing them today might not be quite as joyous as Miller's interpretation, but certainly it is disconcerting, not least, one assumes, to the Porians who must contend with boat-loads of foreigners peering through their windows.

The mainland plays an economic as well as a scenic part in the lives of the islanders. Some of them farm the land on the other side of the straits and "commute" between Poros and the mainland.

Poros is actually two islands, united by a bridge. **Kalavria,** the northern section, is verdant and green, at least 10 times the size of **Sferia,** the volcanic islet on which most of the population lives. Although midway between Ae-

The greenery and pistachio groves of Aegina.

gina and Hydra, this industrious island lacks the glamour of its near neighbours and as a result is less frenzied.

In the last few years the wooded bays of the north have become the destination for British package tour firms, an influence also felt in the town of **Poros** where Union Jacks wave on scores of commercial craft.

Poros is built around several hills, one hill crowned with a blue and white clock tower. The climb to the tower is revealing—melons, grapes and flowers overhang domestic verandas. Staircases which begin with promise are apt to end in a villa-owner's market garden. This disregard for tourism—flotilla notwithstanding—is also evident along the harbour, where pride of place is given to a busy, even smelly, meat market.

On the northern side of town stands the **Naval Training School.** The building was constructed in 1830, the first naval arsenal in Greece. A stroll through this part of Poros can be refreshing on a hot summer afternoon, due to a series of fine family mansions surrounded by well-tended gardens.

The **Monastery of Zoödóchou Pigís** lies 20 minutes by bus from Poros next to a hillside spring. This 18th-century whitewashed building is dedicated to the Virgin of the Life-Giving Spring (Zoödóchou Pigís). Although it is common practice for Greeks to be buried behind the sacred walls of a monastery, Zoödóchou Pigís is exceptional in containing the graves of three foreigners— one English, one Russian and one Italian. The first two were victims of the War of Independence.

The latter was the daughter of the noted painter Raffaelo Ceccoli, who helped to create, among other things, the Athens School of Fine Arts. Ceccoli and his family were living on the island when his daughter fell ill and died at the age of 21. Ceccoli painted the portrait of the Virgin (the Life-Giving Force) inside the monastery near the altar and as a memorial, embellished the painting with the features of his daughter.

HYDRA: Although mentioned by Herodotus in the fifth century B.C. it

The "Flying Dolphin" hydrofoil from Piraeu calls regularly at Poros.

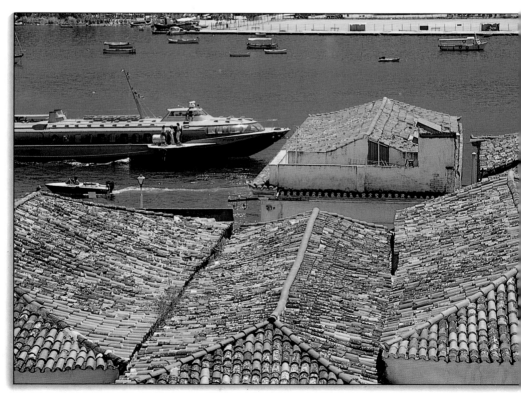

was not until the 17th century that Hydra (Ydra) came to prominence. Shipbuilding brought a welcome and lucrative income and by the next century Hydriots dominated the seas, sailing as far afield as America and bringing back goods of distinction and beauty. Captains built huge mansions in the port to house their booty and the island's experienced seamen made a substantial contribution to the War of Independence in 1821.

In an act of remarkable charity, the people of Hydra offered to shelter the population of nearby Spetsai, an island which suffered greatly in the conflict. Although the offer wasn't taken up, it was a commendable gesture for a people known more for inter-island rivalry than solidarity.

In the 1960s, artists, attracted by the port's symmetry and clear, bright light, took up residence which in turn attracted well-heeled hippies. Hydra became a minor jet-set destination and even today, the movie stars and artists having, for the most part decamped to other resorts, Hydra is a fashionable, expensive place more akin to Athens' Plaka or Mykonos than her nearer Saronic neighbours. Chic boutiques line the quayside (dollars accepted) and cocktail bars overflow with poseurs sporting the best hair-dos to be found in Greece. Cruise passengers and day-trippers add to the general parade and although the atmosphere is far from restful, this onslaught of visitors does not erode the island's charm.

Many of Hydra's *archontika* (Italian-style mansions) have been refurbished in their original style, grey stone on the outside, tastefully furnished on the inside. A branch of the Athens School of Fine Arts is housed in the Tombazis villa; the Merchant Navy Academy in the Tsambadosa mansion. The streets behind the harbour are prettily cobbled, narrow, and twisting. White-washed walls give way to elegant doors (lion's head brass knockers are much in evidence) and small squares provide refuge from the worst of the crowds.

Better still for peace and tranquillity

A 19th-century bridge at Vlichos, Hydra.

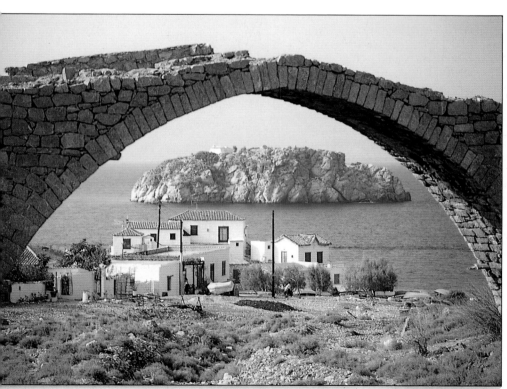

is the rest of the island. The only real town is the capital and port and as cars are banned, the trippers and the trendies rarely venture farther afield than a far-flung café. An hour's walk upwards and inland leads to the **Convent of Ayia Efpraxia** and the **Monastery of Profitis Ilias**, only two of Hydra's many churches. Island beaches, however, are less impressive. One of the few sandy beaches can be found at **Mandraki** just east of the town.

SPETSAI: Just eight sq miles (22 sq km) in area, Spetsai (Spetses) is the birthplace of a national heroine. During the 1821 revolution, Laskarina Bouboulina, as the story is told, was landlocked on Spetsai along with the other women by a Turkish fleet while the men were out at sea. Rather than panic, Bouboulina organised for all the hats available on the island to be gathered together (and there were many, as all Turkish subjects were required to wear a fez) which she then placed on towering plants which grew along the shore.

From the sea the fezzes looked like a platoon of soldiers crouched in the grasses. The Turks fled, the women rejoiced, and the island was saved from invaders. Laskarina, who became a captain on her husband's ship after he was murdered, went on to inspire many poets and writers. The historian Filimonas said of this brave Spetsiot: "She put cowards to shame and brave men made way for her". A rather flattering portrait of Ms Bouboulína can be found on the present-day 50-drachma note.

The 1821 revolution constitutes the most glorious chapter in the island's history. Spetsai was one of the first islands to raise the flag of rebellion and its notable fleet fought with dignity. In the centre of the harbour town, cannons intact, stands the Dapia, the square and fortified point where Spetsiots did battle with the enemy.

Today the **Dapia** is the hub of island life, ringed by tavernas and cafés. Tiny red and white water taxis buzz between the port and the mainland with scenic regularity; there is a slight touch of Venice in the carefree atmosphere. Many of the narrow, cobbled alleyways

threading through the town are inlaid with pebble mosaics, primarily of mythical marine figures. These back streets contain several fine *archontika,* most of which are owned by wealthy Athenians and used as summer homes.

The former Chatzi-Yanni Mexis mansion is the **island museum** where Bouboulina's bones now reside. Her house, too, has been preserved, but is not always open to the public. Just outside the town is a curious phenomenon: a Greek impression of an English public school called the **Anargyrios and Kordialenios College**. The novelist John Fowles taught here and used the island as a setting for his book, *The Magus.*

Boats depart regularly from the Dapia, calling in at several coves sheltered by trees. **Bekiri** cave on the west coast was used as a hiding place by islanders during the war. Further south, at the very tip of Spetsai, looms the hilly terrain of **Spetsopóula.** This well-tended, well-guarded islet is owned by the wealthy Greek shipping magnate, Stavros Niarchos.

The sophistication of the Saronic Gulf islands is mirrored in Spetsai.

PLUMBING AND OTHER PROBLEMS

"Greek loos are dodgy", warned the note behind the bathroom door. "Throw your paper in the bin provided".

Another notice, another place, more to the point: "Don't put anything down the toilet you haven't consumed first." A sobering thought after *kalamaria* and a few ouzos.

In Greece all things lavatorial are a snare and a delusion. Greek plumbing is the eighth wonder of the world. You wonder how it works at all.

Seasoned Grecophiles know all about the no-paper rule, thus avoiding clogging, flood and hysterics from landladies. They also know that it's a good idea to carry tissues, or *hartopetsétes* (napkins) nabbed from taverna tables, just in case. Cramped cubicles at the back of Kostas', Yorgos' or Haris' seldom bear close inspection with overflowing bins, floors awash and no loo roll. *In extremis* the brand-name cry of "Softex" is a nationally recognised distress signal.

Squat-over loos are quite common, especially if they are public conveniences. You might even come across a hole in the floor over the sea for instant and natural flushing. Brace yourself: some toilets can be grim. For reasons known only to themselves—AIDS scares, fear of lavatory seats?—some Greeks prefer to

ignore the pan altogether and use the floor instead. And that's just in the Ladies.

In the main, toilet facilities in most tavernas and restaurants are adequate, with soap, towels and the ever-present bottle of *klorini*. But perhaps the biggest mystery of all is why the Greeks go in for bathroom fittings which are straight out of *Homes and Gardens*.

Visit the remotest of islands, the poorest of village rooms and you can be sure that the *tó loutrón* (bathroom) will be sumptuous. Colours outmoded in more sophisticated countries, like avocado, rose pink or even deep, hard-to-clean maroon, are all the rage. Patterned tiles, the more garish the better, are a must, as are the bidet, shower with backless chair but no curtain, fancy taps and mirror-fronted bathroom cabinet.

The fact that there's rarely a shower tray, just a hole in the uneven floor down which water refuses to drain (you have to urge it along with your loo brush) or that the door won't shut because it's been warped by all this water and the posh fittings have also gone rusty is neither here nor there. The matching suite is essential, especially if your lodgings are eventually to become a dowry for a lucky daughter.

One palatial bathroom encountered had all the mod cons except water. You flushed the loo with a bucket and if you wanted a wash you drew water up from the *sterna* (well) with a Spam tin on a piece of rope.

"Can we drink the water?" is a normal tourist question. "Where can we find the water?" is a specifically Greek inquiry. Lack of fresh water is a giant problem for many islands so you may have to get by with bottled, and wait patiently for the waterboat to arrive.

When the boat comes in there's usually a mad scramble with hosepipes as families fill up their wells, jugs, and containers. You may find you have to make daily trips to the pump or village tap as well. Most countries take old H_2O for granted, but in arid Greece in high summer water is a precious commodity and conservation is the key.

"Save water: shower with a friend", one taverna sticker advised. In the Dodecanese a yachtie almost got lynched by furious villagers for doing his washing at the communal freshwater tap. So be warned, and wash accordingly.

Some islands like Halki, in the Dodecanese, have Heath Robinson water systems relying on pumps, fittings, and a spaghetti junction of bewildering pipework. The natural water supply is brackish but every now and then it can be switched over to fresh for a virtual feast of salt-free washing.

Pondering over pressure, bores, cisterns, pumps and ball-cocks one visitor asked a Greek plumber why he couldn't put paper down the pan. What was the secret of Hellenic plumbing?

The workman scratched his head, sipped his coffee and eventually revealed: "The pipes. She is different size from the rest of Europe. *Ti na kanoume?*" (What can we do?) He wandered off, wrench in hand.

THE CYCLADES ISLANDS

The Cyclades are travel brochure islands. Every cliché, every memory, every dream of a sun-drenched beach can be realised here. The white cubed houses are justifiably famous, inspiring the work of many modern architects, Le Corbusier among them. The beaches are good, the food fresh, fellow travellers companionable, and the ferry connections so organised it is easy to sail to more than one "paradise" while on a relatively short holiday. It is not surprising, then, that for many people the Cyclades *are* Greece; other island chains merely aberrations in national character.

There are 56 Cycladic islands in all, 24 of them inhabited. Their spiritual centre might well be Santorini, for although flung to the south geographically, it is to this dramatic, volcano-created island that most people gravitate before venturing further.

The eastern and central islands fan upwards from Santorini in a loose chain which includes the Naxos/Paros/Mykonos back-packers' beat, takes in little discovered islets like Donoussa and Iraklia, before concluding rather grandly in the rich red soil which is the island of Andros

The western Cyclades form a different chain, a spine of islands self-contained in their unity, sharing a common culture linked by history and ferryboat connections. Odd man out is Kea, popular with Athenians and Archaic stone lions, little known outside the tavernas around the Acropolis.

The Cyclades were inhabited as early as 6000 B.C. The end of the fourth millennium and throughout the third saw an advanced civilisation, with many inroads made in art, craft and commerce. A high standard of living was enjoyed, as anyone who visits the Goulandris Museum in Athens, on Neofytou Douka Street, will appreciate. The museum is the world's first to be devoted exclusively to Cycladic art, exemplified by its long, linear, bright-white sculpture.

This vast backdrop of culture and history might not be evident amidst the gaudy cafés or hedonistic merry-makers of Mykonos, but it is never very far away. One sunset over the Vale of Klima, the valley in Milos where the Louvre's Venus de Milo was discovered, is all that's needed.

Preceding pages: two girls and a buoy; the dovecotes of Tinos. Left, Mykonos.

SANTORINI

On the approach, Santorini (Thira) looks like something out of a science fiction movie: an impossibility. Broken pieces of a volcano's rim form a dark circle around a wide expanse of ocean. Santorini is the longest, easternmost piece of the rim, a half-moon of land whose precipitous inner curve is formed of petrified lava, which, at sunset, seems to reflect a fire from the underworld. **Firá** (Thirá), the capital, sits high on the rim, its white houses protruding from the edge like ancient teeth from an old man's mouth.

To the northeast, the land smoothes out into a fertile apron. A few bare hills push up again in the southeast. One of them is the setting of **Ancient Thira**, a stupendous ruin of a city founded by Dorians in the ninth century B.C. It last supported 5,000 Romans, but was emptied by one of many eruptions that racked the island, aggravated by the clashing of two of the earth's plates which meet beneath it. Further south, **Akrotiri** is an ongoing, multi-tiered excavation of a vast Minoan settlement built over a Cycladic period town. Its proportions are grand, and this "live" excavation is vastly more interesting than the usual piles of rubble left after finds have been dispatched to a museum. (If you plan to visit either of these sites, Firá's Archaeological Museum is highly recommended.)

Today, Santorini is as famous for the rock 'n' roll atmosphere of the main town as for its geography and excavations. Although packed with the jewellers, boutiques, and cave-like discos that are the stock and trade of the more tourist-conscious islands, its beauty hasn't been dampened. The blazing whiteness and sensual lines of Cycladic architecture are doubly disarming against the smoky purple banks of old lava, and from every portside passage there is a sombre, fantastic view of the ocean-bound volcano with "burnt islands" at its centre. Lights twinkle across the strait on the islet of **Thirassia**, sparse in vegetation and inhabitants, as though from some lost planet.

Most people stay in Firá. Consequently, it's relatively easy to find quiet accommodation almost anywhere else. At the island's northernmost tip, **Oia** (Ia) is reachable by bus. For those with time and no cumbersome luggage, the hike along the caldera's edge from Imerovigli (on the bus route north) to Oia brings the cruel reds and purples of the petrified lava and the island's tempestuous geography into sharp focus. The volcano is only dormant, not extinct; earthquakes are always a disturbing possibility.

Oia's beauty is disturbing: in 1956, a severe earthquake sent the uppermost layer of settled lava catapulting down over the houses. Afterward, people dug their way back inside their homes, which now look like squared-off cave-dwellings. A steep walk down twisting stone steps from the western end of town ends at Amoudi beach, overhung by deserted houses. Each year, there are more places to stay in Oia.

eft, the lear, deep ones of santorini. ollowing age, the hurch omes of ia.

Santorini

Thira

Aegean Sea

Santorini

5 km

ap/ Text
hira/ Firá

Kamari and **Perissa** are busy resorts on the east coast. Perissa, with the main campground, has a roasting hot black sand beach. It is also a good point from which to climb to Ancient Thira and then **Mount Profitas Elias**, the next hill inland. Profitas Elias Monastery is a hive of workshops. The monks have mastered everything from shoemaking to winemaking, and although some of the workshops now contain only exhibits, homemade wine and liqueur are still set out for guests. Be sure to check whether the monastery is open, though, before setting out on the climb. The hours Profitas Elias is open to the public tend to be erratic.

It is also possible to walk to the monastery from **Pirgos**, a landlocked village on a central plain which characterises the island's interior. Yellow wheatsheaves, grapevines twisted into wreaths Santorini-style, tiny tomatoes, and riots of spring wildflowers—all growing out of angry-looking pumice soil—make up the island's gentler side. Small caves occasionally yawn up from grassy fields, used as tool sheds, barns, and occasionally, as homes.

The town closest to the airport, **Monolithos** (a 45-minute walk), consists of one grass-roofed taverna furrowed into a hillside on the ocean, plus two houses. The taverna's owners, a sweet older couple who have, sadly, outlived their four children, keep an assortment of dogs. They may open the place up if you happen to arrive at this unlikely outpost after a night flight. The last stretch of road before Monolithos is lined with hollowed out sandstone formations that emit eerie piping noises when the wind rushes through them.

Bus transportation on the island is good, augmented by excursion buses to places like Akrotiri. Near Akrotiri on the sea is a taverna set in caves where sweet, lava-nurtured Santorini wines are served in dented tin jugs.

Most boats put in below Firá at **Skala Firá**, accessible via a stone stairway, donkey, or funicular. But some embark at **Athinios**, further south; clarify when buying tickets, as transport to and from the port can be awkward.

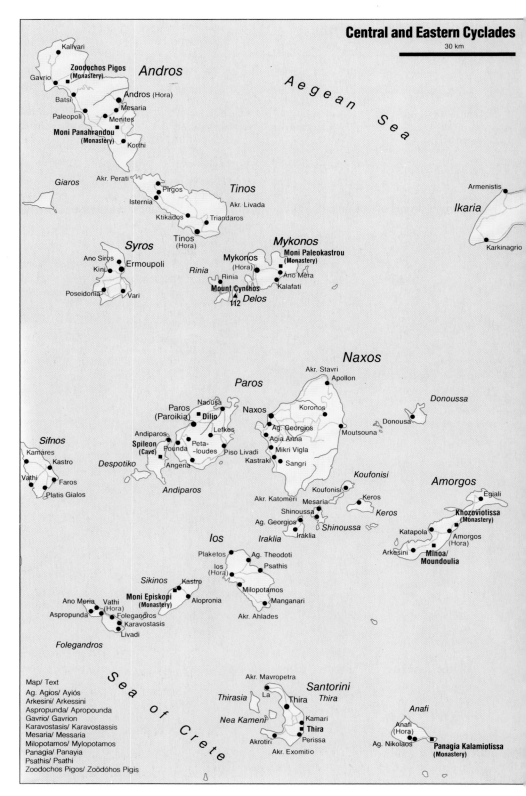

Central and Eastern Cyclades

30 km

Aegean Sea

Kalivari

Zoodochos Pigos (Monastery)

Gavrio

Andros

Batsi

Andros (Hora)

Mesaria

Paleopoli

Menites

Moni Panahrandou (Monastery)

Korthi

Akr. Perati

Giaros

Pirgos

Tinos

Isternia

Akr. Livada

Ktikados

Triandaros

Armenistis

Ikaria

Karkinagrio

Syros

Tinos (Hora)

Mykonos

Ano Siros

Ermoupoli

Mykonos (Hora)

Moni Paleokastrou (Monastery)

Kini

Rinia

Rinia

Ano Mera

Poseidonia

Vari

Mount Cynthos

Kalafati

112

Delos

Naxos

Akr. Stavri

Apollon

Paros

Naousa

Koronos

Donoussa

Paros (Paroikia)

Dilio

Naxos

Donousa

Lefkes

Ag. Georgios

Moutsouna

Sifnos

Andiparos

Spileon (Cave)

Peta-loudes

Pounda

Agia Anna

Kamáres

Kastro

Despotiko

Angeria

Piso Livadi

Mikri Vigla

Kastraki

Sangri

Koufonisi

Amorgos

Egiali

Vathi

Faros

Platis Gialos

Andiparos

Koufonisi

Khozoviotissa (Monastery)

Akr. Katomeri

Mesaria

Keros

Katapola

Shinoussa

Keros

Amorgos (Hora)

Ag. Georgios

Shinoussa

Ios

Iraklia

Iraklia

Arkesini

Minoa/Moundoulia

Plaketos

Ag. Theodoti

Ios (Hora)

Psathis

Sikinos

Kastro

Milopotamos

Ano Meria

Vathi (Hora)

Moni Episkopi (Monastery)

Alopronia

Manganari

Aspropunda

Folegandros

Karavostasis

Akr. Ahlades

Livadi

Folegandros

Sea of Crete

Akr. Mavropetra

La

Santorini

Thirasia

Thira

Thira

Anafi

Nea Kameni

Kamari

Anafi (Hora)

Thira

Akrotiri

Perissa

Ag. Nikolaos

Panagia Kalamiotissa (Monastery)

Akr. Exomitio

Map/ Text
Ag. Agios/ Ayiós
Arkesini/ Arkessini
Aspropunda/ Apropounda
Gavrio/ Gavrion
Karavostasis/ Karavostassis
Mesaria/ Messaria
Milopotamos/ Mylopotamos
Panagia/ Panayia
Psathis/ Psathi
Zoodochos Pigos/ Zoödóhos Pigis

CENTRAL AND EASTERN CYCLADES

ANAFI: In legend, Apollo conjured up Anafi to shelter Jason and the Argonauts when the seas grew rough and they risked losing the Golden Fleece; Apollo's shrine was built here in thanksgiving. Divine intervention has never again been reliable. Earthquakes originating at Santorini usually shiver through Anafi, causing tidal waves and maelstroms of volcanic detritus.

Anafi's appearance has probably not altered much in the interceding years: it still looks like a rough boulder heaved up out of the sea and kept in place only by the goodness of a tenacious god. However, a different god is involved now: the **Panayia Kalamiotissa** monastery was erected over the old shrine in the island's southeast. Patches of worn marble in its walls are believed to be remnants of the old temple.

Under 300 people live on Anafi today, surviving mostly by fishing and subsistence farming. Tourism has not provided much of a boost to the economy, nor has the island made many concessions. There is an occasional caique from Santorini; Dodecanese and Crete-bound ferries call in approximately once a week.

The harbour, **Ayios Nikolaos**, is directly below the **Hora**, (also known as Anafi, or Horio), and has rooms available in summer. Continue up to the Chora for a wider choice and finer setting—a medieval *Kástro* looms over it, and life in the quiet streets has so far been unaltered by the presence of tourists. Feast days on Anafi are an occasion for all-out dancing.

Hikes eastward lead to the beach at **Klisidi** (with seasonal taverna) and then the monastery. The north is virtually empty, except for the rubble of another Venetian castle. Goat paths amble aimlessly, as you may feel like doing... above all, Anafi remains a supreme place to be alone.

FOLEGANDROS: The vaulting steepness of Folegandros's coast has served as a natural deterrent to outside invasion over the centuries and lent security to those who remain within. Despite its tininess—12 sq miles (32 sq km) populated by barely 500 people—its role in very recent history has not been insignificant: many Greeks were exiled here during the country's 1967-74 military rule. Its pre-Christian ties with Crete were strong, and many paintings of the Cretan school can be found in its churches today. In myth, a son of King Minos founded the island.

Folegandros abounds with bays, wild herbs, and grapes. **Karavostassis** (the port), **Vathi**, at the waist of the island on the west shore, and **Apropounda** above it are the little-developed beaches. It is possible to run into a "no rooms" situation in high summer; if this happens there is camping at **Livadi** in the south. There are buses to the Hora, a magnificently-sited, fortified medieval town lodged high above the sea. The second village, **Ano Meria**, comprises stone houses and farms; the surrounding hills are dotted with chapels to which islanders make their way to pray. Historically,

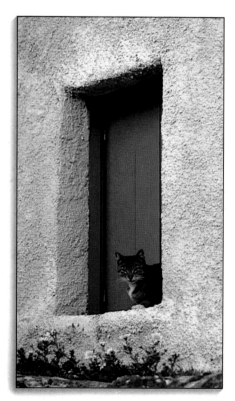

Folegandran supplications were for rain, and still are, for on no other Cycladic island is the pitifully empty rain-barrel so omnipresent.

Chryssopilia, the "golden" cave near the Chora, gapes over the sea. It is rich with stalagmites and stalactites; excavations show this was a place of long-term refuge. Enquire in Hora about caiques to the cave.

SIKINOS: Hotel-less, bankless Sikinos, ever-visible from the west shore of Ios, couldn't be less like its neighbouring island. Although connected to Piraeus and the other Cyclades twice weekly by the Milos Express ferry, and by caique to Ios and Folegandros in summer, the island so far seems to have given tourism a big shrug. It also escapes mention in the history books for long periods of time, but there are antiquities—and as always, churches—to be seen here. The three beaches, Aloproni (also the port), Ayios Nikolau and Yiorgios to the north face Ios.

From Alopronia harbour it is an hour's hike (or mule ride) to **Kástro**, the only town, and the site of **Ancient Sikinos**. (There are as yet no buses but Kástro is still the safest bet for rooms.) An abandoned convent sits above the town. Perhaps even barer than Ios, it is a solitudinous island with few obvious diversions. One site of note, the **Episkopi Monastery** stands on what may have been a temple to Apollo; this is disputed by a theory that what lies below is an elaborate marble tomb, and that the shrine is somewhere south of the town.

Sikinos' old Greek name, Oenoe, testifies to the fact that the island once produced a celebrated wine, but no more. The name Sikinos is mythological: when the banished Limnian, Thoas, was set adrift in a sea-chest by his daughter to save him from death, he washed up here and was taken in by a nymph. Their child was called Sikinos.

IOS: The centre of Ios nightlife shifts constantly. In order to ensure his corner of the market, the owner of the Ios By Night club cooks up a Miss Ios contest each Friday. The prize is 5,000 drach-

Sikinos through the ruined doorway of an 18th-century kastro.

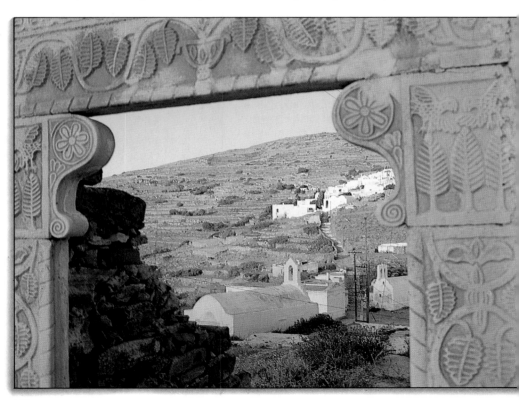

mas and a bottle of champagne. Mr. Ios contests are held only by default, when no girls can be persuaded to participate. In this case, the ringleader shouts: "OK. I guess there are no sexy girls on Ios." No one budges. The men are ready.

Ios has ethos; it is a state of mind. A tiny island with few historic attractions, it has drawn the bandanna-headed hordes in regularly since the 1960s. The current lot, mainly under 25 and a weak echo of their hippie forbears (who encamped the year round), flock here to live cheaply, drink and dry out in the blistering sun.

People still sleep on the beach at **Mylopotas**, although this is now less common. Boutique shopping is minimal. But one thing people are sure to spend money on while here is drinking. Nightclubs stud the hill above Ios harbour, with another large cluster of bars in the Hora. Homemade music strummed on well-travelled guitars, and drugs, former stock items on Ios, aren't much in evidence anymore. After the sun sets, Ios resembles a downmarket, younger Mykonos. At around 11 p.m., the still of the streets is broken by beach stragglers ready for night-time revels (a bus runs regularly between the beach and harbour via the Hora). Once ensconced inside a bar, they could be anywhere in the western world, for there is not a Greek in sight.

The permanent effects of the tourist invasion have been twofold: Ios is no longer poor, and traditional life has virtually disappeared. Hora is the only town; there are no smaller villages to keep up the old ways. As one elderly resident recounts, weddings were once a week-long feast in which everyone participated. Now, unless they are held in the dead of winter, they last a scant half a day, as everyone is too busy tending tourist-related enterprises. Island women even try to avoid summer pregnancies.

Ios is not devoid of natural beauty or charm; even the bleary-eyed can see it. The hilltop Hora, capped by a windmill, blazes with the blue domes of two Byzantine churches. Its layout and the

A pause in the fast pace of Ios.

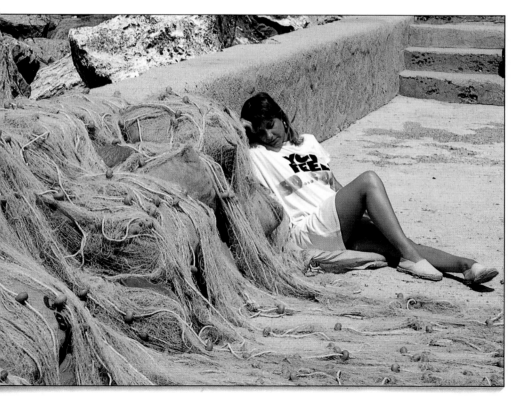

palm trees that flank it give an almost Levantine look to the location. Buses are frequent, and there is a marble stair path from the port. The flat plain north of the harbour is filling up with new houses, and at least one villa complex has been constructed on the main road. Ios has many good swimming beaches, including the nude beaches north of the harbour. There are summer caiques to **Manganari bay** in the south and **Psáthi** in the east.

A half day's walk east ends at **Ayios Theodoti**, with beach and seasonal camping. A traditional *panayiri* is held at Theodoti Church on 8 September, the only festival in which the entire island still participates. Beyond the church is **Paleokastro**, an elevated fortress containing the marble ruins of what must have once been the major town on Ios. At a lonely spot toward the northern tip, in back of the cove at **Plaketos**, is a series of prehistoric graves, one of which the islanders fiercely believe belongs to Homer, who died en route from Samos to Athens.

Kritikakis Travel in Hora, with another office on the port, is one of the most helpful agencies one could hope to find; they also change money.

AMORGOS: Like many of the eastern Cyclades, Amorgos was once thick with oak trees. The forest provided two assets: shade and wood. A 19th-century fire demolished the trees, leaving triple-peaked Amorgos bald as a skull.

The spine of mountains—the tallest is Krikelas, 3,000 ft (900 metres)—precludes expansive views unless you're atop them. The harbour town, **Katapola**, is in the flat hinterland, and green. Trees overhang the quayside, and at the back of the town is a thick fringe of orchards. Unfortunately, new development is encroaching on the older Cycladic structures as Amorgos, though still uncrowded, gets more tourist traffic each year.

Three important ancient cities once thrived here. At **Minoa** (Katapola) are ruins of a gymnasium, stadium, and temple to Apollo. **Arkessini** comprises a burial site and fortification walls. **Egi-**

A man and his puppets on Amorgos.

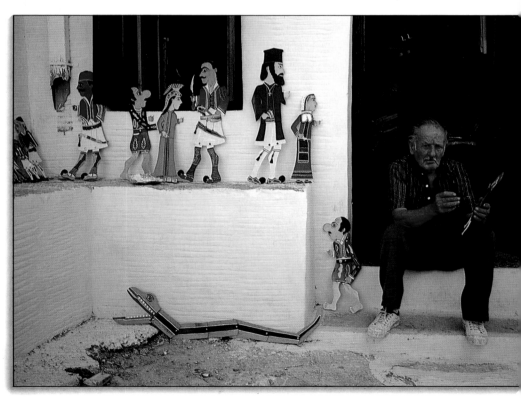

ali, Amorgos's second harbour, was also an ancient colony; now only the ruined fortress is visible.

The elevated Hora, accessible by bus, centres around a 13th-century Venetian castle. Forty churches and chapels nestle inside it, including one that holds only two people. On the town square is a crammed puppetmaker's shop; Mr. Ketabis' creations make a hectic carnival inside. The island's two most famous churches are outside Hora. **St George Balsamite**, two miles (four km) southwest, is on a sacred spring *(ayasma)* once believed to cure lepers. Spilling from a jagged cliff like milk from a jug is white-washed **Khozoviótissa**, home of a revered icon of the Virgin from Palestine. Its sacristy holds myriad religious items. For the miraculous story of the chisel, linked with the vision that inspired the church's building, take a copy of the church pamphlet.

Below Khozoviótissa, Ayia Anna beach beckons. Eastward is an emptier stretch of bathing and sunning turf; a line of windmills edges the ridge above. The coastal ledges are covered with wild thyme and oregano, which release their pungent bouquet when crushed underfoot. The island's southernmost point, below Arkessini, is marked by a Hellenistic tower looking toward Anafi. High-perched villages characterise the north, excepting **Egiali**, a small anchorage with accommodation and swimming. Some ferry boats, plus caiques from elsewhere on Amorgos, put in here. Beyond it is **Tholaria**, surrounded by Roman tomb sites.

Sheer rockfaces notwithstanding, Amorgos is riddled with beaches. Local maps name them all and provide valuable information, couched in comic English and German, about places like Tholaria, the former "valley of the old useless, doomed donkeys".

THE "BACK ISLANDS": Nicknamed the "Back Islands" because they represent the Cycladic back beyond, **Donoussa**, **Iraklia**, **Schinoussa**, and **Koufonissia** were once thickly populated. Now, there are only 100 to 200 inhabitants on each island. **Keros**, virtually empty of human habitation, was excavated to reveal multi-levelled burial sites, scores of votive offerings of marble and clay, and jewellery.

A stay on any of the Back Islands means accommodation with local families and a very low-key existence. Water is scarce on all of them. Hilly Donoussa, with only one town (Donoussa) and one reliable ferry connection per week, is covered with vineyards; views from the harbour take in the barren **Makares** islands, and beyond, the grand profile of Naxos. Iraklia has two settlements; the harbour, **Ayios Georgios**, and Hora above, just over an hour's hike up. Schinoussa's hilltop Hora has a medieval fortress at its back ("Hora" is a generic term for "main village".) **Messaria** is a tiny beach settlement on Schinoussa's north coast. Koufonissia (its neighbour, **Kato Koufonissia**, belongs mainly to the goats) has an actual hotel, and an east coast beach with a seasonal taverna. For Iraklia, Schinoussa, and Koufonissia there's a twice to thrice weekly ferry

Khozoviótissa
Monastery
spills down
the cliff like
milk from a
jug.

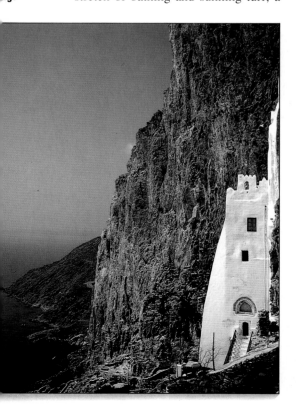

that plies between Naxos and Amorgos. Also, boats bound for the Dodecanese may pick up the Back Islands on their summer schedules. Paros is the best correspondence point; Donoussa has the poorest ferry connections, but is served by caiques from Naxos, Paros, and Santorini in summer. There are no regular services to Keros.

NAXOS: Naxos is a dark horse amongst its showier Cycladic neighbours. It's the largest of the Cyclades, and yet very little is accessible by public transport. It is an extraordinarily mountainous and fertile island, with long beaches easily lending themselves to camping and languishing. Hora is a labyrinthine chaos of old homes complemented by churches, ruins, and an international bookstore. Perhaps the explanation is in the brooding solitude of its interior. Hemmed in by the highest mountains in the Cyclades—**Zas**, the tallest, is over 3,000 ft (1,000 metres)—it is a country unto itself, as shut in and sequestered as some of the more forbidding parts of the Peloponnese.

Near the ferry dock in Hora, a colossal free-standing marble frame marks the entrance to the **Temple of Delian Apollo**—which was never completed. Fully constructed, it would have been the largest temple ever to be erected in ancient Greece.

Naxos' size, natural resources, and the bravery of its warriors have given the island status throughout the centuries. The Venetian Duchy of the Archipelago, which began in 1207 and ended in 1566 with the Ottoman invasion under Selim II, was centred in Naxos. Marco Sanudo, the first Duke of Naxos, began a tradition of allotting surrounding islands as rewards to Venetian nobleman with whom he wanted to curry favour. Naxos also has a long, strong tradition of poets and sculptors. At Delos, many tributes were made to Naxian culture, such as the House of the Naxians, and many of the island's early sculptors are represented there, most notably in the statue of Artemis by Euthycartides.

In myth, Minos's daughter Ariadne

The evocative service at Easter in a church on Naxos.

helped Theseus outwit the Minotaur on Crete. They were married, and called at Naxos on the return to Theseus's home, Athens. Inexplicably, Theseus sailed on without his wife even though she had saved his life. Perhaps Theseus feared bringing the daughter of his father's enemy home with him; other theories hold that Theseus was blown out to sea and couldn't get back to pick her up. Dionysos consoled Ariadne on Naxos. Meanwhile, Theseus forgot to raise his ship's white sail when rounding Cape Sounion. Seeing the black sails against the sea, his father, King Aegeus, assumed Theseus was dead and pitched himself off the cliffs. The Aegean has borne his name ever since.

The Hora is divided into sections, place names reflecting the port's long occupation by the Venetians. The **Metropolitan cathedral** at the back (east) of the town demarcates the Fontana section. The residential Borgo quarter behind the main *plateia* still has a splendidly Venetian aspect. Higher up, surrounding the **Kastro**, is an enclave of Naxian Catholics whose ancestors were converted by the Venetians. Look for their coats of arms over the doorways. The French School, founded in Ottoman times, now houses the **Archaeological Museum**. Just north of Hora is an area known as the Grotta, with ruins of a Mycenaen settlement.

On the northern shore of Naxos is the town of **Apollon**, a one-time hippie enclave. A vast *kouros* representing Apollo lies prone on the hillside above it, abandoned there when the marble from which it was wrought cracked. (Another *kouros* suffering a similar fate lies six miles/10km east of Naxos near the road to **Moni**.) If you hear the sound of jazz floating out of a window in the evening, it's probably one of the hundreds of recordings owned by Dimitrios Kariotos, an Athenian guitarist who turned his uncle's house here into a *pension*. There is a daily bus from Hora, but beware of Sundays, when the Apollon bus goes only to **Koronos**, seven miles (12 km) short of Apollon.

The rest of the island is a sumptuous

Traditional Easter fare: soureki.

wilderness, ripe for exploration by anyone with the time and stamina (or hired means of transport) to do it justice. The rural villages of Naxos are numerous and unpredictable, with reception to foreigners varying enormously from one to another. Olive and fruit trees grow densely around them, concealing Byzantine churches and crumbling Venetian manors. As for beaches, **Ayios Yiorgios** south of the port is serviceable, although the further south you move, the lovelier are the beaches. **Ayia Anna** is a good beach for rooms; **Mikro Vigli** beyond it has a fine taverna, and **Kastraki**, the furthest along, offers the most sand and solitude.

PAROS: This island's open-air cinema, tucked into an uncovered courtyard, has an amazingly good bill of fare. Townspeople, tourists, and laid-over boat passengers sit gazing at a screen under the stars, and somehow the experience feels supremely Greek. Reading Greek subtitles is actually a good way to pick up a few handy phrases—-more so at least than in the bars and crêpe restaurants of **Paroíkia**, Paros's main town. If you arrive at this heavily trafficked island in August, however, expect to sleep under those very same stars— rooms can be scarce.

Paroíkia is as pretty as Mykonos, but not so labyrinthine. A river bed encircles the old town like a moat; bridges hunch over it at intervals. The two main things to see in Paroíkia are the **Ekatontapyliani** (Our Lady of a Hundred Portals) **church**, and the **Archaelogical Museum**, both inland past the post office on the road starting at the quayside windmill. Just north of Paroíkia are remains of an old temple to Aphrodite; for directions, ask in the windmill, which houses the information centre.

Paros is loaded with beaches. **Pisso Livadi** (also called Chrysí Aktí, or Golden Shore) on the east coast is a perennial favourite. Here, a fold of rich Aegean blue separates Paros from the high, dark crags of Naxos. None of the coastal villages are as old or as handsome as Paroíkia or the inland villages, but do serve as good resorts. This island

The church i reflected by contemporar island life.

126

plays a close second to Mykonos in popularity, particularly with the French, whose presence here is signalled by dozens of *crêperies*.

Lefkes is the largest inland village. There are several medieval churches, the two most prominent edged with an opaline-blue wash. It is also a good base for walking excursions, as the area is full of monasteries. One of the best walks is over an old cobbled road leading to the east coast and Pisso Livadi. The sunwashed, church-pocked landscape yields little else in abundance but the brilliant marble for which Paros has always been famous.

Náoussa is a small, once beautiful port on the north coast where the boats in their moorings seem to nudge up right against the old fishermen's houses. Now it's overrun with hotels and villas, although the west side of the bay is still tranquil. The southwestern shore is lined with Athenian-owned villas and is also the site of **Pounda**, the small port servicing the island Antiparos. Near **Angeria** is a convent of nuns whose special craft is weaving. Also in the south is the touted "Valley of the Butterflies", or **Petaloudes**, a verdant area of fruit and olive tree orchards which flutter with pumping butterfly wings in early summer. It's accessible via coach or by foot over dirt roads.

Paros is an invaluable travel correspondence point. Boats connect with Athens (Piraeus, Rafina), the other Cyclades, the Dodecanese, Ikaria, and Samos. The island has an airport, too, though the planes from here are the smallest Olympic Airways runs, and so fill quickly.

ANTIPAROS: This small, pretty island was once joined to Paros. The two are now separated by a narrow channel, plied by frequent caiques bringing tourists to see **Spileon Cave**. The French Marquis de Nointel made the Antiparian cave famous when he led a Christmas Mass inside it in 1673. Cement steps make exploration less of an adventure, but cannot subtract from the cave's primordial beauty; echoes bounce like crazy around the stalag-

The bright, white arches of Paroíkia, Paros.

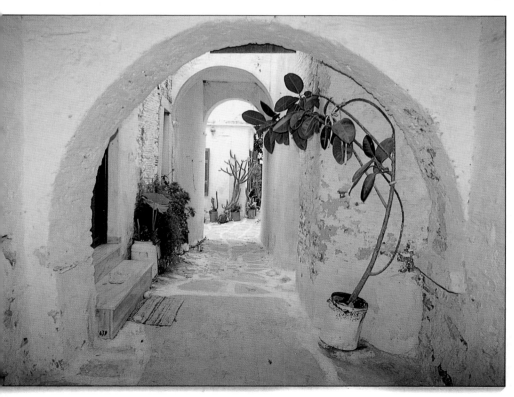

mites and stalactites. Upon entering the cavern, which is adjoined by the Church of St John of the Cave, you will descend over 300 ft (90 metres) before coming to the vaulted chamber where Mass was held. Yes, Lord Byron was here, too.

The cave is a hilly two hours' walk from **Antiparos Town**. Most daytrippers bypass the village for the cave, although it is relatively easy to find rooms here outside of July and August (the newer houses belong to Athenians). There is a beachside campground on **Yialos** bay; it looks out over a snaketail of rocks trailing back toward Paros. Excavations completed in 1964 on one of these islets, **Saliagos**, revealed evidence of Neolithic habitation.

Good beaches and bars have given Antiparos some of Paros's former business. **Soros** is an east coast beach with a taverna; Ayios Yiorgios, on the west coast, has a taverna, too, and faces the islet of **Despotiko**. Antiparos is only seven miles by three miles (11 km by five km), so there are no impossible distances. The only site south of Spileon is **Faneromeni chapel**, standing alone on a southeastern cape.

MYKONOS: If it weren't for Mykonos' twisting dazzles of architecture, its plentiful beaches and chapels, and foremost, its reputation, this small blue and white island would be a drear place. It's rocky, treeless, and there are no ancient sites. Yet people are irresistibly drawn here by the thousands. Why?

Mykonos has glamour appeal. While the other islands share a rugged kind of beauty, Mykonos has smoothed down and refined its natural features and molded them into a tourist-pleasing package which works—making it more expensive than any other Greek island.

Mykonos has its legends, however, which cover and include the beaches, bars, transvestite shows, fur and jewellery shops, and restaurants serving dishes like Lobster Thermidor. The most innocent looking *yia-yia* (grandmother) can be a hustler, charmingly unburdening a load of grapes on you and then demanding twice the going price. But even the smoothest of the

Little Venice, Mykonos.

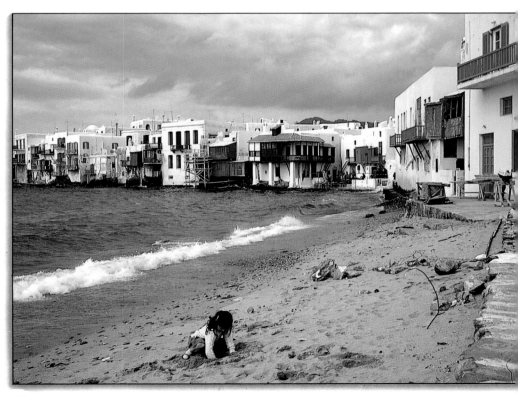

PELICAN POWER ON MYKONOS

Anyone who visits Mykonos, either regularly or even for an hour, returns with clear-cut memories. The string of windmills on the horizon? The sun-bleached cubic houses? The beaches, the bodies, the bars? Perhaps. But for many one of the most enduring memories of Mykonos is Petros the Pelican. How did the island come to have such a high profile mascot?

To unravel this mystery is to come up against two quintessential Greek conundrums: conflicting stories and inter-island rivalry. Mykoniots questioned on the subject of Petros would concur on only two points. First, the original Petros is dead and the bird who now sticks his formidable beak under the elbows of the fishmongers is Petros Two. Second, Petros One went missing one year, and kidnapping was suspected by the islanders of nearby Tinos.

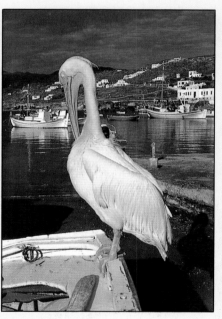

As for the rest of the Petros story, rumours run rife—and foul. Petros One is said to have died at least three different ways. He caught pneumonia and was taken (flown) to a Thessaloniki doctor, who put him down. Or someone strangled him. Or someone tried to bed the poor bird.

The record has now been set straight, and the man to do it, Bo Patrick, sits quietly each afternoon in his Little Venice photo gallery, and almost as quietly behind his bar (Bo's), near the town hall, at night. He has a superb moustache, and squints deeply and thoughtfully at anything beyond the range of the doorway.

Born on Lesvos, Patrick spent much of his childhood and working life (mainly in television production) in America. He returned to Greece in the early 1970s. This time he came to Mykonos, settling into his dual role as photographer/barkeeper. Bo has been happy here, but if it weren't for his dog Phillip, his cat, and other pesky possessions, he'd be off taking photos in India by now, preferably for the rest of his life.

Bo's skills and the fact that he got to know Petros One very well over the years have resulted in a book. It is dedicated to the "young at heart" and told like a child's story. Yet the book is greatly detailed, the tale gleaned from older islanders and then sieved for the facts, not an easy task when dealing with any kind of Greek myth, ancient or otherwise. *Whitewash and Pink Feathers* also has a picture log, and will probably keep the story of the Petros dynasty from sinking deeper into the murk. For seekers of the truth, and for anyone who has admired this proud, handsome bird and wondered about his origins, here is the result of Patrick's research:

Four pelicans left their home near the Black Sea and were travelling to their winter home in Egypt. A storm drove them off course and grounded them on Mykonos. Three of the birds perished, but Petros survived and was adopted by a local fisherman, Théodoros. He lived on the quayside and appeared to bask in the attention, at the same time drawing visitors to the then-quiet island, which had yet to achieve the notoriety of later years.

Mykonos's fame grew. Jackie Onassis, by then a dedicated lover of the islands, even sent two American pelicans to substitute for the ones which died. The birds suffered on the journey, though, and didn't live very long after their introduction to the territorially-minded Petros.

One day, Petros followed a boatload of Mykoniot schoolchildren to Tinos. A malevolent Tiniot fisherman clipped Petros's flight feathers, which turned the bird from a visitor into a hostage. The Tiniot refuted Mykonos's claim to the bird, saying he was theirs. One day Théodoros came over and the bird leapt to his shoulders. Ownership was established, a deal was struck and Petros went home to Mykonos again, to much joyous celebration. Today, Tinos has its own pelican, friendly but not as famous.

Female pelicans were introduced, too. Irini Two (an earlier, French Irini lasted but briefly) and Petros, though they never mated, strutted around together, until 1985, when Petros was hit by a car. Irini is still alive, but after Petros died she withdrew from the quayside to spend her days sleeping on a shaded square. In 1986, Petros Two arrived from Munich, donated by a German travel baron and dedicated to the lovers of Mykonos.

All is now well, as pink feathers litter the quayside once again.

ANCIENT DELOS

Minuscule Delos, southwest of Mykonos, is nirvana for archaeologists. Extensive Greco-Roman ruins, occupying much of the island's 1.5 sq miles (four sq km), make Delos the equal of Delphi and Olympia.

Sufferers of *mal de mer* should remember, before setting forth, that the island is "windy and waste and battered by the sea". The voyage may be only 45 minutes but, as the caique heaves and shudders, it can seem 10 times that long. Dedicated travellers are advised to forego breakfast as an empty stomach is a good way to make the journey less painful; another tip is to take along a sweater or to dress in layers as the sea breeze is very stiff. Having accomplished these preliminaries it's then best to forget the physical and concentrate your mind on the metaphysical.

It was on Delos that Leto, pregnant by Zeus, gave birth to the twins Apollo and Artemis. (Artemis was actually born on the adjacent island of Rhenia, nine days after Apollo—surely a most difficult delivery!) Delos, at that time a floating rock, was rewarded when four diamond pillars stretched up and anchored it in the heart of the Cyclades.

On arriving at Delos, you should immediately orient yourself to avoid getting lost among the ruins. Most of these occupy the two arms of a right angle which immediately faces you. Ahead (southern arm) are the theatre and mainly domestic buildings. To the left, on the west shore, is the sanctuary to which pilgrims from throughout the Mediterranean came bearing votive offerings and sacrificial animals.

For nearly 1,000 years this sanctuary was the political and religious centre of the Aegean and host to the Delian Festival held every four years. This, until the fourth century B.C., was the greatest festival in Greece. The Romans turned it into a grand trade fair and made Delos a free port. It also became the slave market of Greece where 10,000 slaves were said to be sold on any one day.

By the start of the Christian era, the power and glory that was Delos was waning and soon afterwards the island fell into disuse. During the ensuing two millennia the Mute Stones were silent; then, with the arrival of French archaeologists in the 1870s they began to speak.

Unfortunately, now it is Delos' snakes rather than its stones which are deaf—be sure to stamp your feet loudly when walking through little-trafficked areas, for they can nip at the ankles.

Follow the pilgrim route to a ruined monumental gateway which leads into the Sanctuary of Apollo. Within are three temples dedicated to Apollo—there is also a temple dedicated to Artemis—and parts of a colossal marble statue of Apollo which was destroyed when a massive bronze palm tree fell on it. Close by is the Sanctuary of Dionysos with several phalli standing on pedestals with Dionysic friezes. Upstanding is a marble phallic bird symbolising the body's immortality.

Continue to the stunning Lion Terrace where five anorexic, archaic lions squat, apparently ready to pounce. Below this is the Sacred Lake and the palm tree which marks the spot of Apollo's birth.

Most visitors delight in that part of Delos which was occupied by artisans rather than gods. Their houses, close to the port, are a regular warren separated by narrow lanes lined by drains from 2,000 years ago and with niches for oil-lamps which illuminated the streets. The main road leads to the theatre which seated 5,500. It is unimpressive but superb views can be enjoyed from the uppermost of its 43 rows. Close to the theatre are grander houses surrounded by columns and exquisite mosaics, to which they owe their eponymous names, on the floor.

From here a gentle stroll leads to the summit of Mount Kynthos (368 ft/110 metres), from which the views of the ruins and the Cyclades are memorable. Descend by first passing the grotto of Hercules and then stopping at the Sanctuaries to the Foreign Gods.

Remember, Delos was a free port and in classical times practically the entire Levant traded—and probably banked—here under the tutelage of shrines erected to their divinities. All were welcome—as evidenced by the ruined synagogue, erected by the Phoenicians, in the northwest corner of the island.

And so to the waiting caique for the return to Mykonos. Forget the rough waves ahead and dwell on Kazantzákis: "Happy is the man who, before dying, has the good fortune to sail the Aegean Sea. Nowhere else can one pass so easily and serenely from reality to dream."

locals is not truly in form until haggling begins for the fishermen's catch, for which they have to contend with Petros the Pelican. Later in the day, it's back to the tourists again. Luxury liners shimmer on the horizon, turning slowly around their anchor leads while passengers are shipped ashore for shopping sprees, then horn-blasted reluctantly back, laden with sheepskins and gold.

It's possible to eschew all this and still enjoy Mykonos. There is **Delos**, the sacred island around which the Cyclades centre. There is a **Folklore Museum** and an **Archaelogical Museum** at either end of Mykonos's quay. Little Venice, a strip of cafés hanging over the sea behind the Town Hall, is the least frenetic part of town. Or one can strike inland to **Áno Méra**, the only real village, which houses Tourliani monastery, and toward Panormos bay, the 12th-century Paleokastro convent (indefinitely shut due to a collapsed roof).

Áno Méra, a trunk point for Mykonos' quieter beaches like **Kalafati**, has an airiness and lightness unusual for a hill village. As often happens on Mykonos, a British camera crew was here not long ago. They were filming a comedy about an English-Mykoniot marriage. As the wedding scene assembled, the church's courtyard filled with men in balloon-sleeved blousons and black vests and breeches while the women were veiled in gauzy pink gowns, their headpieces encircled by wreaths of tiny roses. Without the presence of cameras, this scene would be unlikely. Then again, traditional events like Greek weddings are not why most people come to Mykonos.

SYROS: The *braggadocio* in Syros's tourist literature must be forgiven: when Syros ceased to be Greece's premier port in the late 1800s, it lost a lot of status, too. The island remained the administrative and cultural capital of the Cyclades but when Piraeus sapped its steam as a trade centre, Syros was cut off and left, as one Greek guide says, "a grand but old-fashioned lady who lives on her memories of the good old days and on her half forgotten glories".

stormy awn on yros.

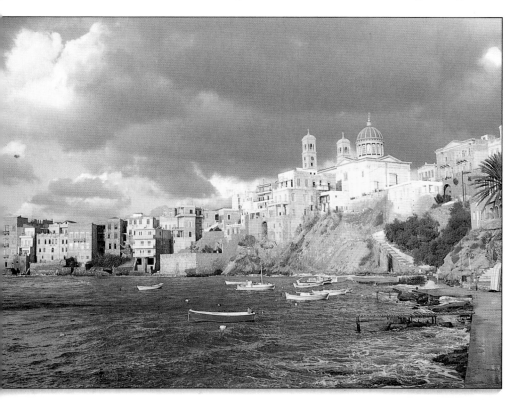

Which is a shame, for with its excellent inter-island ferry links and low-key but useful facilities (launderettes, and dry cleaners), Syros can provide a pleasant alternative to a one or two day stop-over in Piraeus when trying to cadge a ride on one of the eastern-bound boats.

What hurts the island is its modern port area, **Ermoúpolis**, dominated by shipyards. Syros calls itself the "Manchester of Greece", which doesn't help its resort image, either. Yet it does show how proud Syriani are of their industrial importance. Although little seems immediately appealing about Ermoúpolis, the amusement park just off the main pier, and the lights of the quayside tavernas give it a festive air at night. Behind the harbour itself a few grace-notes appear: the area called **Ta Vaporia** ("the ships") is where you'll find old mansions (a few doubling as cheap hotels) and the handier shopping streets. The main square, Plateia Miaoulis, is lined with the dignified, neoclassical hulk of buildings that attest, a little fadedly, to the grandeur Syros once possessed. The Apollon Theatre adjacent to the Town Hall, modeled after La Scala in Milan, is still a point of pride, although in need of a facelift. Ayios Nikolaos church houses the Monument to the Unknown Soldier.

A hilly prominence at the north end of the town, **Vrontdado**, is capped by the Greek Orthodox Anastasias Church; to the right and higher up is **Ano Syros**, the medieval Catholic quarter, dominated by Ayios Yiorgos church (adjacent is a British World War I cemetery). Around late October a joyous *panayiri*, (saint's festival) is celebrated here.

The name Syros may be derived from the name Osiris, a widely worshipped, originally Egyptian god of corn, the harvest, and the floods; scant remains of a temple to Isis, his wife, lie just outside of Ermoúpolis—which was named after an ancient Nile settlement. **Phoenikas**, a beachside town in the southwest, is named for the Phoenicians, who were probably Syros's first inhabitants.

The island's south is softer and greener than the north and has the highest concentration of beaches, namely **Poseidonía**, **Phoenikas**, and **Vári**. At Poseidonía is an Early Cycladic ruin (Ktesios, the father of Odysseus's swineherd, was the king of this city) and a series of churches. Pythagoras's teacher, Pherekydes, inventor of the sundial, was from here; several caves bear his name. Up the west coast, **Gallísas** and **Kini** are emerging resorts. The north of the island is busy with excavations, but thinly inhabited.

Giaros, the empty island to the north, was once an outpost for political exiles.

TINOS: A penchant for neon crosses and a quirky power supply make Hora on Tinos an eerie spectacle at night. When the power is restored after a cut, everyone hoots and cheers as the neon crosses flicker noisily back on as though some crank evangelist had staged a sound and light show for their sole benefit.

Tinos's pandemoniou *panayiri* (holy) days are on 25 March and August 15. Greeks from all walks of life pour off ferryboats to worship an icon of the Virgin within Hora's massive **Panayia**

The doorways and dovecotes of Tinos.

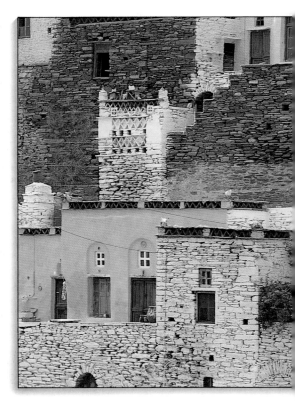

Evangelistria cathedral. In 1833, the icon, which a nun dreamt of, was thought to have been unearthed at the site where the church complex now stands. The marble steps leading to it are carpeted to accommodate those who go on their knees, and even sleep here.

Religion is a cottage industry; antiquity has fallen by the wayside. The site of **Poseidon's temple** opposite Tinos beach, the only known pre-Christian artefact, is neglected. The Tiniots' aesthetic sense has not been totally obscured, however. There is still one non-Christian figure to be found among the clutter of icons, man-sized poles of incense, and plastic holy water bottles for sale in the cathedral quarter: a beatifically stark rendering of the goddess Aphrodite, special to Tiniots in ancient times. Amidst the religious paraphernalia are also locally-produced jewellery and sculpture by Tinos's artistic community, a cut above the factory-made tourist junk.

Tinos's other hallmark is the dovecote. Hundreds of them occupy the empty spaces of its unmitigatedly bald interior, a tradition started by the Venetians. The pattern of triangular windows in the birdhouses is echoed over doorways and in fences and window-shapes, as it is on Mykonos, Andros, Serifos, and Sifnos. It is a pliant symbol which seems to represent anything from the shape of a sail to, certainly in Tinos's case, the Trinity. A bus ride across the island will also reveal some weird, mushroom-shaped, wind-sculpted rocks, and a proliferation of chapels, many newly constructed.

Pirgos, the marbleworkers' village, has a tiny art museum. It is the place to see Tiniot artists at work or hanging out in cafés. Of the several monasteries to see, **Katopoliani**, near **Istérnia**, is exceptional. Abandoned by monks, it's inhabited by a shy farm family whose daughter will heave the old door away from the chapel's entrance for the (very) infrequent visitor.

The south (west) coast settlement **Ormos Isternion** is a fabulous hike from Isternia. Take the marble steps to

Pilgrims journey from all over Greece to worship on Tinos.

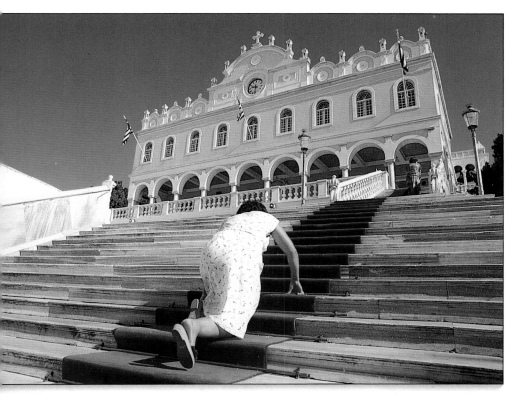

a dirt path which, after 10 minutes of dust and goat blockades, leads to a marble-cobbled path to the sea. Belying its reputation for more sombre attractions, Tinos doesn't lack for beaches; **Ormos Panormou** in the northwest is one of the best. **Kionia** (Tinos beach area) is a long decent stretch of beach, too, but commercialised.

ANDROS: The red Andros soil makes everything glow sienna at sunset, especially on its bare northern heights. Settled centuries ago by Orthodox Albanians who still speak their ancestral tongue, stone huts contrast with the whitewash and red tile of the other villages. Solitary eagles and long-haired goats may be spotted here, too. Farmland is divided by painstakingly built stone walls, unique for the pattern of triangular slates incorporated into them. From **Kalivari**, the northernmost hamlet, roads appear as no more than chalk marks, and a diaphanous blue haze unfolds in the late afternoon to wipe out the distinction between sky and sea.

Tourism is in its infant stages here and the only resort is **Batsí**, on a bay four miles (six km) south of **Gavrion**, the port. Batsí's "Glari" tourist office arranges rooms, as all else is pre-booked by package operators. There are also rooms in Hora, but only in summer. A mix of faded buildings encroached upon by villa developments, Batsí's bland tranquillity is no measure of the rugged grandeur that characterises the rest of Andros.

On the east coast, Andros's Hora, with cliffside promenades and Italianate administrative buildings, looks more Ionian than Cycladic. Its surprise is the Modern Art Museum, a few steps north of the main square. Works by modern Greek sculptors and artists such as Tombros, Bouzianis, and Manolidis, as well as an international group including Braque, are featured. Entrance is free, and the sculpture garden, tiny and exquisite, is imbued with a modernist sense of play.

Between Batsí and **Andros Town** runs a long, deep valley as majestic as the Levantine Bekaa. Terraces run all

Ploughing the red earth in Mesa Vounio, Andros.

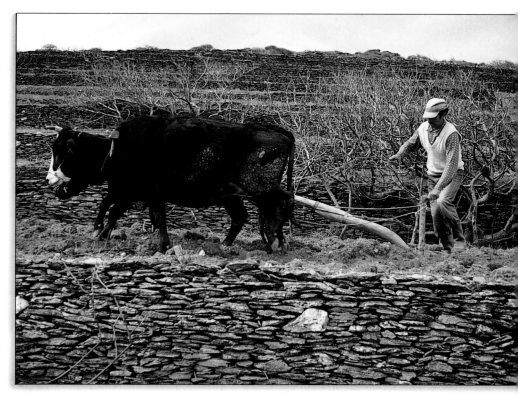

the way up its sides toward the island's highest mountain range, culminating at **Kovari**, 3,000 ft (1,000 metres). Sycamores, mulberries, and fruit tress grow in turn with acres of pine. Feeding all this verdure are a series of springs whirling down from the mountaintops, most notably at **Ménites**, where Panayia ti Koumulous is sited. The spring is considered sacred; possibly there was a major temple to Dionysos here. According to a pan-Cycladic legend, the water turned to wine each year on Dionysos's feast day.

However, Monastery Zöodóchou Pigí (Haghia) also claims to be on the most sacred spot. Situated in the hills northeast of Batsí, it is kept up by a fast-diminishing order of nuns guarding a library of precious sacred manuscripts. Adjacent is a fountain straddling the Zöodóchou Pigiu (life-giving spring).

Northwest of Haghia is the village of **Ayios Petros**, remarkable for its intact Hellenic *pyrgos* (tower). It's negotiated over a series of goat-tracks. Ayios Petros is alternatively reached from

sh.

Gavrion (just over an hour's walk); turn off the main road at "Camping Andros" signs south of the port, then follow the Ayios Petros road).

South of the Paleópoli-Andros road is the most spectacular of Andros' (13) ancient monasteries, **Panahrandou**, just past its 1,000th birthday, which still retains ties with Constantinople. Duration of the round trip on foot is about six hours (four by donkey) from **Messaria**, a valley town with the Byzantine Taxiarchis church; in summer a weekly coach excursion leaves from Batsí.

Paleópolis, the ancient capital, doesn't give much hint of its past; but the Hermes statue discovered here is displayed in Athens' National Museum. Korthí is the only sizeable village in the south, which is as remote, though greener, than the north; tourist accommodation is not commonplace.

There are four major beaches—Nimborion just south of the port, Batsí, Korthi, and Yialia (near **Stenies**)—plus a number of lovely remote coves like Ayios Pellos.

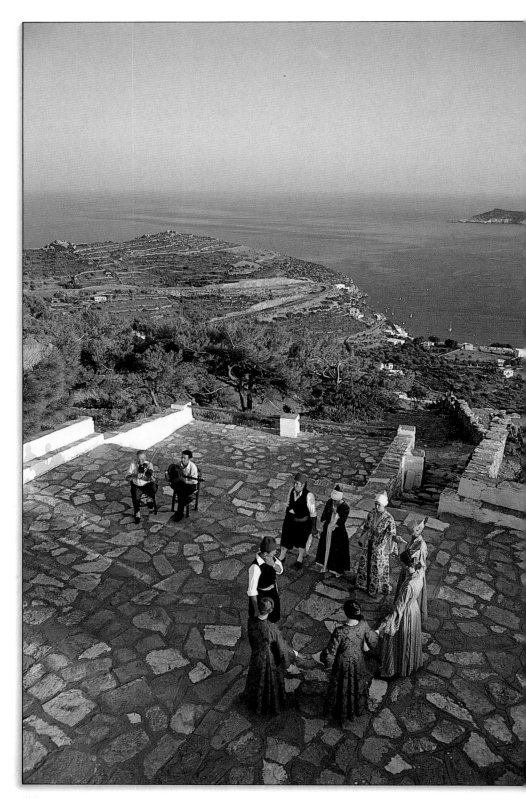

THE WESTERN CYCLADES

MILOS: Most of the island's coastline was formed when legs of lava dribbled from the now dormant volcano. The lava dripped into caves and overhung as it hit the sea, thrusting up weird rock formations that take on animal shapes when caught in the purple shadows of the setting sun. The island has always been extensively mined, once for obsidian, now for china clay. Only a few dusty beaches show the evidence; the landscape is not profoundly scarred.

Milos has graciously adapted to the thin stream of tourism it receives, concentrated in **Ádamas**, the port, and **Apolonía**, a fishing village in the northeast. On the map, Milos resembles a bat in flight; the island's total population is 4,500 but the western wing is nearly deserted.

One way to kill time while waiting for a boat in Ádamas is to take a hot springs bath. The entrance to the spa is a tiny door in the concrete wall near where the boats dock. Inside the Ayia Trianda church in Ádamas, Cretan-style icons dominate; links have always been strong between Milos and "the great island", most recently in World War II when Milos became the largest enclave of Cretan refugees.

The island's capital, **Plaka**, has both an Archaeological and a Folklore museum. The latter, set in an old house, is packed with artefacts from rock specimens and goat horns, to samples of native weaving. A hike to the chapel atop Plaka (follow signs for "Anna's Art Dresses") and the old Kastro walls gives a splendid views of the bay-bound Milos and, on clear days, as far as Paros and Naxos. Southwest of Plaka lies **Ancient Milos**, source of the island's most important artefacts, including the far-famed statue, the Venus de Milo, now found in the Louvre.

Milos was long famous for producing superb statuary, wrought by succeeding generations of a family called Grophon. Their beloved Venus was probably from the first century B.C. Like Tinos,

Milos never quarried its own marble, yet always produced marblework of the highest standard. The marble itself was probably Naxian or Parian. Examples of Miliot sculpting include a (copied) bust of Asclepius in the British Museum, and a Hermes in the Berlin Museum. More examples can be found in the National and Archaelogical Museums in Athens.

Also outstanding are an ancient theatre and early Christian catacombs. This seaside slope, the **Vale of Klima**, is littered with ruins from near Plaka to the hamlet of **Klima** by the sea; and excavations undertaken by the British school in Athens in the late 1800s uncovered a Dionysian altar and an ancient gymnasium.

Follow the catacombs signs, detouring onto the track to the theatre (sign in Greek only). The cavity in the field below marks where, in 1820, a farmer discovered the Venus statue (to the Greeks she was Aphrodite, goddess of beauty). Entrusted to the French consul to keep her safe from Turks, she has

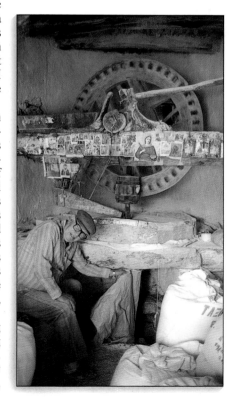

Left, traditional island entertainment. Right, the interior of a windmill.

been a major draw at the Louvre ever since; it is no wonder the Greeks have been unable to get her back.

The Dorian theatre is amazingly well preserved, probably due to its Roman renovation. Below the theatre lies one of the island's prettiest villages, Klima. From the sea, it looks like a minute Venice, with brightly painted boat-houses lining the shore. However, things weren't always so bucolic in the Vale of Klima. When Miliots refused to submit to Athenian rule during the Peloponnesian wars, all male inhabitants were slaughtered. **Tripiti**, meaning "serrated" or "perforated", was so named because it was the ancient burial ground, honeycombed with victims' graves. Those who had escaped returned to resettle the island.

Off the paved Tripiti-Klima road below the theatre turn-off are located the elaborate catacombs. Although cheerily lit by tiny electric lanterns, the frescoes and religious graffiti are hard to discern.

Apolonía, a restful base, is a good starting point for several short walks that give the full measure of Milos' eerie beauty. Just west along the coast (follow the town beach), four volcanic boulders do a ring dance atop a crest of sandstone; the feeling of movement is undeniable, though the rocks were cast and petrified here centuries ago. A half hour's walk away on the Ádamas road is **Filakopí**, the extensive rubble remains of a 4000 to 800 B.C. city whose frescoes are in the National Museum in Athens. Just south of "modern" Filokopí—a settlement of a few houses—is a narrow arm of water lined with widemouthed tunnels and caves. Two tiny sand spits would make the site a fantastic beach encampment, if they weren't in use as garbage tips.

Modern Miliots are possessed of a quiet sophistication and worldliness. (They boast of the first known school for women in the Aegean, no longer extant; no one, however, seems to know its founding date.) As skilled miners, many have travelled widely in pursuit of work, going to live as far afield as Australia, South Africa, and North

Map/ Text
Adamos/ Ádamas
Agios Andreas/ Ayiós Andreas
Apollonia/ Apolonía
Driopis/ Driopida
Galani/ Galini
Hrisopigi/ Hrissopigi
Korissa/ Koressia
Paleokastrou/ Paleokastro
Praso/ Prassa

Western Cyclades

25 km

America as obsidian became a less sought after commodity. But many Miliots come back. Greek Street in London is named for the Miliot ghetto that grew up in Soho, populated by refugees after the islanders were massacred by Turks in the late 1600s.

KIMOLOS: This island is an alluring presence for anyone who has been staying in Apolonía on Milos; the distance between the two is swimmable. Kimolos is a tiny isle—14 sq miles (35 sq km), with a population under 1,000—whose chalky cliffs, mined for Fuller's earth, turn a velvety rose at sunset and then seem to disappear in the evening haze. It takes only 30 minutes to ply the narrow channel between Kimolos and Milos by caique; landings are at Psathí. The Hora is a 20-minute walk inland. Ferryboats stop en route to and from neighbouring Milos.

Kimolos was once known as a pirates' hideout and today it provides refuge from the more crowded islands. Although blessedly undeveloped, it has several beaches with rentable rooms at **Alyki**, **Klima**, **Rima**, **Bonatsi**, and **Mavro Spilia**, and all sites are within easy walking distance. On the west coast is the hulk of the old fortress, Paleokastro, grimacing over Christos Church. To the southwest is **Ayios Andreas**, a now detached piece of Kimolos that has been excavated, revealing a significant and fascinating Mycenaen settlement. Prássa is a harbour-town on the north coast. Hora is the population centre, with only a medieval church and a tiny Folk/Archaelogical Museum for distraction.

SIFNOS: Resplendent with olive trees, bougainvillea, and wind-bent pines, Sifnos may well be the greenest of the Cyclades; it is so touted far and wide. The island's villages are flawlessly pretty, and the valleys surrounding them are filled with dovecotes and monasteries. Even the harbour, **Kamáres**, has a pleasant aspect. Its mouth is narrow, formed by opposing mountain ridges that look as though two dusty-flanked dinosaurs were backing toward each other unaware.

Milos, with the islet Antimilos peeking out behind.

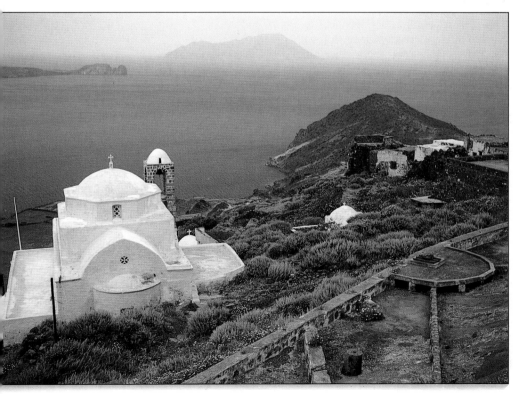

Sifnos's central range of mountains softens as it meanders south; toward the empty north, it spreads into sand-coloured pyramids. The main road strikes through a steep, deep valley from Kamares to sleepy **Apolonía**, the capital. Countless terraces cascade from the mountaintops; the pale soil makes it look as though a golden pudding was poured down over them, cooling in ridges along the way.

There is a tradition of pottery-making on Sifnos; potters still set out long racks of earthenware to dry in the sun. Weaving and jewellery-making are the other crafts, the jewellery-making harkening back to times when Sifnos was rich in gold and silver. According to legend, the Sifniots once neglected to offer the traditional golden egg to Apollo at Delphi. Apollo avenged them by submerging their mines under the sea; from this new paucity Sifnos gets its odd name, which means "emptiness".

Near Apolonía is **Artemonas** (the towns are named for the godly twins Apollo and Artemis), a handsome inland village set on a low escarpment; it is the island's most populous village. The oldest community is seaside **Kastro**. Kastro's sequestered medieval courtyards set it apart from other villages. Catalans and Venetians once ruled the city, and the walls they built are still in evidence, as are some remains of an ancient acropolis.

Sifnos' south shore settlements make tranquil beachside bases, but it is easy to find rooms in inland villages, too. **Faros**, on a clover shaped bay, abounds with pottery and churches. Sifnos's most important church, within **Hrissopigi Monastery**, is situated across a narrow passage of water at the south end of the bay, rejoined to the land by a footbridge. No longer in monastic use, basic rooms are let here in summer. Several of the island's ancient watchtowers flank the bay, one of which was a *faros* (lighthouse). For explanatory literature in English on Hrissopigi's "miraculous" icon and Sifnos's patron saint seek out the bookstore in Apolonía.

Platis Yialos is a beach settlement with a winter population of less than 30 and the place backpackers feel most at home. Camping on the beach may not be welcomed forever, though, as there is now a campground plus a number of pensions. Public notices primly advise that nudism is prohibited and that "cleanliness is the key to civilisation". Many glorious walks into the island's interior begin in this area. Footpaths connect it to Apolonía and **Ayios Andreas**, an excavated prehistoric settlement which is worth visiting.

A red paint-blazed footpath leads from Yialos to **Vathi**, a coastal town excluded from the road system (caiques in summer only). Its sandy-floored bay is edged by a number of small coves, yet it is a man-made feature which makes Vathi so visually stunning: **Taxiarchis Monastery**, poised over the bay as though ready to set sail.

SERIFOS: A long tail of land slashes out to enclose the harbour of Serifos. Consisting of little more than a handful of tavernas and homes (currently the only place to rent rooms), **Livádi** is an

Space beach...

agreeably quiet place to stay, with a necklace of beaches radiating westward from it. Hora clings closely to the mountain above and has a precipitous beauty emphasized by the starker, taller mountains that lead from it into the island's interior.

The only bus service is between Livádi and Hora, although this may someday change. The road is paved as far as **Pirgos**, in the north, and a wide dirt road loops all the way around past the fortified Byzantine **Taxiarhon Monastery**. Inside are a frescoed *katholikon* (chapel) and manuscript library. It is worth asking—at Serifos Travel in Livádi, for example—for someone to phone ahead to make sure the monastery is open. Many of the islanders know the priest personally and will be more than happy to oblige.

Another more scenic and walkable route to the monastery is via a footpath from Hora. It begins coastward from the square in upper Hora (marked "Kentarchos"), and consists of a wide paved and walled path that winds northeast.

Numerous small bays headed by tiny, empty beaches lie below. Habitation is sparse, and there are just a few small farms along the way.

After an hour's walk, the village of **Kallítsos**, or Kendarhos, as it is locally known, appears at the far side of a steep valley. Marigolds and palm trees grow between the older houses; some abandoned stone huts straddle the palisade of rock overlooking the sea. There are no tavernas, but there is a fresh water fountain along the main cement path. A track which later joins the paved road near Pirgos cuts northward from here, leading to Taxiarhon in about half an hour; it sits directly on the roadside, opposite a small chapel.

Galani, **Pirgos**, and **Panayia** are the rustic villages of the magnificent valley beyond Taxiarhon. You can cross this valley over a footpath up the spine of the hill that bisects it, or stick to the road. Panayia church, dedicated to the Virgin, is infamous for its 16 August feast-day *(Xilopanayia)*. Bachelors and maidens used to rush in pairs to be the first to

...and space house, Sifnos.

dance around the church's olive tree, for the first couple on that day to complete the dance would be allowed to marry during the year. The element of choice caused jealousy and feuding, and when the island's youth started beating off unwanted competition with rose-bay switches, a priest put a stop to the fighting but not to the custom: now the priest is always first to circle the tree.

Serifos abounds with beaches, all accessible only on foot, and all fantastically unspoiled. **Mega Livádi** in the southwest is the island's second port (buses cross to it in the summer only).

KITHNOS: After iron mining operations ceased, Kithnos lost its prime source of income, one which has not been supplemented by tourism from abroad. There is, however, a small influx of Athenians to the island each summer. Kithnií (or Kithniots) are mainly dairy and livestock farmers. Elderly residents and visitors frequent the old thermal baths at **Loutra**, on the north coast, therefore Kithnos is a supremely quiet island. It is also quite

barren. Bowers of blossoms cultivated in family gardens provide the only colour against the fawn of the landscape.

With night-time arrival in **Meríhas**, the port town, it is entirely possible everything will be shut. If so, there is a tree-lined beach to sleep on. Except for Loutra, Meríhas appears to be the only place with accommodation on Kithnos, at least for the moment. In summer, a "taxi-boat" runs from Merihas to Episkopi, Apokpousi, and Kolona Kithnos beaches.

Kithnos' landlocked **Hora**, four miles (six km) to the northeast, is exquisite. Whereas most Cycladic towns crawl spiderlike over the area, this Hora is on a rectangular plan. Enclosed wood-beamed bridges span across narrow streets to join two sides of the same house. In the passages underneath, the rock pavements are playfully decorated with whitewash fish leaping from stone to stone. There is a small, sweet-smelling oleander-filled main square. The fields at the back of the town rise gently away, dotted infrequently by farm-

Taxiarhis chapel on the trail between Hora and Driopida, Kithnos.

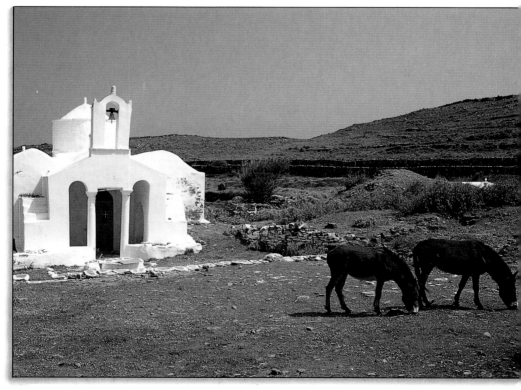

houses and tile-roofed chapels.

Just outside Hora is a "Wind Park", which helps supply the island's power (along with the "Solar Park" on the road to Loutra), and rarely a day passes when its windmills, cranks, and flags aren't spinning and pinging away furiously. A walk to Loutra (three miles/five km from Hora) goes through the rural central plain. Cows sedately cross the road, udders swinging, and long-haired sheep cluster under the rare tree. Above Loutra, at **Maroula**, excavations revealed the earliest known settlement in the Cyclades.

Byrokastro (Ancient Kithnos), is a seaside ruin where the foundations of the old town are visible. It is a two hour walk from Hora but obtain directions locally; the ruin does not appear on any map. A nearby islet fortress, glowering in the direction of Hydra and the Peloponnese, has also been excavated. The presence of so many graves on this islet points to a local belief that ghosts do not cross water. Sillika, the medieval capital, now called **Dryópis**, is split by

A pretty island girl.

a rush of water and has a chambered cave (Katafiki) linked in legend with the nereids.

KEA: The island's main town, **Ioulis** (Hora), rides a rounded ridge overlooking the island's northern reach; it was a spot chosen precisely for its inaccessibility from foreign and mainland marauders. Proximity to Attica signalled constant, if not always happy, relations with Athens. Kea (locally known as Tzia) is now a popular holiday spot with beach-loving Athenians, but its present inaccessibility from the rest of the Western Cyclades makes it a cumbersome destination for the dedicated island-hopper. As a result, little English is spoken and foreigners are welcomed for their novelty value.

Kea-bound boats leave from the mainland port of Lavrion, some 30 miles (50 km) from Athens, and land at **Koressía**, locally called **Livádi**. The jagged west coast has many sandy spits, several impossible to reach. **Pisses** and **Koundouros** are just two of the established resorts which have sprung up to accommodate the Athenian overspill.

Close to Koressía is the bayside village of **Vourkári**, with Ayios Irini church, a Minoan excavation, and an ancient road. The Lion of Kea, about four miles (seven km) southeast of Koressía en route to Ioulis, is a renowned statue carved out of stone, which may or may not date from the Archaic period; opinion is varied. The object of many local legends, the lion is almost 20 ft (six metres) long and has a smile on its face.

Almost all Keans live in Ioulis, the rest of Kea is made up of resorts rather than villages. **Otzias** is the busiest resort and has the pick of beaches. Follow past Otzias to the island's treasured **Kastriani Monastery**. Between them is Cape Kephala, site of the oldest Neolithic settlement in the Cyclades.

The four former Ionian cities—Koressía, Ioulis, Karthea, and Poiessa—testify to Kea's one-time political importance. The first two are near their modern namesakes. Poiessa is near Pisses and Karthea is near **Poles**, south of Kato Meria.

THE SPORADES ISLANDS

The Sporades—in English, "sporadic" or "scattered"—are a group of four, the northernmost Aegean islands on the Greek as opposed to the Turkish coast.

Skyros, the largest and in many ways the most interesting, is detached from the others, and while hopping among Skiathos, Skopelos and Alonissos is very easy, Skyros generally means a special trip to catch a ferry from Kymi on the mainland island Euboea. Skiathos alone among them has an international airport with several (charter) flights daily in summer, mainly from England, Germany and Scandinavia, and domestic connections. Skyros has an airport but other than a feeder service from Athens it is reserved for the Greek Air Force. Ferries and hydrofoils run from Volos and Ayios Konstantinos. Occasionally they will make Skyros their final port of call, but by then passengers will have been on board for some 11 hours and have lost their tempers.

Mainlanders have long recognised Skiathos' beaches as the best in the Aegean and made an annual pilgrimage. They are now outnumbered by foreigners, and the fact that there are shops which sell nothing but expensive fur coats (a little something that in summer one might have forgotten to bring along?) and will accept any conceivable credit card is a forecast of what to expect. In spite of a rich history, Alonissos is the least developed in terms of tourism while Skopelos, more recently and self-consciously the senior partner among the trio, is a compromise. Skyros is like a scaled-down version of Crete. It has an independent spirit and a deeply entrenched local culture impervious to the events swirling around it.

The islands are what's left of a mountain range which snapped away from the mainland in a geological convulsion and "sank". They lie within a narrow band where prevailing winds and other factors produce reliable rainfall and lush vegetation, notably pine forests. The rains do not intrude in summer. Instead, the *meltemi*, a northerly wind, helps to hold temperatures down a little.

The traditional trade route between the Mediterranean and the Black Sea via the Bosphorus passes the Sporades. As they've been ringed on charts since ancient times as possible ports in a storm, bad weather has brought unexpected and often unwanted callers, including distressed invasion fleets (e.g. Xerxes) and pirates. Yet major archaeological sites are surprisingly few.

World War I produced a postscript to the strategic location: it was on a convoy heading for Gallipoli that the poet Rupert Brooke died. Skyros rose into sight, and it was here that they stopped to bury him.

Preceding pages: a somewhat ancient ruin; still-life of a girl. Left, empty cafés are an uncommon sight.

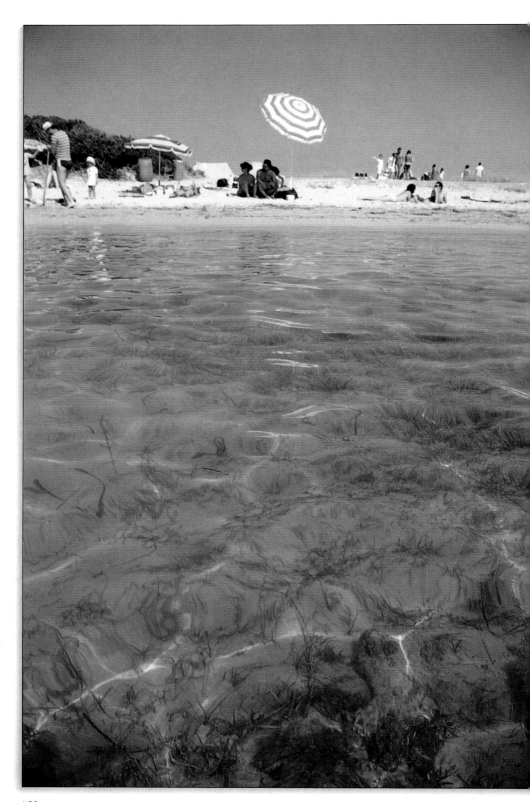

THE SPORADES ISLANDS

SKIATHOS: The scythe of Koukoukanariés is used as evidence on thousands of postcards that the Aegean can produce the kind of beach normally associated with the Caribbean. Propriety would prevent as many postcards from featuring **Krassi** (colloquially, "Banana Beach") because it caters for nudists. The fact that no one cares whether bathers at Banana strip off or not is typical of the easy-going, relaxed nature of Skiathos as a whole.

The island has beaches for all occasions, not least because some will always be sheltered wherever the wind is coming from. **Koukoukanariés** and **Banana** are near neighbours at the end of the twisting 11-mile (18-km) coast road from the town; there are dozens along it, many with a taverna or at least a kiosk selling drinks and sandwiches. A path leading down from the road usually promises a beach at the bottom, possibly the kind of secluded cove which is the stuff of holiday fable.

Round-the-island boat trips pass the rocky and otherwise inaccessible northern shoreline and in particular **Kastro**, the abandoned citadel which for centuries was a haven from predators. The boats stop for swimming and lunch. A moped or hired car—or perhaps a mule and infinite patience—would be necessary to follow the unpaved road looping through the mountains. It provides stunning views as well as the chance to pop into monasteries which, with Kastro, are more or less the only buildings of historic interest.

The bluff above the under-used beach at the end of the very busy airport runway has produced fragments suggesting a pre-historic settlement, but neither it nor the rest of the island has ever been properly excavated.

The port village is lively at night, probably the most important consideration after the beaches for the type of visitor which Skiathos attracts in intimidating numbers in August. The preferences of the fast-living set change constantly, but it is not difficult to spot which places are in vogue at any particular time.

The bright lights are along **Papadiamantis**, the road which dissects the two hills on which the town stands, and along the *Paralia* (pavement) which skirts the fishing port. The cobbled alleys above the port provide more of the same as well as some quieter places.

Expect restaurants rather than tavernas and be prepared to pay accordingly. Plate-smashing and other forms of sociable anarchy are at a safe distance out of town; to the fury of taxi drivers and the regular bus operators, the tavernas concerned lay on special transport from the ferry terminal. Nothing happens on Skiathos that Dimitris Mathinos, a retired sea captain, doesn't know about or can't fix. He has an office at the foot of Papadiamantis.

The permanent population of 4,500 includes an expatriate colony in lovely houses on the **Kanapitsa peninsula**. The fact that they want nothing done to improve the deplorable state of the access road says something, as do doubts about the new—and larger—airport terminal building.

The island hardly needs to be able to admit more visitors than already arrive between mid-July and mid-September. Skiathos has many devotees who return year after year—they know better and adjust their timing to suit.

SKOPELOS: An enduring image of Skopelos, for anyone who has been there in August, is the way in which the famous local plum is picked, examined, wiped and, before being popped into the mouth, given a final polish with the thumb. And who, on sailing or driving along the coast between Glóssa and Skopelos town and knowing a local tale, would not be on the look-out for the spot which best fitted the dénouement?

It seems that a rampaging dragon had proved itself to be invulnerable to conventional weapons. The local priest, one Yorgios, was implored to direct a sermon at the beast, the islanders having heard enough of them to think that it might do the trick. Finding itself as bored as they had been, the dragon reared away and fled until it could go no further. The pious Yorgios followed doggedly and, on cornering his quarry on a cliff-top, prepared to deliver another one. Despairing at the prospect, the dragon dived off, and the impact on landing created one of the indentations which are characteristic of the deeply rugged coastline.

Visitors waiting in Volos for the ferry to Skopelos (the alternative is to fly to Skiathos and catch a ferry from there) could usefully call at the **island museum** to look at the contents of a grave discovered on the island fairly recently. The gold crown and ornate weapons almost certainly belonged to Stafylos, a Cretan who colonised the island and went on to become its king.

The island's distinguished past is not so much demonstrated by prominent historical sites as by the exceptionally fine houses in **Skopelos Town**, a handsome amphitheatre around a harbour which, unfortunately, can let off ferocious smells.

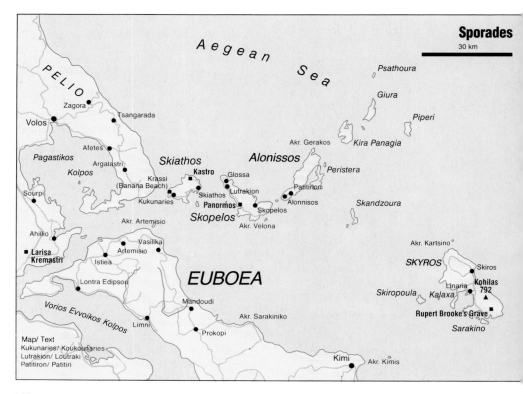

152

Glóssa, the island's other town, is something of an oddity in that the inhabitants have a pronounced dialect which, together with houses whose features are not like other island architecture, suggests that at some time they immigrated from Thessaly. They seem to have made themselves welcome; other islanders refer approvingly to their "exaggerated hospitality".

The only road on the island runs between the port of **Loutraki**, where Glóssa used to stand before it moved up the mountain for safety's sake, and Skopelos Town. It is an attractive run which includes a number of hamlets and **Panormos Bay**, where there are a few remains of a city which probably existed in 500 BC. The wise money is on the dragon having made its desperate departure somewhere around Panormos Bay.

ALONISSOS: This island is full of ghosts whispering what might have been. On the hill above **Patitiri**, the port where the ferries from the other islands land, is the Hora (also called **Alonis-**

sos), the former capital destroyed by an earthquake in 1965. Nearly a quarter of a century afterwards, mundane possessions like broken kettles were still visible among the ruins, ghoulishly reminiscent of the Marie Celeste.

Alonissos seems to have been ever thus: the previous capital, Ikos, the name by which the island as a whole was known in classical times, literally disappeared when the ground on which it stood toppled into the sea. The submerged remains off Kokkinokastro beach are an important part of a "marine conservation park" which may be explored with a snorkel but not with scuba tanks (a general rule in the Aegean to prevent pilfering).

Of the famous wines which were once shipped all over ancient Greece in urns stamped "Ikos", there is no longer any trace. Yet in 1970, paleolithic traces were found which could mean that Alonissos was singled out for habitation before any other island in the Aegean, perhaps as early as 100,000 B.C., and it was considered a prize over which

A boat under construction; Skopelos is in the background.

THE FALTAITS MUSEUM

The Faltaits Museum is located near the northeastern edge of Skyros, high on a ridge atop massive stone fortifications built thousands of years before the founding of Rome. The museum is housed in a mansion built as the Faltaits family home in the late 1800s near to the original site of a temple to the goddess Astarte (Ashtar).

It seems only fitting that it is here that the oldest of the old *megala strata* (upper class families), on an island even Homer and Plutarch referred to as "ancient", should have collected innumerable artefacts which eloquently present the history, tradition, and mythology of Skyros.

Manos Faltaits founded the museum in 1964. A well-known sociologist, painter, poet, writer, and peace activist, he has written several pamphlets and a fascinating book about the island. Manos has also conducted seminars about future community life based on traditional life, and his family home has become a base and a working monument to these ideals.

"Huddled on the northern tip of the island," a 19th-century visitor to Skyros noted, "the inhabitants think only of how best to safeguard themselves against their [Turkish] masters' greed and against piracy, which is hereditary to the Greeks." The solution was to have a second house within the city fortress used exclusively "for storing personal belongings...whole rooms filled to capacity with copper and earthenware."

The rooms of the Faltaits Museum are laid out in a similar fashion, the size and design resembling that used by Skyrians today. Fine porcelain plates decorate shelves and hang on walls, but the most distinctive features in the museum's first room are the tiny wooden tables surrounded by miniature, intricately carved wooden chairs. Skyrians were, and still are, craftsmen of renown. Walk down any village street today and, through lace curtains, one can glimpse household items carved with immaculate skill.

Some of the older, better pieces have been collected and are scattered throughout the museum. One superb example is found in the next room, the kitchen and above that, the sleeping area, both of which are framed by carved wood. Traditional clothing, normally stored in chests, is displayed on the walls here: the silken garb of upper class men, baggy pantaloons still worn by Skyrian shepherds, and the richly embroidered wedding and bridesmaid dresses with cuffs and hemlines sewn in golden threads.

Skyrian embroideries are particularly distinctive and, as such, are respected throughout Greece. A glass case in the central room shows them at their finest—at once colourful, imaginative, fanciful and serious.

Designs are deeply symbolic: the pomegranate, representing fertility because of its many seeds; or interwined snakes, symbolising protection because they are so feared. The tree of life, the church, the fountain of immortality, the ship, the nymph, and the wedding couple are others, each carrying powerful messages of Skyrian history, legend, mythology, religion, or superstition. Other glass cases contain carved wooden spindles and spoons and bread stamps, or lavish jewellery fit for royalty.

The last room records, in photographs and paintings, the Skyrian goat dance, part of the three-week festival which takes place in the marketplace and back streets of the capital. The most important feature of this room is, however, a remarkable collection of rare books, the oldest dated 1503, about 50 years after movable type was first used.

A professor of Greek archaeology at Cambridge who visited the Faltaits Museum called it a "splendid collection," and another from Oxford referred to it as "most intriguing, truly superb." But the real voice of authority is the museum itself, one of the finest small folklore museums in Greece. The workshop produces hand-painted plates depicting designs of the Skyrian embroideries as well as pillowcases and tablecloths with these designs.

Visitors can sit and chat with Manos Faltaits and his elegant wife Anastasia on the terrace which overlooks the clear and still clean Aegean. Ask Manos about *Daismos*, an ancient way of community living—and more, and an intellectually challenging dialogue is sure to develop.

Philip of Macedon and the Athenians fought bitterly. An airport which might have transformed the island by opening it up to international tourism stands forlornly unfinished.

The way the island has adjusted to its unrealised potential and bad luck is something for which many visitors should be grateful. It is the least developed of the Sporades, a much quieter island surrounded by an interesting collection of islets. One of them, **Youra**, is home to a unique breed of wild goat and has a cave full of stalactites and stalagmites which it pleases the islanders to believe was once occupied by a protective cyclops.

The fishing is excellent too, and many of the swordfish which provide some of the best eating in the Sporades are taken in the waters around Alonissos. In the absence of proper roads, apart from the one built to serve the ill-fated airport, caiques are the most practical form of transport. The terrain is rugged and walking accordingly quite demanding.

The route from Patitiri up to the site of

the 1965 earthquake looks and is steep, but there is a taverna with a large verandah halfway up which, for the view alone, makes the effort worthwhile. Should you go by taxi, the driver might well pop into the taverna along with you for a snack and a song.

SKYROS: The main character in Skyros's Carnival goat dance, staged just before Easter, is a *yeros* (old man) who wears a mask made out of goat skin and by shaking his hips makes some kind of music—he thinks—out of about 60 sheep bells hanging from his waist. The second figure is a young man dressed up and behaving as a woman.

Foreign visitors enjoying the spectacle ought to know that the third figure, a buffoon who has a large bell strapped to his back and blows into a sea shell, represents, well, a foreigner. Islanders might politely add that he is specifically a western European of the 17th century.

Visitors should not take the mockery to heart. Skyros does not have to put up with so many of them that their presence becomes intrusive, and in many ways

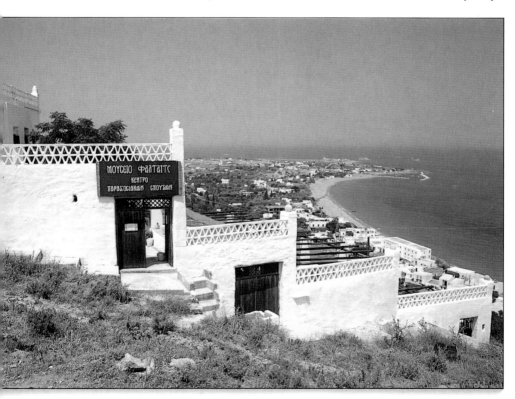

the island goes on as it has always done.

Until recently, there were islanders who would not eat beef, and there are still some who won't drink cows' milk. The origins of this ancient taboo lie in a pagan ox-cult.

Although the presence of the Greek Air Force does not intrude upon the visitor, Skyrians are adamantly against the military being on their island. Frequent demonstrations in the square and petitions passed round any local gathering attest to a fairly united front on this topic. In **Aspous**, a village of about 30 people, three ship owners went on strike for two hours recently and put up signs saying that they did so to protest what they see as the increasing militarisation of their homeland.

Skyros has a unique breed of miniature horse, about the same size as the Shetland pony, which is thought to have existed for 17 million years. They used to roam wild except when needed to help with the threshing, the signal for a battle of wits with nominal owners who first had to find them and then rope them

in. These tiny animals make improbable entries in horse races which—when they happen at all on Skyros—are usually staged in July.

Older islanders will still wear traditional clothes as a matter of course, and behind their characteristic pebbled entrances the cubist houses contain amazing collections of craft work and other prized objects, many of them originally piratical booty. Carved wooden furniture is often, like the horses, rather too small to be practical, which the islanders themselves seem to acknowledge by hanging a lot of it on the wall.

The ancient Greeks knew Skyros well, and it has a walk-on part in mythology as the place where Theseus was thrown to his death—off the rock which is the landmark of **Skyros Town**—and the baby Achilles was brought up disguised as a girl. He did not carry off the role very well, giving himself away when offered, while in the company of female playmates, the choice between jewellery and a sword.

Skyros was probably two islands originally, the halves joining where there is now a road linking **Lináría**, the port, with Skyros Town. The southern sector is barren, and visitors are unlikely to venture into it unless in search of a quiet beach or to see **Rupert Brooke's grave** at **Tris Bóukies**. Day trips to Brooke's grave can sometimes be arranged from the capital.

Life in the town is played out on what is effectively a stage, a raised square where there is the option of joining the promenade or finding a table, ordering a drink, and watching it. This takes place within the shadow of the Gibraltarian rock which was Theseus' undoing. As an obvious stronghold, it was adopted for use by whomever ruled Skyros, and the evidence of their presence lies like layers of a cake.

The ruins are inanimate, however, while the little horses, the shadow of the cult of the ox, the crafts and even the fun still to be derived from an absurd 17th-century western European all show the extent to which Skyros' strong sense of identity has so far, at least, resisted foreign blandishments.

Left and right, characters from the Skyros carnival.

156

ΚΥΡΙΕ ΙΗCΟΥ ΧΡΙCΤΕ
ΕΛΕΗCΟΝ ΜΕ

THE NORTHEAST AEGEAN ISLANDS

The islands of the northeast Aegean are grouped together for geographical convenience. The islands to the north, Thassos, Samothraki, and Limnos, bear scant resemblance to their grander neighbours to the east, and have little in common with each other either. Thassos belongs to the Prefecture of Kavala on the mainland, Samothraki to that of Evros, and Limnos to that of Lesvos. These islands for the most part look to mainland Greece for culture, history and now, food or supplies.

The eastern islands of Samos, Hios, and Lesvos at one time played a leading role on the world's stage, providing much-needed links between Asia Minor and western civilisation. Samos and Hios were in fact, once joined to the coast of Asia Minor and even today only a light craft is need to sail between Greece and Turkey. Politically, however, the waters are deep and it is best to tread warily if wishing to visit both countries within a short time span.

The eastern islanders were superb sailors and merchants, establishing trading stations throughout the Mediterranean. The arts and sciences flourished. Sappho of Lesvos and Pythagoras of Samos are only two who achieved world-wide prominence.

Today it is transport rather than culture which divides the islands. Limnos, Samothraki, Hios, and remote Ikaria are served by few ferries; as a result, they are comparatively free of tourists. Samos, on the other hand, could be classed as an honorary Dodecanese island due to its popular caique service to and from the holy—and very much visited—island of Patmos. As air links with the rest of Europe become more commonplace; so too will the islands with well-placed international airports. Lesvos already is a favourite with discerning package tour companies although it is fairly safe to say that the islands of the northeast—scattered, far-flung, and fiercely independent—will remain free from all but the more adventurous tourists for some time to come.

Preceding pages: A monastery on Hios; tomatoes strung up to dry in Pirgi, Hios. Left, an old woman meditates on her past.

THE NORTHEAST AEGEAN ISLANDS

THASSOS: The ancient claim to fame of the small, green island of Thassos is the "black" wine that disabled brutish Cyclops, allowing Odysseus to escape him. Gold, silver, and even amethyst and opal were once mined here. Marble, which is still actively excavated, and honey, are the island's other notable resources. The island also claims to be the birthplace of Demeter, goddess of the harvest.

Thassos, technically part of (East) Macedonia, was once a centre of panhellenistic worship, evidenced by a string of ruins adjoining modern **Thassos Town** (Limenas). Signposts point the way first to the Hellenistic theatre (ancient dramas every Saturday in summer), on to a Genoese fort and hilltop sanctuaries to Apollo, Athena, and Pan; "secret stairs" snake back down to Hercules's and Dionysos' temples, and the Agora.

Further along are a shrine to Artemis and a Roman road. The relics fill Thassos' **Archaeological Museum**.

Thassos is popular with (German) caravan tourists, but they congregate mainly in a small west coast area, leaving ample stretches of the island peaceful and wild. In the north, olive trees spread across the lower valleys, beehives humming beneath them, while the mountain slopes are grasshopper-green with pine trees.

Travel around the island is inevitably clockwise or counter-clockwise, since only one road rings it. The first town clockwise from Thassos, **Panayía**, is filled with fountains carved from plane trees, and rests above a long, gold stripe of **Chyrssi Ammoudis beach**.

The riot of conifers and fruit trees then fades, for in 1986, southern Thassos' forest land was destroyed by fire. Some think it was maliciously set by hotel developers looking for cheap land clearance. The villages and a thin fringe of vegetation around them were saved; the rest is wasteland.

Alyki, a fisherman's cove with a small neck of beach, encompasses an ancient marble quarry and shrine. Down the coast is the startlingly modern **Monastery Archangelou**. Both **Potos** and **Limenária** (constructed for German mining engineers brought by the Turks around 1900) are large, new towns given over to tourism. Macedonian **Theologos** and **Maries** in the mountains, laden with flowers and grapes, are dominated by scallop-cut slate roofs.

Theologos was the medieval capital (and home to the island's liberation leader, Hadzigiorgis), for inland towns were safer from pirates than coastal villages. The collective memory of invasion is so potent that villagers still affix bars to their windows for extra protection. The burnt areas shimmer with strange green insects with opal wings which love to sun on the rocks.

Thassos' edges are unevenly fluted with beaches, and dolphins play off the east coast. Divers may want to check out the claim that Thassos harbour's floor is sheer marble. Thassos is accessible only by boat from Kavala and Keramoti, on the mainland.

SAMOTHRAKI: Also known as Samothrace, this is the island from which Poseidon is said to have watched the Peloponnesian wars. The forest has since receded from the top of **Mount Fengári**, Poseidon's watchpoint, leaving a bald, craggy pate exposed to the rough winds that dance up its north face. Yet the steep ascent up Fengári (5,400 ft/1,650 metres), from Therma is largely sheltered by plane and fruit trees, and supplied with water from the cataracts that spin down its sides. The summit view—if the haze isn't too thick—extends to Athos and the Ida mountains of Turkey.

From Kavala on the mainland (the only link), ferries stop at **Kamariótissa**, a stepping stone to the older Hora (Samothraki) three miles (five km) to the east. The houses are densely packed, but many of them are occupied by pigs and goats. Shaped roughly like an aspen leaf, the island is sparsely inhabited; only the western half has a paved road. The northwest is most heavily popu-

Left, a baptism is a community event.

lated; the road fades at the **Therma** turn-off, a spa town shaded by a thick web of planes. One German and one Bulgarian doctor treat the rheumatics who bathe in its springs.

Among the permanent residents are several Russian-born Greeks who arrived in the 1920s ethnic exchanges; the women wear a distinctive black wimple. One man plays a goatskin bagpipe for villagers, who gaily dance on arthritic feet. The coast beyond Therma is flat and wooded, making it prime camping turf for young Greeks in souped-up Volkswagen buses, many of them artists and musicians.

Just west of Therma is **Paleopoli** (which means old city), site of the Great Sanctuary of the Gods and source of the celebrated statue Nike, the "Winged Victory of Samothrace". The statue resides at the Louvre, but there is a reproduction in the site's museum (closed Tuesdays). The sanctuary yielded a trove of archaeological finds charting early Greek religious practices. Its excellent condition—the old-

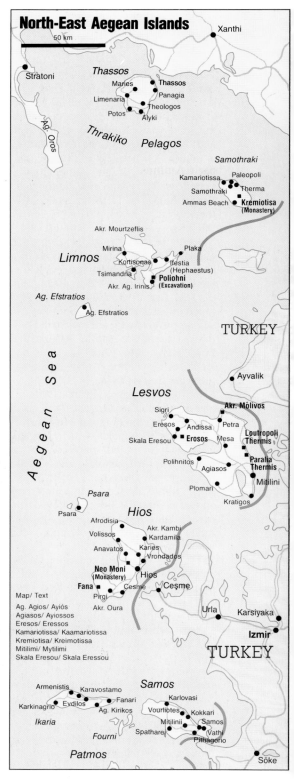

North-East Aegean Islands

50 km

Xanthi

Stratoni

Thassos

Maries · Thassos
Panagia
Limenaria
Theologos
Potos
Alyki

Thrakiko Pelagos

Ag. Oros

Samothraki

Kamariotissa · Paleopoli
Samothraki · Therma
Ammas Beach · **Kremiotisa**
(Monastery)

Akr. Mourtzeflis

Mirina · Plaka
Limnos Kortisonas · Ifestia
(Hephaestus)
Tsimandria · **Poliohni**
Akr. Ag. Irinis · **(Excavation)**

Ag. Efstratios

· Ag. Efstratios

TURKEY

Aegean Sea

· Ayvalik

Lesvos

Sigri
Eresos · Andissa · Petra · **Akr. Mólivos**
Skala Eresou · **Erosos** · Mesa · **Loutropoli Thermis**

Polihnitos · **Paralia Thermis**
Agiasos
Mitilini
Plomari

Kratigos

Psara

Psara

Hios

Afrodisia
Volissos · Akr. Kambi
Kardamila
Anavatos · Karies
Vrondados
Neo Moni
(Monastery) · Hios
Fana · Cesme · **Çeşme**
Map/ Text · Pirgi
Ag. Agios/ Ayiós · Akr. Oura
Agiasos/ Ayiossos
Eresos/ Eressos · Urla · Karsiyaka
Kamariotissa/ Kaamariotissa
Kremiotissa/ Kreimiotissa · **Izmir**
Mitilimi/ Mytilimi
Skala Eresou/ Skala Eressou · **TURKEY**

Samos

Armenistis · Karavostamo · Karlovasi
Karkinagrio · Evdilos · Fanari
Ag. Kirikos · Vourliotes · Kokkari
Ikaria · Mitilinii · Samos
Fourni · Spatharei · Vathi
Pithagorio

Patmos · Söke

166

est artefacts date to 700 B.C.—shows earlier Roman refurbishment.

The villages of the south coast rarely see visitors. Olives, onions, and grapes are cultivated under the rocky glare of Fengári. The older olive trees' trunks have turned spongy and hollow, and it's not uncommon to see four or five sheep grazing with their heads stuck inside them. A haul over the dirt extension passing these villages ends at an idyllic beach, **Ammos**.

There is no settlement here; only caves, and a taverna which is sometimes open. However, Samothrakians make an occasional pilgrimage (five hours by foot from the nearest town, a rough 90 minutes by car or motorbike) to give thanks at nearby **Kremiotissa**, an 11th-century chapel perched on a high rock shelf. A series of smaller hills spans the distance between it and Ammos, and it's possible to climb to the church in about two hours.

LIMNOS: Except for the alluvial plains of Thessaly, Limnos may be one of the flattest patches of Greece to be found. A few hills hug the bays around **Mírina**, the main town; otherwise, Limnos is full of military posts and grain fields; wheat, tobacco and cotton grow here.

On a tour of the island, it's impossible to miss the garish scarecrows, dressed like medieval knights or Hell's Angels, the totem of Limnian agriculture. Typical of the Hellespont region (the Dardanelles), the island gets a great deal of wind and cloud—but not much rain. Shellfish, ouzo, and merchant shipping are sources of income.

There is not much of substance to hold tourists' interest, despite Limnos's rich history. Jason and the Argonauts stopped here and their sojourn is intertwined with island lore. Just before their arrival, as a punishment for forgetting Aphrodite, the women were cursed with an odour so repulsive the men planned to seek new wives. The outraged females slaughtered their male relatives, but Hypsipyle hid her father, and was castigated for it. She alone welcomed the Argonauts, and later bore Jason's son, Euneus, the island's future king.

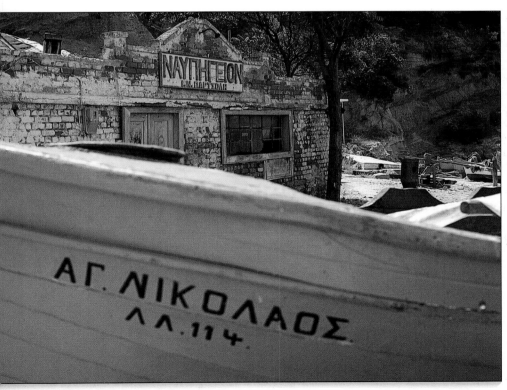

Marulla was a 19th-century woman agitator against the Turks; her statue is at **Kotsinas**. The Poliohni excavation, on the east coast, shows evidence of Limnian life as early as 4000 B.C. (a local shepherd unofficially keeps the gate). A remote temple to Hephaestus, god of the forge fire, sits near his namesake town in the northeast.

Limnos also worshipped the Kaberoi, obscure demigods believed to protect sailors. Hephaestus' Kaberoion is claimed as Greece's oldest sanctuary. Mírina's **Archaeological Museum** displays all local finds.

Mírina's festive market street leads to the 1000 B.C. **fortress**, where 15th-century Venetians fought Suleiman. Beaches edge the island's southwest claw (the best is just southeast of Mírina), and there are spas at **Therma** and **Plaka**. **Tsimandria**, 14 miles (22 km) to the east, has some basic resort accoutrements; the rest of the island is grimly unappealing and public transportation is almost non-existent.

AYIOS EFSTRATIOS: Limnos is the source of vital supplies to this lonely wedge of land in an unsettled reach of the Aegean. Everything from diesel fuel to fresh melons is imported on Ayios Efstratios.

The island is really just a single village which comprises 200 residents, 10 soldiers, two cars, one café, and one taverna. In 1968, a severe earthquake split the island, killing half the population and levelling most buildings; hence the uncharacteristic rows of identical housing, provided as emergency aid.

Farming is nearly impossible, but the Manicakis family have arable land in the throat of the valley adjacent to the town, orchards, and a vegetable and flower garden. Thyme and basil spout wild from the stone walls. Vasilis is retired now, but spent his youth working on passenger ships, as many islanders once did. Now, the younger generation has generally deserted Ayios Efstratios, including Vasilis' children. His wife smiles as a neighbour leads a newborn colt past her hedge, and sets aside the vegetables to sell to the grocer.

Vasilis Manicakis with Ayios Efstratios in the background.

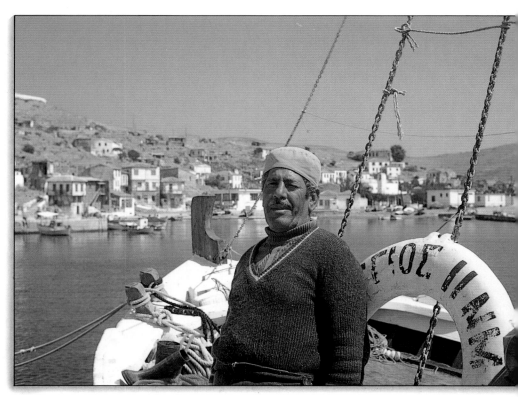

Goats and hens have taken over the shell of the enormous old school. Now classes are held in a private house; the children throw a party each year to welcome the teacher from Limnos.

No one has excavated Ayios Efstratios as the island's ruins are painfully recent. The village chapel's graves all date after 1968, the earlier ones destroyed in the earthquake. An odd pair of monuments occupy a nearby hillock: a shrine to the perished islanders, and a German soldier's grave.

Merchant shipping and fishing are the island's lifeblood. Tourists are an oddity, and must inevitably stay in the one hotel. Neither of the two beaches, 15 and 90 minutes' walk south respectively, will likely contain another soul.

LESVOS: Mytilíni, the capital of Lesvos (natives now call the entire island Mytilíni or Mytilene), has a charged, metropolitan atmosphere, and is a good place to get a reading on the temper of this proud island. There's always been a separateness—if not arrogance—about Mytilíni, the island: its tallest mountain at 3,300 ft (1,000 metres) is called Olympus.

Old Mytilíni seems little changed since the 18th century, when it grew to house the pasha's shipyard workers. Its focal point, the **Old Market**, is a long, dusty street crammed with tiny shops. However, on Sunday afternoons, when spates of laughter issue from within the shuttered houses, it's only the televised antics of the "Pink Panther" film character tickling the collective funnybone.

The enormity of the island (Greece's third largest) means far-flung villages. Between them lie 11 million olive trees producing 45,000 liquid tonnes of oil yearly. Shipbuilding, carpentry, and ceramics are still important, but none rival the olive, especially as it complements Mytilíni's second industry: tourism. The nets are laid out in autumn, and as soon as the tourists leave, Mytilíni's black gold begins to drop.

Mytilíni's **Archaeological Museum** sorts the puzzle of its past, along with the **Byzantine** and **Popular Art Museums**. They might be useful, therefore, in planning tours. The northern coastal villages and their beaches draw the most visitors. **Mólivos** (Mithímna), wrapped around the foot of a Genoese castle, was once graphite-rich. Its homes, built of stone (Macedonian style) with pine window jambs, have frescoed or carved wood ceilings. Guided and unguided donkey treks leave from Mólivos weekly in summer.

The towers of **Thermís'** natural spas make it architecturally unique. In **Petra**, an arty beach town, the Women's Agricultural/Touristic Cooperative promotes women's financial independence, and arranges accommodation in rural spots.

Further west, **Eressós** (the best beach is Skala Eressóu) was the home of Sappho. The inhabitants of Andissa supposedly buried Orpheus's head when it washed ashore with his lyre. The Petrified Forest around **Sígri** was transformed by lava; the ash-dusted, hardened stumps are scattered, but the enriched soil produces wildflowers that attract furious clouds of butterflies to the area. **Ayiossos**, a medieval hill vil-

The beach at Gera, Lesvos.

LITERARY LESVOS

Up at the Genoese castle a group of strolling players were doing Chekhov in Greek under floodlights. The following week, according to posters, there would be a touch of Dario Fo. Not quite what you would expect at a package holiday resort. But this was Mólivos, magnet for culture vultures, on Lesvos, the cradle of the arts.

A kind of Hellenic St Ives, the village has long attracted writers, poets, artists and thinkers, reflecting the island's intellectual heritage. Beguiling as Circe, Lesvos gives off a very special vibe, an inspirational magic.

Mytilíni, "where burning Sappho loved and sung" is of course best known as the birthplace of the extraordinary poetess, the original Lesbian. Sappho (*Sapfo* in Greek) was born in Eressós, a well-educated aristocrat and a free-thinking woman—remarkable elsewhere in Greece, around 600 B.C. But Lesvos, known as the Red Island by other Greeks because of its leanings towards Communism, has always had a history of democratic ideals; a quest for knowledge and literary freedom.

Plato called Sappho the tenth muse. Her lyrical outpourings and erotica, usually written to the women at her academy, however, were deemed too hot to handle by Pittacus, the contemporary ruler. Her work was ordered to be burned and only fragments of her nine books of poetry have survived, although some of her writings were discovered among papyrus rolls in Egypt only a hundred years ago.

The Greeks say she had a bad Press. Her condemnation was political: she was too smart for comfort, a threat to democratic reforms. Who knows? She and her pupils followed Aphrodite, warrior as well as love goddess. Whatever her sexual proclivities, Sappho was way before her time, introducing new poetic metre and, with the poet Alcaeus, giving lyric verse new depths. Alas—she threw herself from a rock for the love of a young man. A statue of her stands in the harbour at the main port while gay women pay homage to her at Eressós.

Lesvos has always been a cultural oasis, according to the Ionian poet Anacreon: "An island with a touch of class". Mytilíni people—they don't like being called Lesvians—seem to have an almost Celtic temperament. Like the Welsh or Irish they burst into song, or tears, or dance at the drop of a hat. They are great dancers and musicians. Forget tourist Greek nights. Here it's all for real, an explosion of exuberance and heart-felt emotion. If you have the chance to go to a *paniyiri*, don't miss it.

If Sappho is the first lady of literary Lesvos then her male counterpart must surely be Aesop, he of the fables. The island also boasts the poet-musicians Arion and Terpandros, while Aristotle and Epicurus often gave lecturs to students at the famous local School of Philosophy.

The Nobel prize-winning poet Odysseus Elytis came from Lesvos as did the novelist Stratis Myrivilis. Myrivilis lived in the fishing village of Skala Sikaminias near Mólivos. You'll find a plaque to him on the trunk of the mulberry tree in the village square; apparently the writer used to sleep in the branches on hot summer nights. The tiny chapel to the Mermaid Madonna immortalised in his prose, is across the harbour.

From literature to art and the village of Petra is famous for the primitive painter Theophilos. A wandering tramp, he would paint murals to earn a crust. Discovered by a French critic who lived on the island, his works were exhibited in the Louvre, but he died in poverty nonetheless. Most of his paintings can be seen at the Theophilos Museum at Varia, just out of town.

Poetry is alive in the mountain village of Ayiossos. Famous for its pottery, too, the villagers wear traditional costume and uphold the old oral traditions at their fiestas. On Shrove Monday, *(Kathara Theftera* in Greek), there is a custom known as *Vallia* which involves impromptu exchanges of satirical verse, one poet picking up the thread from the other.

Albert Camus planned to build a house overlooking Sígri, in the north. Songwriter and national hero Mikis Theodorakis is a regular visitor. Once visited, Lesvos lures you back. The Muses still haunt the olive groves.

lage, produces traditional pottery.

Check tourist information (Mytilíni and Mólivos) for local feast days. Ayiossos, on 15 August, has one of the most vivid; there's also a carnival, with improvised poetry and masked jesters. Gypsies and Turks can also be seen on the island.

In fact, many Mytilínians were born in Turkey (their parents fled here when the pasha monopolised the olive trees), returning in the 1920s ethnic exchanges. Occasionally, they now cross over to find their childhood homes. Usually, they are welcomed, despite political tension between the countries (in the 1970s, after the Cyprus invasion, all of Mytilíni's beaches were closed for security reasons).

PSARA: Minute Psara has been on the political map since antiquity, and is first mentioned by Homer, who may have stumbled on Psara first when he left his native island of Hios. Further, Independence hero Kanaris, who destroyed the Turkish flagship in 1822, was born here and exemplifies the courage of the islanders. Psara aided Hydra and Spetsai in rebelling against the Ottomans in 1821. When 14,000 Turks came to avenge them, inhabitants blew themselves up inside a powder-packed magazine on the harbour.

This magazine has been restored by the tourist office and turned into a taverna (run by two Psarans with 20 years of New York restaurant experience); the tourist office also subsidises the mini-ferry ride from Hios (twice weekly) during certain months. There are only 300 inhabitants on Psara; a tale is told that they are the progeny of the men who were fighting elsewhere when the Turks landed.

It is a prosperous, one-village island that makes a good living off the sea and is amused by the few tourists that trickle over from Hios. Homes are perpetually being improved, in a style that is somewhat between Cycladic and Dodecanesian, yet is neither. Whitewashed plaster predominates, set off by the sizzling sky blue of the principal cathedral.

Psara is covered with dry, thorny

eft,
ainting by
lk artist
heophilos.
elow,
ytilíni
arbour is
e island's
ommercial
istrict.

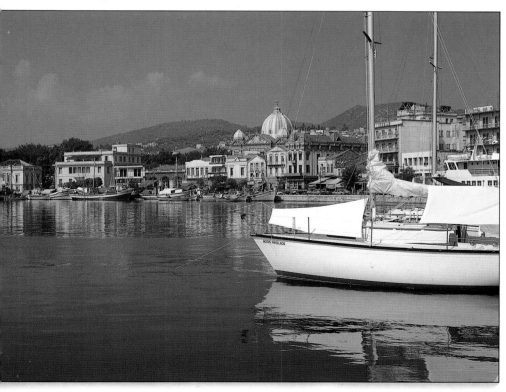

stubble. Fig trees provide virtually the only greenery. The coastal cliffs resemble petrified wood, with narrow outcrops of red-veined marble pushing through. The coastline is pocked with caves which once made Psara popular with pirates. Just past the electric plant is a handsome beach with a smooth, sandy seafloor. Twenty minutes' walk into the interior and a left turn reveals a longer beach, graced by a wreath of tiny islands offshore; on the largest is perched a **fisherman's chapel**.

The climb to the highest summit at 1,750 ft (530 metres) is a dusty, windy one; the view will confirm Psara's nakedness, broken by one green plain on the west coast where corn is grown. There is a tiny monastery called **Theotokou** at the island's northern extreme. The wind-buffeted beaches are covered with chalk-white seagrass and minute nautilus shells.

One of the boats that plies between here and the rest of the world (i.e. Hios) is owned by Captain Stamatis, who was decorated for his courage in fighting for the Allies in World War II.

HIOS: This island (also spelled Chios) has a bitter past. In 1822, at least 30,000 islanders were executed by the Sultan's men, while the terrified villagers of Anavatos dove from the clifftops in a Masada-like act of mass suicide. An additional 40,000 men and women were shipped to Constantinople to be sold as slaves. No one who was found was spared. It is no wonder that local residents are prickly; even those returning from Australia and North America are treated warily.

In the centuries preceding this bloodbath, Hios was a highly Europeanised island. The Korais family established a library in the capital in 1792. The **Argenti Museum** was later annexed to it, a vivid collection of folk art, costumes (each town had its own distinct dress), and tools. There is also a reproduction of Delacroix's *Massacre at Hios* now found in the Louvre.

The best of **Hios Town** lies within the old citadel—peaceful, dilapidated, and a little bit smelly. From atop the walls

Residents join in the activity of stringing tomatoes at Pírgi, Hios.

one sees windmills strung along the coast. Surprisingly, a mosque still stands nearby, but is being joined with the **Archaeological Museum**.

No two villages on Hios are alike. The southern region is called **Masti-choria**, after the mastic trees which yield gum and derivatives used in industrial production. The mastic's vaunted sweet smell is undetectable, despite claims to the contrary. The *xysta* ("grating"—geometric etchings in plaster) that adorn the houses of **Pírgi** are singular.

Walled **Mésta** is a weird labyrinth of a town with only one way in and one way out. **Kámbos** is an enclave of the island's wealthiest families. Some towns are built in roseate granite, while others are plasterwork, painted in deep ochres and pastels.

The Byzantine monastery, **Nea Moni** (due west of the capital and constructed in 1049), was built on a spot where Mary is said to have appeared in a myrtle tree. Nea Moni seems to be run single-handedly by an ancient nun, daintily proud of the brilliant mosaics that escaped ruin by the Turks. There is a local bus here only once or twice a week; otherwise, follow the woodland path from **Karies** which should take under two hours to walk.

Once weekly, the bus continues to stony **Anavatos**, the scene of the island's greatest tragedy. In the empty northwest is **Vólissos**, said to be Homer's birthplace and served by one bus daily. Homer's "teaching stone" lies near **Vrondados** on the east coast, where most of the island's best beaches and fishing villages can be found.

IKARIA: Except for the brief flurry when a ferry arrives at Ikaria's main port, the traffic of **Ayios Kirikos** consists mainly of towel-draped elderly people streaming down the stairs from the nearby hot springs. On the bus to **Armenistis**, endpoint of Ikaria's only paved road, islanders disembark into what seems complete wilderness. Far-flung villages and the steep pitch of the island—the 3,300-ft (1,000-metre) **Athenas mountain** covers its length—

makes some villages (like Karkinagri) more easily accessible by caique.

The wing-shaped island is named after mythical Ikaros, who fell into the sea when his wax wings melted. It is one of the most unharassed islands in the Aegean today. **Armenistis** and **Nas**, both prime beaches, lack the packaged resort feel many travellers dread. An offshore chapel marks Armenistis' eastern reach. The Naiads were believed to have lived at Nas, a deep-cut cove between two mountainous vertebrae; Artemis's temple near **Tavropolion** is the island's most significant prehistoric ruin.

In the mountain towns *(Rahes)* around **Christos Rachon**, dominoes rather than *tavli* is played, and people carry their belongings in hairy goatskin rucksacks. Southwestward, the roads become demoniacally rough. Many minor roads aren't on the map, making for navigational Russian roulette.

The uplands' naked towers of boulders are inhabited only by russet-chested hawks. Lower down, yews, beards of heather, and the exotic autumn crocus grow. Stone walls weave senselessly up empty mountainsides near the coast, but weirdest of all are the Stone Age-like dwellings with slabs of rock forming their roofs and walls. Toward **Evdilos** (the second port and capital), at **Kambos**, are remnants of the early medieval city of Oenoe; Kambos' museum displays the finds.

Xylosirti Monastery and **Therma**'s **springs** are the outstanding south coast sites; Hellenistic **Fanari Castle** at the eastern tip looks toward Samos, the island's long-time ally. Songs about historic sieges still survive, accompanied by violin and bone flutes.

The biggest feast day is 17 July (the day of St Marina). On the same date in 1912, Ikarian Dr. Malachias declared the island a republic; until Greek unification in October, Ikaria made its own coins and stamps. In subsequent years the island's independence and remoteness attracted thousands of Communist exiles, a presence still strongly felt.

SAMOS: The dense forests may re-

A remote chapel on remote Ikaria.

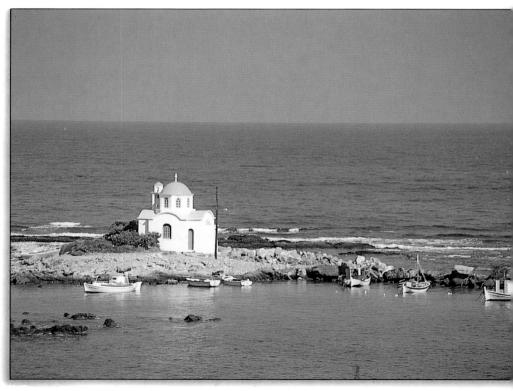

cently have been ravaged by fires, but Samos's distinctive red-roofed houses, the variety to be found in both town and countryside, the proximity of the exotic east (Turkey lies little more than a mile off its coast) plus the pleasures of the world-famous Samian wine bring many visitors to this island year after year.

Samos Town (Vathí) has an elegance rare in most sizeable Greek towns today. Tourism is concentrated in other parts of the island, which leaves Vathí free to concentrate on civic and domestic life. Its quiet suburbs at the foot of Mount Thio—a few minutes' walk from the harbour—make a convenient, restful base. The standout diversion is the **Archaeological Museum**, featuring the finds from Hera's Temple near Pithagório, the former capital.

Pithagório is a cluttered resort, but this cannot dim its historical importance. Named after its most famous resident Pythagoras, the town teems with archaeological activity as experts dig for more finds (an enormous *ágora* is now being unearthed).

An example of Samos' green landscape near Vourliotes.

Highlights include: the **Eupalinios Tunnel**, an ancient mountain-bound aqueduct which can be visited on Mondays, Wednesdays and Thursdays; **Spiliani Monastery**, with its chapel set deep inside a dripping crevasse; the ancient breakwater built by Lesvian slaves; and **Hera's Temple**, a profuse wonderland of devotion on the Tiganiou Gulf with shrines to Hera, Hermes, Aphrodite, Apollo, and Artemis.

A Roman settlement borders the Sacred Way. Riveting on its own, the place jumps to life with a visit to the **museum**, with exhibitions of votive offerings like pomegranates, pinecones, poppies, and palm fronds, plus tales of degenerates and a tax scandal.

New roadsigns announce that Samos is "unnuclear". Most of the mountain villages are undramatic, although **Spatherei** offers fine views across the island to Turkey. **Mytilini**, near Samos, has a fossil museum. Acres of pines, pierced by cypresses, undulate over most of the island. There are several deep gorges in the western half; roads are often unpaved and small coves, perfect for swimming, can be reached only on foot.

More accessible beaches lie on the south coast; a north coast favourite is **Kokari**, and the island's most luxuriant mountain valley rises above it toward **Ampelos**. Follow the road to **Vourliotes** for **Vronda Monastery**, the island's oldest, built in 1566 with vast courtyards. The footpath from Kokari emerges inside a long storage chamber filled with firewood and tyres. Only one monk lives in the monastery now.

Below Vourliotes, a tiny hamlet called **Pnaca** hangs over a shaded gush of water. A stone road from the coast leads past Pnaca to Vourliotes through terraced fields devoted to the grape of that celebrated Samian wine. Dark, orangey Samian tea is another recommended indulgence.

Karlóvassi is the other major port. Behind the serviceable waterfront area, it resembles Samos Town with its graceful turn-of-the-century houses, funded by profits made from the local tanning industry.

THE DODECANESE ISLANDS

The term "Dodecanese" is relatively new to the Greek vocabulary. For the 450 years that these far-flung islands were ruled by the Turks, they were known, incongruously, as the Southern Sporades. At the beginning of the 20th century 12 islands (*dódeka nisiá*) banded together to protest the harsh rule of the Ottomans. The rebellion failed although the name stuck—hence the Dodecanese.

In fact, there are and always have been more than 12 islands in this archipelago. Depending on the source, 14, 18 or even 27 islands comprise this chain. The only fact on which everyone seems to agree is the number of inhabited islands is never lower than 12.

The 17 principal islands included in this chapter are divided into three sections. Rhodes is the first, for it is the capital, the administrative, and the economic centre of the Prefecture. The collective term "Southern Dodecanese" has been coined to include the islands which fan out in all directions from Rhodes, and for which the capital is the main port of call. "Northern Dodecanese" islands, on the other hand, use Kos as a transport hub or are serenely self-contained, like the holy island Patmos or the proverbial "inset island" Astipalea, rarely included on any map of Greece except as a boxed insertion.

During the eighth century B.C. several of the islands enjoyed a period of intellectual and economic growth, sending scholars to the West and founding prosperous colonies. Two centuries later the three cities of Rhodes (Ialyssós, Lindos, and Kámeiros) comprised, along with Kos, Halicarnassus and Cnidus, the influential Dorian Hexapolis. Periods of wealth and domination alternated with capitulation for the next 2,000 years.

The Dodecanese were Greece's final territorial acquisition, completing the tourist map we know today as recently as 1948. Before the Greeks came (briefly) the British; before the British but after the Turks came a reign of brutal occupation by the Italians. To walk the streets of Kos or Rhodes is to piece together a geographical and cultural jig-saw; a minaret on one corner, an Italian villa on another. As always, though, it is the sea which provides the most lasting continuity for the islands known as the Dodecanese.

Preceding pages: priests on Patmos often vie with tourists for places on the buses; twilight at the port entrance to Rhodes Town. Left, Lindos beach is one of the best on Rhodes.

RHODES

The capital of the Dodecanese and fourth largest Greek island, **Rhodes** (Rodos) has long been on the package tour trail. But the Island of Eternal Summer, smiled on by Helios the sun god almost all year round, still holds colossal surprises.

It's a duty-free port, thronged in high summer by Scandinavians in search of Valhalla via cheap booze. *Smörgåsbord* is as common as *souvlaki* and the Post Office even has a separate box for Sweden. Stylish Italians swarm the steets in August and the British beer and *bouzouki* brigade also abound, propping up the hundreds of bars in town and the built-up outskirts.

Rhodes spells fun for the young, free and single. But not far from the madding crowds in Mandraki Harbour and the serried ranks of umbrellas and sunbeds on the town beaches, you can find the peaceful, unspoiled face of the island.

Hop on a bus—frequent services run down the east and west coasts from the main town of Mandraki—and you can get off the beaten track in under half an hour. It's worth hiring a car—plenty of buggies and jeeps available—or a bike if you really want to explore.

The island offers deserted sweeps of shingle with deep aquamarine waters; rocky coves scented with pine; castles perched above lemon groves; sylvan glades with strutting peacocks. This Rhodes is light years away from the "No Problem, No AIDS" teeshirts and tawdry knick-knacks of the town.

Patchwork history: The legacy of ancient Greeks, besieging Turks, crusading knights and occupying Italians forms a fascinating architectural patchwork in Rhodes town, from the turrets of the castle to the ancient city walls. There are Doric pillars and Byzantine churches; mosques and minarets, plus the twin bronze deer guarding the waters of Mandraki Harbour where the Colossus once stood.

In mythology, when Zeus shared out the world, he forgot Helios the sun god. Helios settled for newly-erupted Rodos as his prize. He fell in love with the nymph Roda, the island's namesake, daughter of Poseidon, and their grandsons Lindos, Kámeiros and Ialyssós founded the triple Doric cities which joined forces in 408 B.C. to form the city of Rhodes.

Rhodes was once plagued by snakes, and Forvas of Thessaly was brought in to do a Pied Piper. Helped by local stags, who speared the serpents with their antlers, he did the trick and a deer has been the civic symbol ever since.

From the fifth to the third centuries B.C. Rhodes was the major commercial force in the Aegean, founding colonies, minting coins and introducing maritime law. Sport and theatre flourished and the School of Rhetoric, founded in Rodini Park in 303 B.C., was attended by great orators like Julius Caesar, Brutus and Cassius.

Under Alexander the Great, Rhodes forged links with the Ptolemies, so the Rhodians refused to fight the Egyptians alongside King Antigonos. Angry, the

eft, wheels
rn in
hodes
arbour.

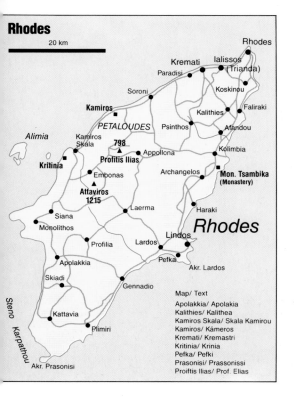

Rhodes

20 km

Rhodes

Kremati   Ialissos
Paradisi   (Trianda)

Soroni   Koskinou

Kamiros

PETALOUDES   Kalithies   Faliraki

Alimia   Kamiros   Psinthos   Afandou
Skala   798

Appollona   Kolimbia
Kritinia   Profitis Ilias

Embonas   Archangelos   Mon. Tsambika
(Monastery)

Attaviros
1215   Laerma   Haraki

Siana   *Rhodes*
Monolithos
Profilia   Lardos   Lindos

Apolakkia   Pefka
Akr. Lardos
Skiadi

Gennadio
Map/ Text
Apolakkia/ Apolakia
Kattavia   Kalithies/ Kalithea
Kamiros Skala/ Skala Kamirou
Plimiri   Kamiros/ Kámeros
Kremati/ Kremastri
Kritinia/ Krinia
Pefka/ Pefki
Prasonisi/ Prassonissi
Akr. Prasonisi   Proiftis Ilias/ Prof. Elias

Steno
Karpathou

King sent his son Dimitrios the Beseiger, plus 40,000 men to attack the city with all the latest weaponry. He failed after a year of siege and a peace treaty was signed in 304 B.C.

The assorted military hardware left over was melted down or sold to make the island's most famous landmark, the giant Colossus of Rhodes. The work of a local sculptor named Charis of Lindos, this wondrous statue stood 98 to 120 ft (27 to 37 metres) high, and was a representation of Apollo. Impressive by any standards, rumour made it even more so by describing the figure standing with one foot on either side of the harbour entrance so that ships passed between its legs. But to do so it would have to have been over ten times its original size, an impossible architectural feat. Nonetheless this beacon to passing ships and monument to peaceful prosperity stood for over a century before it fell to the ground during an earthquake in 226 B.C. The bronze was later sold off for scrap by the Saracens.

Rhodes remained at peace until, ironically, she tried to reconcile warring Romans and Macedonians only to have Rome take revenge in 168 B.C. by declaring Delos an open port and ceding it to Athens. Rhodes lost 15 percent of its trade. This punishment forced Rhodes to give up much of its independence and become subservient to Rome. Rhodes' trading partners took a dim view of her alliance with the trouble-making Romans.

In one chapter of Roman intrigue, Rhodes sided with Julius Caesar only to have Caius, after Caesar's murder, destroy her fleet, plunder the city and fill up Rome with her treasures. Two years later in 42 B.C. Octavius triumphed over Caius who committed suicide and Rhodes regained much of its autonomy. However, its fleet was gone as was much of its wealth. But Rhodes did regain cultural influence and for three centuries was the place where many statesmen and literary leaders of the age received their education.

In A.D. 43 the Apostle Paul landed at Lindos, bringing Christianity, and in

A mere shadow of a girl.

A.D. 395 the island came under Byzantine rule.

In 1306 Rhodes was taken over by its most influential masters when the Admiral of Byzantium sold the island to the Knights of St John who had fled Jerusalem via Cyprus. The Knights ruled for 213 years under 19 Grand Masters, fortifying the city against the Turks. But in 1522 they were overwhelmed by Suleiman the Magnificent, who had 100,000 warriors against their 650 knights.

The Grand Master plus 180 brethren surrendered, and the Turks held the island for 390 years. Churches became mosques and Greeks were banned from living within Rhodes' city walls.

In 1912 Italy occupied Rhodes while at war with Turkey. The castle later became Mussolini's summer palace. When Italy fell in 1943 during World War II the Germans took over.

The Mosque of Suleiman in the Old City.

Rhodes was liberated by the Allies in 1945 and the Greek flag hoisted in 1948 when the Dodecanese became united with Greece. These days, the island is still besieged—by tourists.

The present town of Rhodes divides neatly into the New Town and the Old City. Neon, fast food, designer clothes and disco beat versus quaint medieval streets and a time warp.

The New Town: This is designer territory, full of smart shops. Lacoste, Trussardi, and Benetton abound. Umbrellas are big business and you can have any logo, from YSL to Dior.

Rhodes Romeos *(kamákia)* are known as Princes because of the brand of Danish cigarettes they smoke. Coolest—but expensive—place to hang out for coffee is Dolce Italia, on the corner up from the bus stops in Mandraki.

You can sit and watch the world go by and the yachts bobbing at one of the pricey and touristy pavement cafés in **Mandraki**. Better, and cheaper are those inside the market amongst the fishmongers, butchers and the wonderful arrays of fruit and vegetables. Little *kafeneía* echoing the owner's origins like the Symi and Halki bars, are seemingly open all hours. The market stalls

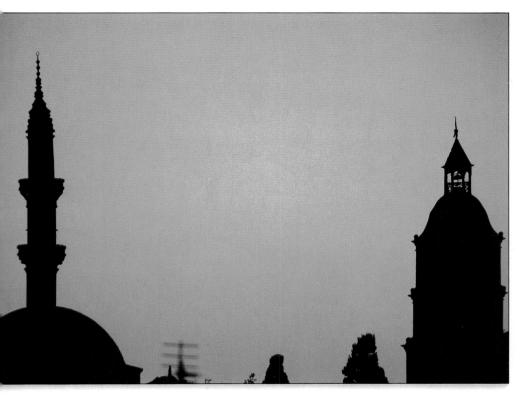

offer cheap *souvlakia* and *pitta*, freshly squeezed orange juice and there's a good bakery for early morning *psomakia* (bread rolls) or *koulouria* (biscuit rings), plus very fattening doughnuts for late morning breakfast.

The harbour front buzzes night and day with artists, popcorn vendors, sponge sellers and agents hawking their daily boat trips. Most boats leave at 9 a.m. for the island of Symi, calling at Panormitis Monastery, or down the east coast to Lindos. You can also go on barbecue cruises or take the hydrofoil to Kos. Inter-island ferries leave from the commercial harbour a short walk away.

The harbour, guarded by twin deer where the Colossus once stood, is also part of the smart international yachting scene, like a mini Cannes, with boats for charter. In the evening it's packed with tourists taking a pre-dinner *volta* (stroll) past the windmills down to the old **fortress of St Nichólas**. At the northern end of the harbour is the picturesque **Governor's House** with its Venetian Gothic arches. Next door is the **Bishop's Palace** and the **Church of the Annunciation** (Evangelismou), a 1925 replica of the old church of the Knights of St John.

A stroll along the waterfront from here towards Elli beach finds the grandly named **Hydrobiological Institute** at the northern tip, apparently the only aquarium of its kind in Greece. It boasts 39 tanks of regional fish, a female seal from Britain called Katerina, and assorted natural phenomena including an eight-legged calf.

Opposite the harbour are the Italianate public buildings. The **Post Office** and **OTE** (the Telephone Exchange—the Telegraph Office is round the back at 25 Martiou Street); the court, the town hall, the police station and the national theatre—featuring Rhodian character plays—are all in a convenient row, with the **Mosque of Mourad Reis** with its graceful minaret next door. The Aliens Bureau, Ministry of Public Order, is behind the Post Office should you wish to stay more than three months and need a permit.

The Knights' Hospital is now a museum.

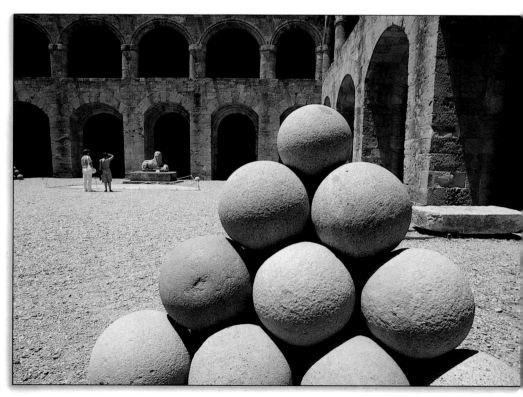

Palm trees wave in the municipal gardens beneath the imposing **Palace of the Grand Masters** where there are *son et lumière* performances every evening, re-enacting the siege of Suleiman the Magnificent. Pay as you enter and check with the person in the box office for your particular language.

Buses for Lindos and the east coast leave from outside the *son et lumière* and the new Rhodes Tourist Information Office is also along here, next to the taxi rank. The National Tourist Organisation and Tourist Police are on Papagou St, while the Olympic Airways Office is on Amerikis. For flights, ferry guides, sight-seeing tours and other Rhodes information Triton Holidays just off Mandraki at Plastira Street is an extra nice and helpful company.

The New Town throbs with nightlife, revellers spilling out of the bars onto the pavements in high season. One pub points out: "A balanced diet is a drink in each hand". Big spenders can head for the Casino at the Grand Hotel Astir Palace, 7 p.m. to 3 a.m., where smart

dress and passports are required.

Just out of town, **Rodini Park**, home of the ancient school of rhetoric, turns up some interesting modern babble from July to September with a wine festival every evening. Entrance fee covers all the wine you can drink. There are lovely rose gardens, lakes and bridges, Hellenistic tombs and the grave of Ptolemy.

Monte Smith, more correctly, the **Hill of Ayios Stephanos**, offers panoramic views over Rhodes. Named after Admiral Sir Sydney Smith, who kept watch there for the Napoleonic fleet in 1802, the hill is also the site of the ancient Acropolis with the ruined temples of Athena and Zeus.

In an olive grove on the east side are the restored **Temple of Pythian Apollo**, the third-century B.C. stadium and the theatre.

The Old City: The medieval walled citadel, with its ramparts, turrets and narrow cobbled streets, is so well preserved a visitor half expects to bump into a crusader. Step through the **Free-**

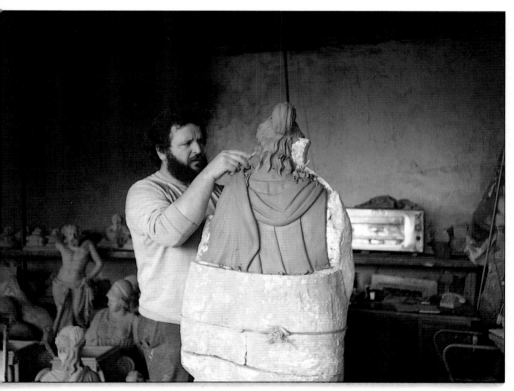

dom Gate (Pyli Elefterias) into Symi Square to view the remains of the **Temple of Aphrodite** and **Inn of the Order of Auvergne**. There's a giant map of the old town at this point behind some newly laid pebble mosaics. In the corner of Argyrokastrou Square the **Museum of Decorative Arts** is well worth a visit for its display of Dodecanese costumes, folk art—especially ceramic plates—and interiors of Rhodian houses.

The **Byzantine Museum** is opposite, situated in the former Cathedral of the Knights, later a mosque. Next stop is the 15th-century Knights Hospital, now the **Archaelogical Museum**. Full of the hospitallers' relics plus ceramics, coins and ornaments from Mycenean graves at Ialyssós, its most famous exhibit is the lovely Aphrodite of Rhodes, the Marine Venus.

From here the **Avenue of the Knights** (Ipoton St) stretches to the Palace of the Grand Masters in medieval splendour. Narrow and cobbled, the thoroughfare houses the inns of the various knightly orders emblazoned with heraldry and escutcheons of the Grand Masters. The Inn of the Order of France is outstanding. There are also small churches, a Turkish school and odd piles of cannon balls.

The **Palace of the Grand Masters**, is at the top of the street, its turreted towers as perfect as they were back in the 14th century. Destroyed when an arms store in the nearby Church of St John exploded in 1856, it was rebuilt by the Italians and was the summer retreat of King Victor Emmanuel and Mussolini.

Inside it boasts marble staircases and mosaics snaffled from the island of Kos.

For an excellent view of much of Rhodes, walk the **City Walls** from the entrance to the Grand Masters' Palace at 4 p.m. most afternoons.

The main street of the Old City is **Socratous**, the Golden Mile, packed with fur and leather, jewellers, lace and embroidery stalls, ceramic stores and all kinds of tourist paraphernalia. You can see carpets being woven—rugs are generally good buys. (Don't forget to

Rhodes caters to th masses...

haggle.) You can also pick up good bedcovers, table linen and pottery, and, of course, gold.

Socratous leads from the **Castellania** in Hippocrates Square with its impressive fountain up to the pink **Mosque of Suleiman**, conqueror of Rhodes.

Deep in the heart of the Turkish quarter with its mazes of winding alleys, it is easy to get lost. East meets west here and, with Asia Minor just 11 miles (17 km) across the sea, it's very much the gateway to the Levant. Minutes away from the crowds you can find tiny churches with taverna tablecloths on the altars, while cobblers tap industriously away at shoes next door.

Rooms are reasonable to rent in the old town. You can also take the plunge in the **Turkish baths of Hammam** on Archelaou St.

Sample real Greek dancing at the **Nelly Dimoglou Theatre**, behind the baths on Andronicou and Antiothiou Streets. The garden is open all day for refreshments and there are traditional folk dance performances nightly, except Saturdays. There are also dance courses from June to September.

West Coast: Travelling along the west coast, **Ixiá** is the first resort, all high-rise hotels and a sandy beach packed with sardine sunbathers and early morning joggers. By night there are neon signs and discos galore.

Ixiá blends into **Ialyssós**, also called Triánda, similarly commercialised. Above town, the **Filerimos Plateau** is the site of the ancient city of Ialyssós, with ruins of Doric temples. The restored **monastery**, open only to the modestly dressed, is based on a Byzantine basilica and features the Road of Passion with 14 icons of the Stations of the Cross plus a Doric fountain. The monks sell the local *sette* herb, made from seven different varieties. Stunning views abound; a must for photographers. You can get here by bus.

Kremastí, further along the coast, is famous for its festival of the Virgin on 15 August, otherwise notable for the Greek Army barracks and a few nice tavernas. Next stop is the international

.or to those eeking olitude.

airport, frenetic on Wednesdays and Saturdays, main transfer days. The village of **Paradisi**, on the flight path, is hardly heaven but a good place for cheap rooms on arrival.

Rhodes is also called the Island of the Butterflies and the reason why is **Petaloudes**, the Butterfly Valley, the island's most famous beauty spot. Well worth a visit, the narrow valley with its gentle stream, criss-crossed by rickety rustic bridges like something out of *Indiana Jones*, teems with butterflies from June to September. Dull spotty grey when at rest, the rare species Quadrina rise in clouds of vermilion as you pass. They are attracted by the vanilla-smelling storax trees, used in making frankincense. Although the scene is blissfully bucolic, under no circumstances should you drink the water from the stream.

The bus stops in the middle of the valley. Turn right and you head down to the restaurant; turn left and past the gift stalls at the end of the valley you can walk through the woods to the Monastery of the **Virgin Mary of Kalopetra**, a tranquil resting place with stunning views over the plains.

A wooded trail from here leads to the monastery of **Ayios Soulas** (about four miles/six km from Soroni on the coast road) which has a giant fiesta on 30 July with donkey races and folk dances.

The other big tourist attraction just off the coastal road is **Ancient Kámeiros**, the remains of the flourishing city excavated in 1929. Many of its treasures are in the British Museum, but you can see the sixth-century Temple of Athena, a water basin holding enough for 400 families, public baths, the altar to Elios and ruined houses. There are frequent buses from Mandraki, 17 miles (27km) up the coast.

High above Kámeiros, **Profites Elías** is the nearest thing to Greek Switzerland, 2,400 ft (720 metres) up with Alpine scenery. There's a monastery and a hotel and lodge, The Elafos and Elafina, deer and doe, built in chalet style. A stay restores body and soul.

Back on the coast **Skala Kámirov**

Ancient Kámeiros.

(also Kámiros Skala) is a pretty fishing harbour now being enlarged, with good fish tavernas. Small ferries leave daily for the unspoilt island of Halki opposite.

Junoesque women: Nearby **Kritinia Castle** is well worth a visit for its breathtaking views over the rugged vineyards and lemon groves. The village itself, founded by Cretans, is a cluster of white houses on the hillside. Above is **Embonas** on the slopes of Mount Attaviros, famous for its fruit with vineyards, olive groves and to-bacco plantations. Very traditional, many of the villagers wear national costume with long boots. The women are Junoesque and great dancers; festi-vals at Embonas are not to be missed.

Through wild scenery and herb-clad hills to the pretty village of **Siana,** famous for its honey and *suma*—a fire-brand spirit like schnapps. You can sample both here at the *kaféneia*. Old houses have clay roofs.

Further south, **Monolithos**, and its crusader castle perched on a single rock, has one of the most spectacular views on Rhodes. The path climbs up to the tiny chapel, then there's a sheer 800-ft (250-metre) drop.

The west coast is windy and hence undeveloped for mass tourism. There are miles of unspoilt beaches and the **Bay of Apolakia** is wild and undis-covered. The village is unexceptional but **Skiadi Monastery,** seven miles (11 km) away, has a revered collection of icons worth seeing.

Roads are little more than tracks here, so it's unwise to "do" the island by motorbike unless the machine is strong and reliable. Check insurance before you set off. Some car hire firms are touchy about damage caused by at-tempts at motocross.

Katavia has a petrol station if you're exploring by car. It also has a church with remarkable frescoes and niches containing ancient sculptures. From here you can get down to the southern-most tip, **Prassonissi**, or Leek Island, joined by a narrow sandy neck of beach—one side windy, the other calm.

East Coast: Although the east coast is

Roasting a lamb for Easter in a field on Rhodes.

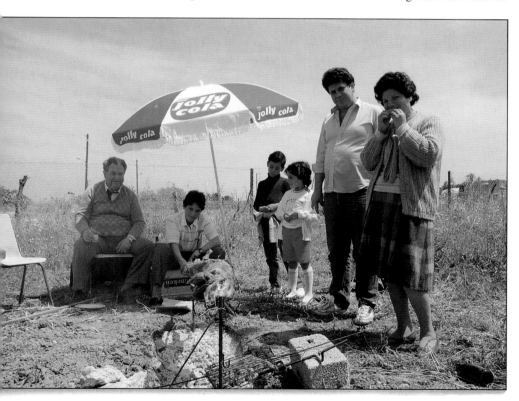

far more developed than the west, it is possible to still find unspoiled beaches, remote countryside and beauty spots, particularly beyond Lindos.

Koskinou is worth a stop for its intricate pebble mosaic courtyards. Then head down through the pines to **Kalithéa** (Thermes Kallithéas), with splendid arches and domed pavilions built in Moorish style by the Italians. There's a *lido* area here beneath the palm trees plus a scuba-diving school. It's rocky, but great for snorkelling; popular with nudists, too.

Sadly the magnificent spa buildings have long since been abandoned, and you can no longer drink the healing waters. But the attractive landscaped gardens still offer welcome shade.

Wall-to-wall hotels lead to **Faliráki**, the popular package resort bursting with the young, free and single. Also known as Fairly Crappy, there are hordes of eateries, discos, mini golf, and swinging night life. The long sandy beach offers para-gliding and all kinds of watersports.

Back on the coast, past the quaintly named Anthony Queen (*sic*) cove where Quinn filmed *The Guns of Navarone*, you come to **Afandou**, which has a long shingle beach and caves. There's a campsite on the way from Faliráki. Popular with barbecue cruise boats, the beach has enough space for glorious seclusion. The 18-hole Rhodes golf course is here, plus a castle and the church of Panayia Katholiki with many frescoes. The village is famous for its apricots and lovely hand-woven carpets.

From here, it's easy to go "over the top" via **Psinthos** to the Butterfly Valley and west coast road. A little past **Kolimbia,** a sandy beach with plenty of sports facilities, you'll come to the leafy glades of *Epta Piges* (Seven Springs). It is one of the island's most popular beauty spots. Peacocks strut beside the gurgling streams and waterfalls which run to a central lake.

You can either hit the woodland trail to the lake fed by the said seven springs, or shuffle ankle-deep in dank water

Rhodes is one of the few Greek islands to house a Turkish cemetery.

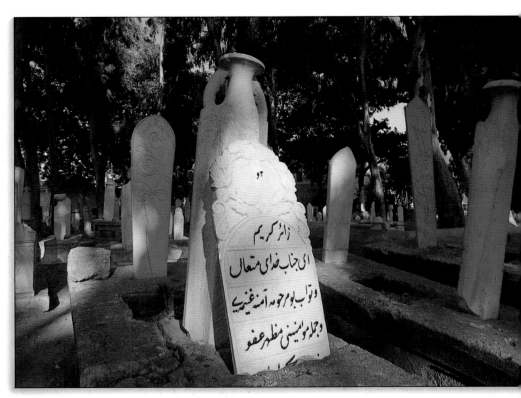

192

down a very narrow, pitch-dark tunnel. It's quite a spooky experience and not for the tall or claustrophobic. As a reward for this ordeal, sample charcoal-grilled meats at the taverna under the shady plane trees.

The Greek answer to fertility drugs, **Tsambika Monastery** is perched high on the mountain opposite, overlooking the sandy beach. The tiny white Byzantine church is a magnet for childless women who walk barefoot to pray for fertility at its festival on 8 September. If the stork calls, they pledge to call the child Tsambikos or Tsambika—names unique to Rhodes—in gratitude to the Virgin Mary. There are daily boat trips here from Mandraki.

It's well worth calling in at **Archangelos**, the island's largest village, famous for soft leather peasant boots and hand-thrown ceramics. You can visit the potteries—traditional plates are good buys. The graveyard boasts tombs painted blue and white—patriotic to the end.

The Knights' castle of **Faraclos**, apparently a kind of Colditz, looks down over **Haráki**, a fishing village with good beach tavernas. There's a vast sweep of empty beach from here to Lindos. Pick your way down through the vineyards for tranquil sunsoaking. **Vlixa bay**, further along is sandy and ideal for families with safe swimming and bustling tavernas.

With its peppermint houses huddled beneath a crusader castle **Lindos** is the dream Greek village. Stunningly beautiful, with a fascinating history, its houses have magnificent doorways and mosaic courtyards. The hottest spot on Rhodes—temperature and nightlife-wise—its cobbled streets teem with trippers in high season. Donkeys (Lindian taxis) heave tourists up the steep hill from Pallas Beach to the **Acropolis** and **Temple of Lindian Athena**. It's the temple of tourism now, with women selling lace on the way up. Sensible shoes are a must.

Lindos dates back to the Bronze Age. With the exception of Mandraki in Rhodes Town it is the only natural har-

LEISURELY LINDOS

Lindos is the last place to visit in Greece. This aphorism was endorsed in the 1960s and 1970s by a score of ex-patriates who found in this beautiful resort a nirvana where they would write that great novel, compose that immortal sonnet or paint that ultimate canvas. Most were British, most were in their thirties, most had had a previous career and some had enjoyed limited artistic success—a published novel, an article in a glossy magazine.

Then there were young hippies—British, Australian, American and German—to whom the mere thought of ever holding down a job was anathema. All these ex-pats lived in modest Greek houses and were fortunate in that Costas, the corner grocer, permitted them to buy "on tick".

Rounding off the scene were transient ex-patriates. These included a publisher, an opera star, an art historian, and a couple of architects. They had purchased as holiday homes the magnificent old sea-captains' houses which grace Lindos.

Ars longa, vita brevis could have been the motto of the "drop-outs" and, in the privacy of their homes, pot accompanied *ouzo* and the *ménage à trois* was not unknown. Pot was tolerated by the authorities except when Greta, a German student enjoying a long vacation and really not part of the ex-pat community, was imprisoned for possession. The consensus was that she was incarcerated because she refused the advances of the police sergeant. Imagine the horror of her parents when they arrived to join their daughter in her Greek idyll and found her in a rural island jail.

So was any work accomplished? Did anyone make a sale?

One day Willard, an enthusiastic snorkler who, years previously had sold a novel but had since collected rejection slips, struck gold. A visiting German television producer was looking for a diving "buddy". Diving over, Klaus read Willard's short stories, and knew instantly they would make great television plays. Willard now spends a lot of time in Hollywood.

And then there was David, who appeared waving a cheque for US$5,000 and smiling broadly. And Tiger with rings (made of hand-painted pebbles from the beach) on her fingers and rings on her toes; and...

Flash-back to the 1960s.

bour on the island. The Acropolis has two re-erected classical temples and later Byzantine and Frankish elements. Near the main square is a beautiful Byzantine church with well-preserved frescoes. The water in the fountain still runs through the original pipes.

Lindos' large harbour with long sandy beaches adds the finishing touch. However, it is the light that has made Lindos famous. The jagged mountains which surround the town reflect both sun and shade in a dazzling display. The Italian and German painters were the first to rediscover Lindos; some moved here for good and lived a life much like the hippies of the 1960s. In addition to Lindos' better known attractions, don't miss the Tomb of Kleovoulos, the philosopher king, and the 17th-century houses preserved to show Lindian life.

Lindos is now a shrine to sun, sea and sex. The beach is a watersports playground and at night the village really rocks with numerous bars and discos.

Once super-smart and home of the astrologer Patric Walker and various members of the Pink Floyd pop group, Lindos is now overrun with visitors. Supermarkets cater for your every need and tavernas even do sweets. It's hard to believe you're in Greece.

Still, the view over St Paul's Bay, where the Apostle landed to bring Christianity, makes up for all the tourist tat. The tiny church dedicated to him celebrates with a giant fiesta on 28 June. There's a good bus service to Lindos from Mandraki, which lies 35 miles (56 km) up the coast, but it's far better to take a boat from the capital to enjoy the splendid scenery.

Down the road, **Pefki** (Pefkos) is less frenetic than Lindos; it has a long sandy beach plus handy *cantina* and several good fish tavernas.

Head south far from the madding crowd. Camping is permitted at **Lardos**, and the bay, miles of shingle with sand dunes as far as Gennadi, is largely deserted. However, it's earmarked for development as a major resort, so go now. **Plimiri** is really remote and from here rough tracks lead to **Prassonissi**.

ull moon
sing over
indos.

THE SOUTHERN DODECANESE

KARPATHOS: Wild, rugged and unspoiled, Karpathos is the second largest island in the Dodecanese and a mix of Crete and Corsica, as yet untouched by mass tourism.

With miles of white sandy beaches, usually deserted, and craggy cloud-topped mountains soaring to 4,000 ft, (1,200 metres) it's a walker's paradise, especially with wild flowers and village gardens full of Madonna lilies.

Pighadia, the main town, (also known as Karpathos) is plain and workaday with few concessions to visitors, although there are good fish tavernas in the harbour. Completely uncommercialised, Karpathos doesn't pander to tourists and the people can seem a bit dour, even unfriendly. Most families have sought their fortunes in America, and you're as likely to hear: "Have a nice day" as *"Kalimera"*.

Property is handed down the female line. As men could not marry before their sisters, hundreds of Karpathians were driven abroad to work and many now live back home on U.S. pensions.

Exploring can be difficult. Roads are rough, often with sheer drops down to the sea, and with the *meltemi* wind buffeting the west coast mopeds should be avoided. There are buses and taxis—expensive—to less remote mountain villages like **Menetes** with vine-covered streets; **Aperi**, the elegant former capital; and **Othos** where an old Karpathian house serves as a craft museum. Best way to see the island is to take a boat to **Diafani** in the northeast, visit the remote and eerie village of Olympos, then travel back overland along the mountainous backbone, where the pine forests still bear the scars of the vast 1983 fire, with blackened stumps like Ikebana arrangements.

Olympos (Olimbos) is the island's famous beauty spot. Clinging to the mountainside 2,000 ft (600 metres) up, the village was cut off from the rest of the world until the road was pushed through from Diafani. The women still wear their traditional costume (intricately embroidered jackets, scarves and pinafores, heavy collars of gold coins) for festivals. They bake bread and *koulouria* biscuits outside in communal ovens from flour still ground in the village's medieval windmills.

The old houses here are simply one divided room, built around a central wooden pole or "pillar of the house". On a raised wooden platform, behind an intricate rail, are rolled mattresses, plus dowry chests of clothes. The pole is covered in embroideries and usually a wedding portrait of the home-owners with their *stefana* or wedding wreaths.

The rest of the room is packed with plates, lace, crochet, souvenirs and knick-knacks—a kitsch explosion of fairground colours—gathered by seafaring relatives from ports world-wide. Even modern villas are decked out in the same way with the TV draped in garish, glittery mats, a shrine for family photos and icons.

Olympos is in a time-warp and the people still speak a form of Dorian

Greek. They are getting used to visitors now, but life goes on and you'll see *Olymbisses* (Olympos women) in their long leather boots carrying reluctant goats along from Diafani below.

Because the harbour is too shallow for the big inter-island ferries, you go ashore by caique, often with a gaggle of Olympos grannies, cartons of disposable nappies and bunches of flowers. It's worth taking rooms here to explore the northernmost point, **Vroukounda**, with an old castle and graves hewn into the rock. The cave shrine to St John is here with a major festival on 29 August, while half of Greece flocks to Olympos for the Festival of the Virgin Mary, *Panayia*, on 15 August. (The other half travels to Tinos in the Cyclades).

Just out of Karpathos Town, the sandy **Vronti** beach—fringed by trees and surprisingly uncrowded—sweeps down to the island's main classical ruin, the fifth-century basilica of Ayia Fotini. Otherwise you can trek over the headland through the olive groves to **Amopi** with three sandy beaches, the third for nudists, which is the nearest thing to an organised resort on the island. Taxis are also available.

Karpathos is supposed to be the site of the legendary Clash of the Titans. The dramatic gorges and rock formations around **Apella** on the east coast are doubtless the giants' leftovers. **Ahata** and **Kira Panayia**, with its lovely pink-domed church, are also spectacular beaches. **Arkassa** on the west side, site of a Mycenaen fort, is wild and wind-swept, but **Lefkas**, up the coast boasts three horseshoe bays of pure white sand, azure seas and a taverna which grows its own vegetables.

Direct flights are available to Karpathos now; the alternative is planes or ferry from Rhodes. Walking routes and general information can be obtained from Possi Travel in Pighadia.

KASSOS: Just three miles (two km) away from Karpathos, Kassos is the southernmost Dodecanese. Remote, gaunt and barren, it's largely depopulated, with abandoned houses crumbling in its five villages where families have left to seek work. The people are

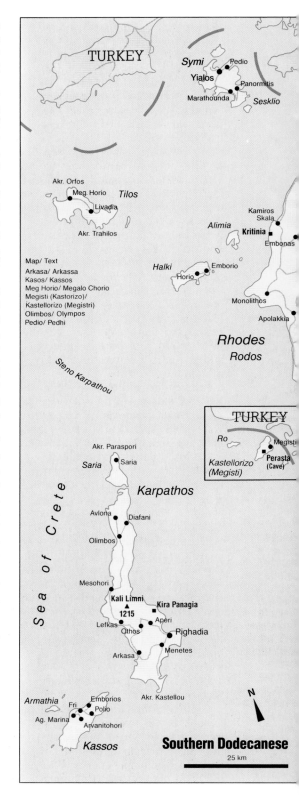

Map/ Text
Arkasa/ Arkassa
Kasos/ Kassos
Meg Horio/ Megalo Chorio
Megisti (Kastorizo)/
Kastellorizo (Megistri)
Olimbos/ Olympos
Pedio/ Pedhi

Southern Dodecanese

25 km

keen to welcome tourists, especially on 17 July, *Agyia Marina*, when there's a big festival and women wear colourful costumes in traditional patterns.

The capital, **Fri**, is a charming fishing port, set against a mountain backdrop, with a couple of hotels and tavernas, while **Emborios** across the bay is also picturesque. Don't miss the cave at **Selai**, near **Ayia Marina**, filled with stalactites. Rough roads lead to the hill villages of **Arvanitohori**, **Panayia** and **Polio** and there's a local bus service.

With orange and lemon trees, sheltered gardens and wildflowers, Kassos is perfect for travellers seeking rural calm. It's great walking country (stout shoes essential) and you can walk across the island through olive groves to the beach at **Khelathros** or get a fisherman to take you to the islet of **Armathia** which has a spectacular beach.

Fri has a tiny airstrip with planes to Rhodes, Karpathos and Crete, although tickets are limited and the planes often full. Inter-island ferries call in at Piraeus, Crete, Karpathos and Rhodes.

KASTELLORIZO: (Also known as **Megísti**). Kastellorizo is laughingly called "the Biggest". The tiny island is first—or last—in Europe, only a mile across from Turkey where locals go shopping or to have a meal.

The smallest in the Dodecanese chain, Megísti, its harbour fringed with red-roofed houses, is topped by a red-stone crusader castle which gives the island its Italianate name. The beautiful island, home these days to Australian Greeks from Perth, has a rocky coastline and no beaches to speak of apart from a pebble one at **Ayios Stephanos**. But the famous Blue Grotto of **Perasta**, with stalactites and basking seals, rivals that of Capri. The cave is about 80 ft (24 metres) high and the rays of the rising sun turn the water opaline. The round island boat trip takes about three hours.

Also worth seeing is the Church of **Ayios Constantinos**, with paintings and mosaics, and the **Turkish mosque**, now a museum. Don't go if you're in a hurry. Kastellorizo is 70 miles (110 km) from Rhodes and ferries can be erratic,

Kastellorizo: this tiny island is laughingly called "the Biggest".

although occasionally free in a government bid to boost tourism. There's a tiny air strip with planes to Rhodes; plus one hotel and a few *pensions*.

HALKI: Designated the Island of Peace and Friendship by the Greek government, Halki, an hour and a half by boat from Kamiros Skala on Rhodes, is pretty, welcoming and unspoiled. The neo-classical houses are being restored under a UNESCO funded scheme. **Emborio** (Halki), the fishing harbour and only settlement, has four tavernas and a hotel for visiting scheme groups. The island's only sandy beach is **Pondamos** with safe swimming and a good taverna. The old **Hora** is now deserted but with spectacular views from its crusader castle complete with frescoes.

The Boulevard Tarpon Springs, built with money from Halki sponge fishermen who went to Florida, is being pushed through to the monastery of **Ayios Ioannis** on the other side of the island, otherwise a good three-hour walk up. The church of **Ayios Nicólas** has the highest bell tower in the Dodecanese. There is virtually no traffic, so beaches like **Areta** and **Trachia** are reached by boat or you can walk to **Iali**, **Arous** or **Kania.** Having no fresh water supply, the island is barren and harsh—but still magical.

ALIMIA: The island of Alimia is deserted. The people fled to Halki following wartime Gestapo raids when the deep waters housed Italian submarine pens. With a **Byzantine castle**, pretty church, pebbly beaches, clear waters and ruined barracks strafed by bullet holes, the island is now a popular picnic spot, and home to Halkian sheep.

TILOS: Home of the poetess Erinna, rival to Sappho, Tilos is just waking up to tourism. It's a pretty, fertile island—lovely in spring with orchards in blossom on the way to the main town of **Megálo Horio**. The port of **Livadiá** has a long shingle beach with good tavernas and a new hotel.

Tranquil and unspoiled, it has 10,000 goats but only about 200 people. You can see fossilised elephant bones in the grotto of **Harcadio** in **Misaria**, while at

Fresh vegetables often have to be imported from larger islands by ferry.

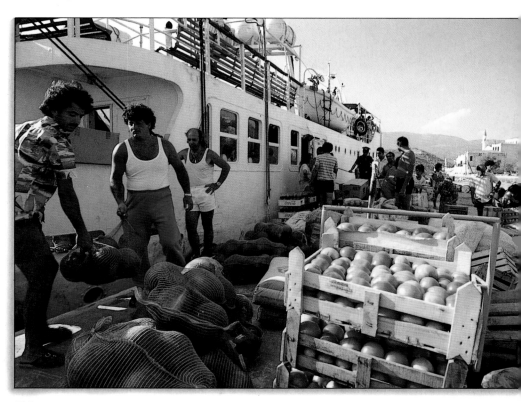

Aghios Antonis beach the sea covers the petrified remains of three sailors.

The monastery of **St Panteleimon** is well worth the journey across the island's rocky, spectacular scenery. The monastery has a beautiful fountain flanked by basil pots, and the church has important paintings and carvings. The three-day festival runs from 25 July with the famous Dance of the Cup. Ayios Nicólas church at **Politissa** has a festival on 23 August with special boats from Rhodes the previous day.

SYMI: As you approach Symi on a day-trip boat from Rhodes, flotillas of little caiques flee the port of **Yialós** (Symi) for the beaches round the island. The foreign "residents" and those who claim the island as their own are escaping the daily droves of tourists.

Symi, one of the most stunning sights in Greece with its tiers of sugar-almond houses, has two (if not three) faces. When the tour boats hoot, Yialós becomes a mini-Rhodes with tavernas touting for business and stalls selling local herbs, sponges and knick-knacks.

As soon as the trippers leave, peace is restored—there's room to walk on the streets and you'll get stronger *ouzo*.

Up the 357 steps of the **Kali Strata** is the other face of the high town or **Hora**. Even further up the maze of streets they say there are old ladies who have never been down to the bottom. On Symi you either stay up or down, or over at **Pedhi**, a pretty sandy bay now being developed. Daily caiques like the *Triton* sail to beaches for barbecues from Yialós. The fit can walk with Hugo, an Englishman married to a local girl and an island legend, who takes guided walks to meet up with the boat.

There is also a boat from Pedhi to **Ayios Nicólas**, where you can have a good beach barbecue. For walkers there's a well-marked track—follow the red road—over the headland.

The town beach is **Nos**, with a disco, and it's also worth walking to **Nimborio**. The most important monastery is **Panormítis** in the south, a place of pilgrimage for Greeks world-wide. Very rich, and very like a movie star's bungalow in appearance, the church is packed with votive offerings from sailors. Things are tranquil again when the tour boats have gone, and you can rent a cell for whatever you wish to pay. But, if you're a woman travelling alone, beware. The priest will insist you sleep inside the enclave and the doors are locked at 9.30 p.m. sharp.

Symians are famous as boatbuilders—they built the *Argo* for Jason—and you can still see boats taking shape on the way to Nos. The Treaty of the Dodecanese (when Symi became part of Greece again after the Italian occupation) was signed in Les Katerinettes restaurant in 1945.

There are boat trips to the beach at **Marathounda** plus the island of **Sesklia**. Yialós, in a bowl and steaming hot in high summer, is beautiful at night, reflecting the myriad lights from the houses above. Smart, popular with the yachting fraternity, but still unspoiled, Symi has plenty of bars and tavernas downtown and uptown. It's not, however, an island for the unfit, elderly or very young.

Yialós, Symi: one of the most stunning island ports.

204

THE NORTHERN DODECANESE

NISSIROS: Legend has it that Nissiros (Nisyros) was once joined to its larger neighbour Kos, but Poseidon, in pursuit of a giant, tore the two islands apart. This same legend credits the giant Polybetes with the creation of Nissiros' most impressive feature, a volcano 850 feet (260 m) in diameter. Although the volcano is now extinct, its presence dominates the island, from the black pebbles which comprise several of the beaches to the spas with their therapeutic sulphurous springs.

The crater lies on the **Lakki plateau** in the heart of the island, approximately six miles (10 km) south of the harbour town, Mandraki. Steps lead from the rim down into the volcano, but be sure to wear sensible shoes, sun-glasses and a hat, for the temperature is hot in the centre. The air is pungent, acrid, and the floor so soft rocks must be used as stepping stones. Canary-yellow stalagmites emit a low, deep roar like Hades calling from the underworld.

Two sparsely-populated villages are perched on the ridge of the crater. **Emborios** is surrounded by greenery while the larger **Níkia**, further on, has a round *plateía* and a café. Just outside the harbour where the ferries and caiques arrive lies the old spa of **Loutra**. Since antiquity visitors have been coming to bask in its healing waters; now it is hoped they will flock to the vast new spa which has been built near the fishing village **Paloi** on the north coast.

Mandraki is the highly attractive capital and principal port. White-washed buildings sparkle next to others painted in bright colours and both are in contrast to the dark volcanic boulders which hug the shore and on which fishing nets are laid out to dry. A rambling promenade extends along the waterfront while behind are streets so densely constructed that the balconies of opposing houses meet up to filter the worst of the sun's rays.

In one of the cafés, be sure to order *soumada*, the drink made from locally grown almonds. If you prefer to buy in quantity *soumada* can also be bought in rather lethal-looking unmarked bottles which belie its alcohol-free status. Overlooking both the capital and the sparkling sea are two fortresses. Hanging onto the very edge of the cliff and within the boundaries of one of them is the small church of the **Virgin Spilianí** which is worth a visit.

In the springtime much of the island is green and covered with wildflowers. Buses and taxis, as well as organised (expensive) excursion parties from Kos make the journey from Mandraki to the volcano. But the best way to appreciate Nissiros' rich island smells (almonds and figs) is by walking.

ASTIPALEA: This small, rocky outcrop is destined to be an "inset island," specially inserted on any Greek map. Falling mid-way between the Dodecanese and the Cyclades, Astipalea, with just over 1,000 inhabitants, technically belongs to the former island chain, yet in architecture and in culture bears more resemblance to the latter. On a clear day

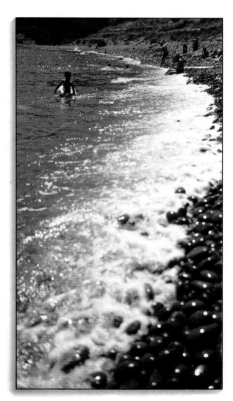

Left, fish is often sent directly from the islands to Athenian food markets. Right, the white-hot, black volcanic beach at Nissiros.

it is possible to see both Amorgos and Santorini on the horizon.

For years Astipalea was most closely observed through binoculars. Scores of visitors, enroute from Piraeus to Kos or Rhodes, would stand on the top deck of a ferryboat and subject all activity in Astipalea's harbour to a seven-minute scrutiny, the approximate time it takes to sail past without stopping. Now, boats call in more frequently, hotels have been built, discerning tour companies offer rooms on a package basis, and Athenians have discovered that a house near the **Xokastra** (old town) can be a desirable summer residence.

So far this development has had only a minor effect. The food in the tavernas and the one paved road have improved, and the houses now dazzle with even more coats of whitewash. If subsequent changes remain as modest, a pleasing time is assured.

Astipalea is shaped like the wings of a butterfly, linked by a narrow isthmus only about 300 ft (100 metres) wide. The village on the isthmus, **Maltezanas** (also called Analipsi) is said to have been named after Maltese pirates who once sought shelter in the tiny fishing harbour. Most people stay in the principal port **Pera Yalos**, with its tavernas, cafés and seasonal *bouzouki* club.

A long flight of stairs connects **Skala** (as the port is known locally) with the old town of Astipalea, or Kastro and the ninth-century **castle of Ayios Ioannis** which dominates the hilltop. The castle is entered from the southwest and within its confines are two churches, the **Annunciation** and the church of **St George**.

In stark contrast to the whitewashed chapels is the sombre brown wall which encircles the castle, which once provided homes for the islanders. Strung out along the crest of a hill is a series of windmills in various states of disrepair. From the sea the Kastro, the windmills and the stark cubic houses provide an enchanting picture. Another fine church, dedicated to the Virgin Portaitissa, should not be missed.

Buses run from Skala to **Livadia**, a resort just over the brow of the hill. The

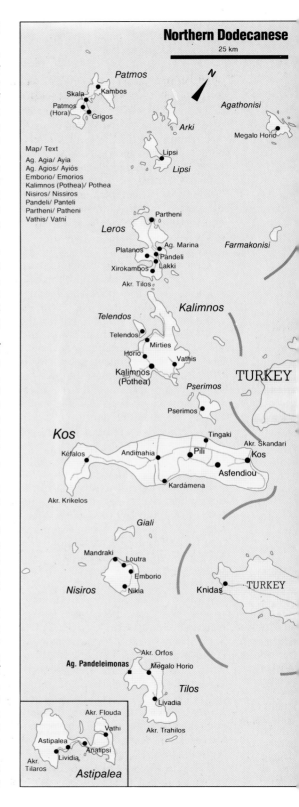

Map/ Text
Ag. Agia/ Ayia
Ag. Agios/ Ayiós
Emborio/ Emorios
Kalimnos (Pothea)/ Pothea
Nisiros/ Nissiros
Pandeli/ Panteli
Partheni/ Patheni
Vathis/ Vatni

beach, backed by citrus orchards, attracts insects and seaweed, but is wonderfully long. Several coves and beaches along the coastline can be reached on foot or by taxi, but the town of **Vathí**, 12 miles (19 km) northwest of Astipalea, is best visited by boat.

KOS: With an international airport, daily ferry connections with Piraeus, and an extensive system of boats, hydrofoils and caiques to neighbouring islands, Kos might well be considered the "hub" of the northern Dodecanese. The cacophony of tourists, souvenir vendors and market pedlars threatens to swamp the atmosphere of this lush, historic island; even in late spring or early autumn the buzzing of mopeds and the wail of disco music reverberates through Kos Town.

The south coast with its excellent beaches has been taken over almost exclusively by developers; hotels, pubs and cafés serving "Zombie" and "Orgasm" cocktails are much in evidence. Travellers seeking solitude should head for one of the villages in the folds of

Mount **Díktaio** or for the final destination on the bus line, ancient **Kéfalos** in the southwest peninsula, but even here bungalows and hotels blur the striking view of Turkey on the horizon.

For those who enjoy the company of other foreigners, Kos' over-development has compensations. The road system is excellent, there is variety to the restaurants in Kos Town, and the range of sports facilities on the beaches—from wind-surfing to water-skiing—is good. History buffs in search of tranquillity might care to stay on one of Kos Town's tree-lined back streets in order to visit the important antiquities, then take advantage of Kos' travel communications by journeying to a satellite island like Pserimos or Nissiros.

Kos is best known as the birthplace of Hippocrates, the father of modern medical science. But traces found at the cave of Aspropetro in the village of Kéfalos bear witness that the island has been inhabited since Neolithic times. From the 15th through the 11th centuries B.C. Kos, from its ancient capital

stipalea
een through
e vaulting
a
enoese
astle.

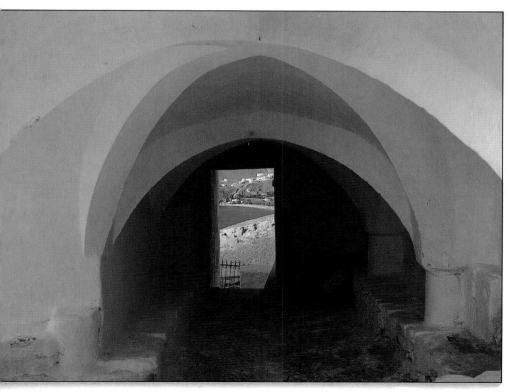

Astypalaia near Kéfalos, took part in the Trojan War and grew into a major, influential naval power.

Together with Rhodes the island developed colonies in southern Italy and was influential in commerce and the arts. Plutarch testifies that during the seventh and sixth centuries B.C. the Koans continued to prosper, joining the holy alliance of the Dorian Hexapolis. Kos surrendered to the Persians towards the end of the sixth century, but by 480 B.C. the island was delivered of the Persian yoke and soon after became a member of the Athenian League.

Twin calamities forced the relocation of the capital to its present position at the other end of the island. Astyochos, Admiral of the Spartans, occupied and then sacked the old capital Astypalaia. Shortly after, an earthquake devastated the same site. Many citizens left to settle on another island which, in remembrance, was named Astipalea. Others transferred to the northern promontory and began to construct temples and beautiful buildings. The historian Strabo wrote of this new town: "She was not large but inhabited in the best way possible and to the people visiting her by sea pleasant to behold."

Cooled by sea breezes and fringed with palms, **Kos Town**'s skyline is a gracious mixture of minarets, towers and round, domed mosques. Its oldest existing quarters are those around the almost circular harbour built by the Knights of St John. The narrow neck of the harbour is guarded by the **Castle of the Knights**, most probably on the site of an older structure. Palm trees are now planted in the moat, while inside the fortified walls (a second wall was completed in 1514 after an unsuccessful raid by the Turks) can be found some remains from ancient sites.

Situated in **Lozia Square** which adjoins the Castle is the **plane tree of Hippocrates**, a handsome, gnarled tree supported by planks. According to tradition the Father of Medicine, who was born on Kos in 460 B.C., used to write and teach his students under its spreading branches. This story, although delightful, is untrue, for the island capital was still located in Astypalaia during the time Hippocrates lived. Nevertheless, this magnificent specimen might live up to its other, less fanciful sobriquet, "the oldest tree in Europe".

Kos's **Archaeological Museum** is located at the Piazza of Eleftheria opposite the **Defterdar mosque**. Although some of its items have been transferred to Rhodes (notably statues and mosaic floors) its three rooms of antiquities provide an important respite away from the heat. Do not miss the regal statue of Hippocrates.

It is impossible to stroll through the streets of Kos without chancing across the island's numerous archaeological sites. Serious students will probably want to visit the ruins at mid-day, when the town slows down and contemplation is possible in relative peace.

The **portico** of the fourth or third century B.C., and its restored columns, the **ancient agora**, the **Roman baths**, and the **gymnasium of Xystos** are among the most notable. Theatrical performances of ancient legends are

Relatively speaking, Greek to Greek in Kos's Archaeological Museum.

occasionally held in the beautiful **odeon**, with its marble steps leading to a well-preserved amphitheatre.

Although the excavations can be loosely grouped into eastern, western and central zones, a more traditional way to view them is to follow the Greek custom of treating the sites casually. To spread a picnic with wine on a collapsed marble column and to consume lunch within the walls of history is perhaps the greatest pleasure one can find on any of the islands.

Situated in a grove of cypress trees three miles (five km) southwest of Kos Town are the ruins of the **Asklépieion**, a healing institution similar to our modern hospitals. There were 300 known *aesculapiums* in antiquity; the most respected being Epidaurus and Trikki in Thessaly where the worship of the god Asklépios originated.

This sanctuary is constructed on several terraces, and the uppermost terrace offers wonderful views of Kos, Pserimos, Kalimnos and, northeast, the coast of Turkey. Appropriately, a temple to

Apollo is thought to have stood near this spot, for it was Apollo who allegedly taught his son Asklepios the practice of therapeutic healing, an art Hippocrates and other scientists incorporated into their researches.

The oldest temple in the sanctuary is the Ionic Temple in **Antis** on the middle terrace, dating from the late fourth and early third centuries B.C. In front of the temple is a great altar in the form of a Greek letter. The upper terrace consists of a great Doric temple to Asklepios which stands on a base of three steps, one of which is black marble.

Throughout the site are chambers from the Roman and Christian eras. Along the exterior walls are two underground chambers, easily overlooked. A notable but unsubstantiated theory places them as treatment rooms for venereal disease, complete with a temple to Venus and a statue of the semi-nude goddess.

Of the other towns on the island, **Kardámena**, 15 miles (25 km) from Kos on the south coast, is the island's

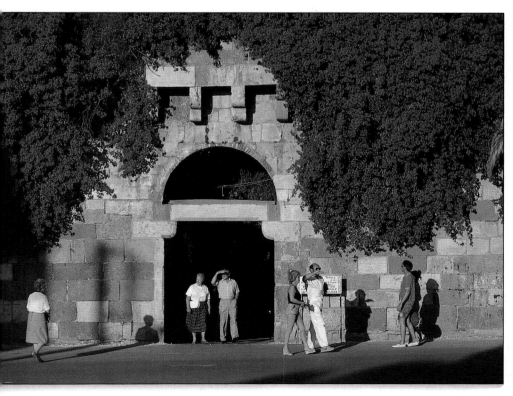

FESTIVE OCCASIONS

It seemed as if the whole village had crushed into the tiny church. The air was heavy with the scent of basil framing the icon of the Virgin Mary. Hundreds of candles flickered, boosting the heat of the midsummer night, while the sweet voices of the choir—specially hired for the occasion—fought to be heard above the congregation.

The priest called for hush, largely ignored. Children shoved through the crowd for their chunks of holy bread, sliced with gusto by the local taverna owner. The greengrocer's wife, dressed in her best, handed out candles and guarded the brimming collection plate.

The Assumption of the Virgin Mary, the *Panayia*, on 15 August is the most important festival in Greece (after Easter). From mainland to islands people flock home for the celebrations, or *paniyiria*, with feasting and dancing, often all night, following the religious ceremony.

The Greeks have a great knack of mixing piety with pleasure. Sombre, moving moments soon give way to rambunctious carousing. Grannies, toddlers, and teenagers all join in while the macho *pallikaria*, brave young men, try to outdance each other.

The festival marks the reception of the Holy Mother into Heaven. Every island has its own celebrations for the national holiday, but at most *paniyiria* the icon of the Virgin, often framed in gold or silver, or encrusted in jewels, is paraded aloft during the feast. The faithful queue up to kiss the Holy image—slipping money into the collection plate for the privilege, of course—or snatch sprigs of basil for good luck throughout the year. *Vasiliko*, the royal herb, isn't used for cooking here but to adorn the church. The Greeks believe it is sacred as it grew on the tomb of Christ.

Paniyiria, equal to our *fêtes* or country fairs, stem from pagan times when ancient Greeks honoured the Gods with orgies, feasting and fertility rites, plus a bit of buying and selling. From the fourth century the *paniyiri fora* celebrated the Christian martyrs. The church frowned on the commercial aspect, although these days you'll find peddlers and market stalls selling everything from balloons to catapults, icons to amulets, crucifixes to tracts on the saints. Condoms have also been spotted among the fairground novelties. In olden times there was often a baby boom nine months after the festival. The word stems from *pan* (all) and *agora* (marketplace), suggesting a public assembly. But the present Greek word to celebrate, *paniyirizo*, *pan* (all) and *yirizo* (return) seems nearer the mark when you see the exiles and expats pouring off the ferries to their islands for the big day.

On 15 August Greeks make pilgrimages to Tinos in the Cyclades where the icon of the Panayia Evangelistria is said to work miracles. Pilgrims flock to Patmos, too, where St John wrote the book of Revelation. But perhaps the most colourful celebrations of the feast of the *Panayia* are at Olympos on Karpathos.

The village clings to the hillside almost locked away in a time warp, and until recently cut off from the world. People still speak a form of Dorian Greek and women wear their traditional costumes every day. The black, elaborately embroidered tunic, with matching headscarf—apparently imported from Ireland—and long leather boots or *stivalia* are the hallmark of the true *Olymbissa* (Olympos women).

At festival time the *koppeles*, girls of marriageable age, wear swirling skirts of vivid satin in pink, blue or green, topped by black cut-away jackets, often woven by their families. Everything is smothered in embroidery, or decked with braiding, sequins and tassels. But the *pièce de résistance* is a heavy collar of gold coins, a wearable dowry, which shows prospective suitors what the girl is worth literally.

On festival day musicians gather beneath the village church playing traditional Karpathian music on the *tsambouna* (goatskin bagpipes). The village men lead the dancing and as they wend their way down the narrow streets the girls join in, the slow *mantinades* giving way to the fleet-footed *sousta*. Old ladies hand out almonds in twists of net and the usual revelry ensues.

The festival attracts throngs of visitors, so beware. Transport and rooms are scarce, so if you plan to attend, plan to stay awhile.

second largest tourist centre. Its beach is long, sandy and very crowded. Within walking distance is a fortress built around 1500 on the site of an older Byzantine fortress.

From **Pili**, in the centre, a track running for just over two miles (three km) leads to **old Pylai** and a hill with the remains of another Byzantine castle. The church has well-preserved frescoes from the 14th century. The remains of a Hellenistic Doric temple and a theatre can be found in the southwest near **Kéfalos**, 27 miles (43 km) from Kos. This is the area where Astypalaia once stood, although the precise location of the ancient capital is unclear.

The beach most easily reached from Kos Town is broad, sandy **Tingáki** on the north coast. Just a cycle ride away, it is protected from northernly gales by umbrellas.

PSERIMOS: Tiny, golden Pserimos can be reached by caique from both Kos and Kalimnos. With a population of just 72 people and a main street which is actually a beach, this gem of a place is the perfect solution to the crowds and noise of Kos. At night the only sound is that of the wind rustling through bamboo groves, or the tinny tinkle of goat bells. At sunset, after the excursion boats depart, local women wade fully dressed into the sea, skirts held high, in rarely seen relaxation. The sea is perfect for children, for several hundred feet away from the shore the water is still only shoulder-deep.

A path behind the harbour leads to a simple church; a free-standing bell tower is the island's monument. The interior of the church is solemn and perfumed. Wooden carvings and icons adorned with gold watches are reflected in the light from candles which appear to remain permanently lit. Outside, beyond the tower, the cemetery chronicles Pserimos' most recent history. Beside each grave is a glass box containing plastic flowers, a photograph of the deceased, and a candle.

KALIMNOS: A reasonably prosperous island where wealth is not dependent solely on tourism, Kalimnos' income is

Left, lighting the candles at midnight on the eve of Easter Sunday. Below, a Greek Orthodox wedding.

derived from sponge-diving. Although the industry is no longer thriving—the Aegean seabed is being stripped bare due to demand—the absence of men in the main harbour, **Pothea**, signals that a fleet has departed for the annual, six-month working trip. (Female travellers might care to enquire as to the date of expected return. The port's bars and cafés become very rowdy, and plans to disappear—or participate—can then be made accordingly.)

The latter stages of the sponge-making process can be observed by asking to be escorted to a factory. If the site is an old one the operation looks medieval: under large wooden eaves stone tanks of salt water, or huge vats of scalding acid stand which bubble and steam. When the sponges are gathered they are black and contain impurities.

Men in wide-brimmed hats (or, if at sea, the divers' themselves) walk on the sponges to "milk" them of any unwanted substances. The sponges are then cleaned in the salt water tanks, bleached in acid to the soft ochre colour

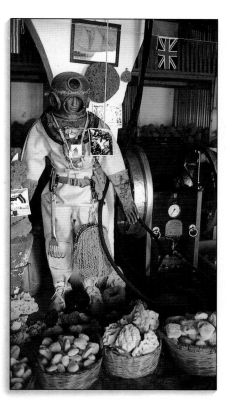

required by tourists (which, incidentally, weakens the fibre), then cleaned once again with salt water. Laid out to dry in a factory's courtyard, the acres of irregularly-shaped sponges make one long for a bubble bath.

Pothea itself rises steeply up a mountain ending in a religious cross. Houses tend to be three or four stories in height with balconies looking out to sea. One church near the top has five silver domes which dazzle in the sun.

Horio, the old capital, contains a ruined castle thought to have been built by the Knights of St John. The road north runs through barren hills; visual relief is provided only by the blue wooden boxes on the slopes which are used to house honey-bees. The greyness of the landscape makes the first view of Vathí a delightful surprise. Rounding a hilltop the town appears, far below, nestled in a green fertile valley on a turquoise arm of water leading out to sea.

Vathí (which means "deep") might well be the sweetest-smelling village in the Aegean. Its principal industry is the growing and exportation of mandarin oranges, and cargo boats ply back and forth along the sparkling water with picturesque industry. Houses are white, built in the Italian style and sparkling whitewashed walls lead to a tiny chapel.

From Vathí it is a long walk or a pleasant boatride to the **Cave of the Nymphs**; in antiquity a place of worship and in more modern times a place of refuge from the Italians. During the last occupation, when the teaching of Greek was forbidden, it is said that secret classes were held in the cave to school the island's children in their native tongue.

Back in Pothea the route west to Mírties is green and lined with trees. Architecture is scenic and varied: windmills, ruined fortresses, a couple of private houses which resemble churches. **Mírties** itself is a busy and highly attractive resort perched on a wide bay overlooking the island Telendos.

Tavernas and *pensions* sport grape arbours and palm trees and the road to the sea, which winds through the village, is adorned with hibiscus and other

Kalimnos is a prosperous island due to the sponge industry.

flowers. The beach tends to overflow with Greek tourists as do the other two beaches at **Masóuri** and **Pánormos.** Intrepid bathers might like to try their luck at **Emborios**, 12 miles (20 km) northeast of Porthea, in the northern peninsula. Crowds are virtually non-existent, but so too is public transport.

TELENDOS: Until the sixth century B.C. Telendos was joined to the island Kalimnos. It was only after one of the Dodecanese's numerous earthquakes (535 B.C.) that this towering rock of an island became a separate entity. A township sank into the sea at the same time and it is claimed that the water is so clear that ancient city walls can occasionally be seen in the narrow strip between the two islands.

The caique from Mírties on Kalimnos runs every 20 minutes in the summer and (optimistically) once or twice daily in the winter. Prepare to share the boat with bulky boxes of tomatoes, loads of blankets, and other household goods. The fishermen who are the most frequent passengers are graced with wonderful manners; even if three times younger, a lady will not be allowed to stand while they remain seated.

The only hamlet, **Telendos**, lies huddled under mammoth **Mt Rathi** which rises to 1,500 ft (458 metres). A small peninsula of pine trees attached to one side of the hill gives the impression, when approaching by boat, that the island is shaped like a gigantic snail. Telendos is more upmarket than its equally tiny neighbour Pserimos; tavernas are chic and colourful, shaded by pine trees and roofs made of straw. *Pensions* have interior marble steps and modern bathrooms.

The cafés are enormously pleasant; sit at one on the harbour to admire the attractive contours of Mírties on the other side of the channel, or watch the spectacle of a man in rolled-up trousers and wide-brimmed hat bashing an octopus against the wharf, presumably for someone's dinner. Three beaches lie only a five-minute walk away. **Hohlakas** is sandy and sign-posted. The two shingle beaches to the west consist of smooth, flat rocks the size of coins.

The island's houses are neat, almost suburban, decorated with trim boxes of carnations or violets. Walk through whitewashed alleyways to the church which is petite and painted pale colours; inside, the incense is overpowering after the fresh scent of flowers in town. The cool interior is dominated by a golden chandelier and 12 hand-painted saints on the wall. One of the painted panels opens to reveal an inner sanctuary for private meditation.

On the north side of the island, best reached by boat, stands a chapel of St Constantine (also known as **Ayios Vassileos**) and the abandoned ruins of a **medieval castle**.

LEROS: If given a choice, arrive by ferry at **Lakki** around midnight for a glamourous experience. The town served as a naval base during the Italian occupation and the new residents built enormous offices in the contemporary style, art deco. Towering palm trees line the harbour-front and to walk along the echoing streets, the magnificent ochre buildings illuminated by indirect light,

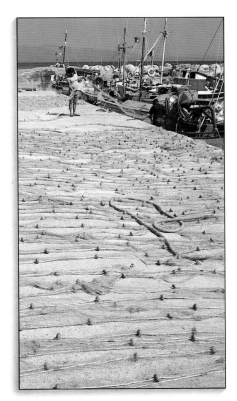

Nets drying in the sun are a common Mediterranean sight.

is to feel like an intruder on the set of a melancholy Fred Astaire movie.

In daylight, Lakki's elegance is shabbier and the streets teem with naval personnel. Still, the broad avenues and little squares tucked behind the harbour offer a faded grandeur rarely seen on Greek islands.

Leros is less popular than most islands for a variety of reasons. Mainland Greeks make crude jokes about its name (the word *"lera"* connotes dirt and unsavoury activities). Its principal business, although worthy, lacks holiday flair: Leros is the centre for the institutional care of both retarded children and intractable psychiatric cases.

Foreign visitors, seduced by the attractions of near-by Patmos and Kos, sail straight past on the ferry, eagerly awaiting more familiar pleasures. Which means, in the end, that Leros suffers little from the ravages of tourism which blight so many of its neighbours. Although it's true that Leros enjoys a respite from souvenir shops, hawkers, and tacky cocktail bars, neither does it sparkle with tourist highlights like ancient ruins or dazzling beaches.

Its massive fortress contains an attractive church of the **Virgin of the Kastro**, but little else of singular importance. Charm lies in its friendly people and a work-a-day ambience.

The island's capital, **Platanos**, snuggled under the fortress, has spread in both directions to include the villages **Panteli** and **Ayia Marina**, names by which it is also called.

The town hall, the island museum and all the necessary shops can be found near the square. Ayia Marina is perhaps the prettiest of the three villages, approached by a steep road from Platanos which leads to a harbour fringed by fragrant pine trees.

On the way to **Alínda**, three miles (five km) northwest, is a cemetery for British soldiers killed during World War II. Leros' strategic position earned it the soubriquet "the Gibraltar of the Med" and it was the base in turn of the navies of Italy, Germany and Britain. Alínda is a developed resort with a long

Twilight over Telendos.

beach and tourist facilities but the best beach is further on past Patheni at **Blefountis bay.**

Patheni is thought to have derived its name from the ancient word *parthenos* (chaste), an epithet of Artemis, goddess and protectress of women, who was worshipped here. The women of Leros, happily, are still protected; the ownership of all island property is inherited through the female line.

LIPSI: Also known as Leipsoi, this sparkling jewel in the Aegean is a gypsy island. Reached by daily caique (summer only) from Patmos or by an erratic ferry service in winter, the cubic houses of its one village, **Lipsi,** have been painted bright colours which emphasise its rakish appeal. The colours, however, change frequently; one topic during the long winter months is when, and what shade to decorate each exterior, right down to the gargoyles on the façades which can be startling in reds or vivid yellows.

Lipsi's harbour-front, however, remains dignified; from the sea the town rises like a mirage. Crowned by a church with three turquoise domes, these shapes and colours are mirrored in a series of small chapels perched on the promontory. Development has meant the widening of the harbour-front and the encroachment of tourism to cater to the Patmos overspill, so Lipsi is best appreciated after the day trippers have left on the afternoon boat.

Its beaches are sandy, the residents hospitable, and its caves a delight to explore. As the island allows few cars (although noisy farm equipment is in evidence during the day) nights are given over to the sound of the lapping sea, the crowing of errant roosters, or the occasional *bouzouki* binge.

Three satellite islands in the area are even less developed and can be reached from Patmos or, occasionally, Lipsi. **Arkoi** has only 68 inhabitants but nice beaches and rooms to let; **Agathonisi** has two villages, Megalo Horio and Mikro Horio. **Marathi** should only be attempted by arrangement as its facilities are seasonal and transport erratic.

Two island pastimes: smoking cigarettes and sitting at cafés.

PATMOS: If Delos, the holy island in the Cyclades, was the sacred place of worship for the ancients, its modern equivalent must surely be Patmos. Patmos has long been a place of pilgrimage for those who believe that this rocky island is where St John the Divine is said to have dictated the text of Revelation to his pupil Prochoros in A.D. 95.

Tradition identifies St John with the Apostle John although this has never been proved. Nevertheless, in 1088 the monk Christodoulos Latrenos founded a great, fortified monastery in honour of St John, and it has been a place of scholarship and religious enlightenment ever since. At Easter and on the blessed Saint's Day, 21 May, the faithful flock to its shores to worship and give thanks.

Although the island is no longer ruled by monks, their presence, along with the fortress which looms into view at almost every turning, tempers the rowdier elements found on most holiday islands. Tourists are much in evidence, but those who elect to stay (as opposed to those who arrive by hydrofoil from Kos or Rhodes) appreciate the unique, even spiritual, atmosphere which Patmos exudes. Conversations in the cafés tend to be elevated, night sounds are muted, and many people return season after season to enjoy what one resident calls "the classical life".

Skala is the main harbour, best appreciated late at night when crickets serenade and the sailboats are illuminated against a dark sky. The lights of Hora on the hill above are indistinguishable from the stars. A few paces from the sea lies a tiny cemetery. Its symmetrical tombstones, when lit by candles, provide a ghostly spectacle.

In the daytime Skala loses charm but gains in efficiency; all island commerce is here, from shops to banks to ferryboat agencies. Buses leave regularly from the main square for Hora and the monastery. Bearded priests in long, hot cassocks vie for seats on the bus with tourists in sandals and shorts; the priests, long familiar with this summer tussle, usually win the race.

The Monastery of St John the Theologian.

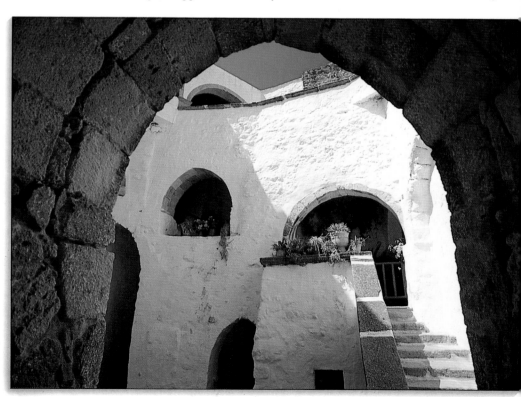

216

Halfway between Skala and Hora is the **Cave of the Apocalypse**. A silver band marks the spot in the wall where St John is said to have composed Revelation; just at the mouth of the grotto is a great cleft in the rock through which the voice of God spoke.

The bus stops again at the monastery terrace where there is an unrivalled view of the Aegean. On a cloudless day it is possible to see, not only nearby Samos, Ikaria, Kalimnos and Leros but also the far-away Cycladic isles Amorgos, Paros, Naxos and Mykonos.

The **Monastery of St John the Theologian** is built at Hora's highest point. A brooding fortress surrounded by defensive walls, just inside is a stall where monks sell illustrated guides, well worth buying for a comprehensive interpretation. Within one of its five chapels are the relics of the Blessed Christodoulos, the monastery's founder, who lies in a marble sarcophagus. The Treasury houses the most impressive monastic collection in Greece outside Mt Athos; priceless icons and jewellery can be viewed, even handled, by special appointment.

Of invaluable importance to scholars is the library which contains 2,000 volumes or manuscripts. It, too, requires special permission to enter but the greatest treasure, 33 leaves of the *Codex Porphyrius*, embellished with gold and silver, can be seen in the public part of the Treasury. Written in the sixth century on purple vellum, the book contains most of St Mark's Gospel.

The silent, shuttered windows in many of **Hora's** villas highlight the fact that they are owned by Athenians. For this reason rooms are hard to come by, but Hora's discreet restaurants and, at night, silent, echoing streets are worth savouring. Taxis can be found for the return trip to Skala.

Most of the island can be visited in a day, but the most scenic way is on foot. Buses connect with the beach resort **Groikos** and the fertile village **Kambos**; caiques from Skala call in at beaches at the **bay of Lambi, Livadi ton Kalogiron,** and **Merika.**

Young monk at St John's.

CRETE

Crete, claimed by many Greeks to be the most authentic of islands, is by far the largest. This "other continent" lies in the middle of the eastern Mediterranean and provides a stepping stone between Europe and Africa. *Megalonissos* ("Great Island") is what Cretans call their home and "great" refers to much more than size.

"Great" can certainly be applied to Minoan, the first civilisation in Europe and one with which Crete is inexorably entwined. Visitors by the thousands pour into the ruins of Knossos, Phaistós, Mállia and Káto Zákros, before heading towards one of the scores of excellent beaches. With two major airports Crete could hardly be classified as undiscovered, but its size and scale manage to contain the crowds and to please visitors with divergent tastes. A car is essential for discovering the best of the island, but car hire is, unfortunately, expensive. Crete's gently shelving coastline also make it a popular choice for those holidaying with children.

Most of Crete's 500,000 people live in the north. The mountains to the south nurture a proud, rugged, independent people whose fierce mustachioed menfolk still dress in jodhpurs, black leather knee-boots and black headscarves. The mountains are honey-combed with caves—it is claimed there are more than 3,000—with which many myths are associated. The Diktaian and the Idaian caves both claim to be the birthplace of Zeus: each has champions and detractors. The Tourist Organisation has resolved the conflict with the wisdom of a Solomon, the cunning of Byzantium and the acumen of an Onassis. The conclusion? Zeus was born in the Diktaian cave and reared in the Idaian.

Unlike more integrated islands, Crete has its own songs, charac-terised by the *mantinades* and its own dances, among them the spectacular *pentozali*. These are almost invariably accompanied by the lyra, a ubiquitous Cretan instrument.

Mountains and beaches. Ancient ruins and modern culture. For many people Crete is the quintessential Greek island.

Preceding pages: a heavenly view of the Cretan mountains; migrant fishermen. Left, a pretty girl.

CRETE

The Aegean's "great island" has an east-west orientation, is 173 miles (277 km) long and has a width of between eight and 38 miles (13 and 61 km). A massive mountainous backbone with peaks stretching skywards to over 8,000 ft (2,400 metres) dominates. In the north the mountains fall gently giving rise to fertile plains while in the south they plunge precipitously into the sea.

Deep gorges divide Crete (Kriti) into four main regions. Many gorges are now penetrated by roads which link the north and south. However, it is best to measure journeys in hours rather than in distance. (An average of 30 miles/48 km an hour is good going.)

Infinite variety: For most of the year snow lies on the highest peaks which, in spring, provide a dramatic backdrop to verdant meadows ablaze with flowers. This, as botanists and ornithologists well know, is *the* time to visit. The former arrive to view more than 100 species which are unique to the island while the latter are thrilled by more than 250 types of birds on their way north.

These transients join such rare permanent residents as Bonelli's eagle and Eleonara's falcon. And it is in spring that the island is redolent with sage, thyme and oregano. However, *the* endemic herb is dittany. (Did you know that bathing in an infusion of dittany increases sexual desires?)

Crete, much more than other Greek islands, is a place for sight-seeing as well as for being on the beach. Minoan ruins are the major magnet but there are Greek, Roman and Venetian remains for which many tourist authorities would give their eye teeth. And, what other island has a score of museums?

There are also literally hundreds of Byzantine churches, many with rare and precious frescoes. These frescoes often have a distinct Cretan style recognisable by elongated figures and attention to detail. (Many churches are locked. Enquire at the nearest café for the key. Even if you fail in your quest you will enjoy the opportunity to meet the locals.)

Dozens of monasteries have fallen into disuse but others still function and have rich treasures and histories. All occupy sites which are a real estate agent's dream. (When visiting be sure to observe a sensible dress code or you will be denied entry.)

Homer's "island of 100 towns" can also be called one of 100 beaches—the coast line is 636 miles (1,050 km) long. However, a beach is a place where a boat can be beached and not necessarily a paradise of golden sands. Yet "search and ye shall find": Crete does have superb beaches. On a few nudity, although not officially sanctioned, is tolerated. The season is long—stretching from Easter until nearly Christmas.

Minoan glory: The division of the one-and-a-half millennia of Minoan glory into several periods still causes much controversy among scholars but all agree that the apogee was the neopalatial era (1700-1380 B.C.). Most of the ruins visited at such renowned sites as Knossos, Phaistós, Mállia and Káto Zákros are from this period when great unfortified palaces, brilliantly decorated, were built and when beautiful pottery and magnificent jewellery, used for both religious purposes and personal adornment, was produced.

The neopalatial period had been preceded by the protopalatial (2000-1700 B.C.) which, in turn, had followed the prepalatial period (2600-2000 B.C.). The first palaces, which were built during the protopalatial period and of which exiguous remains can still be seen, are generally thought to have been destroyed by an earthquake. Debate still rages as to what brought the neopalatial era to an end.

By the postpalatial period (1300-1100 B.C.) the Minoan leadership in the eastern Mediterranean was waning and by the Early Iron Age (1100-650 B.C.) Crete was under the sway of mainland Greece. Surviving Minoans, Etocretans, retired to the mountains and continued to maintain their old traditions.

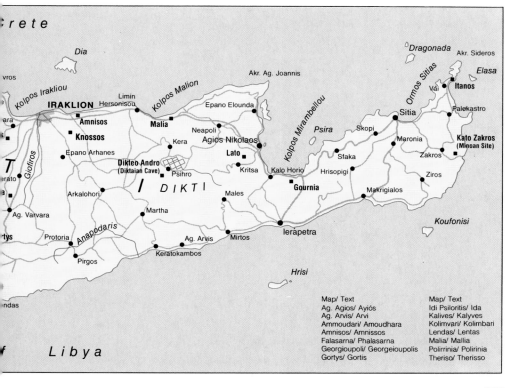

Map/ Text		Map/ Text	
Ag. Agios/ Ayiós		Idi Psiloritis/ Ida	
Ag. Arvis/ Arvi		Kalives/ Kalyves	
Ammoudari/ Amoudhara		Kolimvari/ Kolimbari	
Amnisos/ Amnissos		Lendas/ Lentas	
Falasarna/ Phalasarna		Malia/ Mallia	
Georgioupoli/ Georgeioupolis		Polirrinia/ Polirinia	
Gortys/ Gortis		Theriso/ Therisso	

Iráklion (Iráklio, Heráklion): The capital of Crete since 1971, this city has a population of 125,000 and is the fifth largest in Greece. It boasts the highest *per capita* income of any Greek city. However, look not for elegance: much of Iráklion resembles a building site because of the propensity of its inhabitants to spend money on starting a building—knowing that they lack the capital to complete it—rather than paying taxes on that money.

Iráklion's major attractions, other than the outstanding **Archaeological Museum** and the Minoan ruins of **Knossos**, are from the Venetian era testifying that this was the most prosperous period in Crete's modern history. Visit the **restored fort** at the old harbour, whose three high reliefs of the Lion of St Mark announce its provenance, and the **Venetian arsenal**. Observe in the background Mount Júfktas which bears a resemblance to a recumbent figure, claimed to be Zeus.

Challenging and rewarding is a complete circumambulation of the 15th-century **city walls** which, in their day, were the most formidable in the Mediterranean world. The walls stretch for nearly three miles (four km) and, in parts, are 95 feet (29 metres) thick. Visit also the **Historical and Ethnographic** and the **Religious Art museums**. The latter, housed in the church of Ayia Ekaterini which is near the cathedral, contains some exquisite icons, six of which are the work of the 16th-century master, Mikhail Damaskinós.

From here, stroll north through the market redolent with tantalising smells, jammed with people and resonant with decibels. En route, stop to savour an inexpensive meal at one of the dozen tavernas which block "Dirty Alley".

Much more upmarket are the cafés and restaurants of **Venizélou** (Fountain) **Square** which gains its eponymous name from the charming 17th-century Morosini fountain with its guardian marble lions. Overlooking the square is the handsome Venetian *loggia* flanked by the churches of **Ayios Markos** and **Ayios Titos**. All three buildings have been heavily restored.

Since 1966, when it was returned from St Marks in Venice, Ayios Titos has housed the skull of St Titus, who was St Paul's apostle to Crete and the island's first bishop. Across town, close to the Archaeological Museum, is the less intimate **Eleftherías Square**, choc-a-bloc with cafés which are popular with both locals and tourists.

The best beaches near Iráklion are at **Amoudara**, immediately to the west and at **Amnissos** to the east. The latter, which was a port for Knossos, has the better sands and ambience.

Several short excursions from Iráklion will delight the collector of Minoan sites and provide the opportunity to view the lovely countryside and to savour village life. **Tilissos**, (eight miles/13 km) southwest of Iráklion, boasts three well-preserved small palaces or large villas. Further west, the bipartite village of **Anogia**, where wool is spun and dried and where many homes have looms, is a weaving and embroidery centre. Many Anogians

wear native dress with the picture-book men looking like rebels in search of a cause. This is no stage setting: Anogia has a long tradition of resistance and revolt and its men are among the fiercest and bravest in Crete.

From Anogia the road climbs to the magnificent **Nida plateau** from where it is a 20-minute stroll to the **Idaian Cave** which was the nursery, if not the birthplace, of Zeus. Here the god was guarded by the Kouretes, who clashed their weapons to drown his cries, while he was suckled by the goat-nymph Amaltheai. Climbers might wish to push on to the summit of **Mount Ida**, at 8,178 feet (2,456 metres), the highest point on Crete. A guide is advisable: allow eight hours for the round-trip.

In and around the large village of **Arhanes**, five miles (eight km) south of Knossos, are three churches with interesting frescoes and icons and three Minoan sites. **Turkoyeitoniá** has a Minoan palace: **Phourní** boasts the outstanding cemetery in the prehistoric Aegean and **Anemóspilia** has a temple.

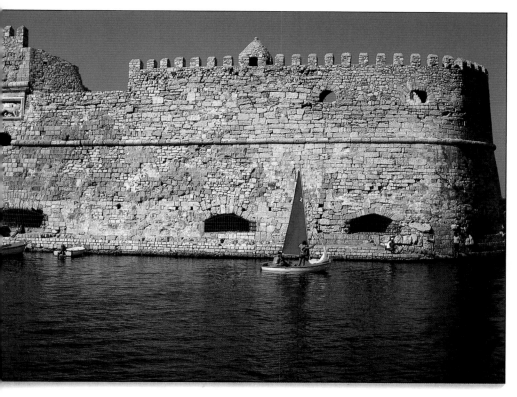

KNOSSOS

Where else but in Crete can the visitor board a local bus in a thriving, bustling, modern city—in this case the No. 2 in Iráklion—and, 20 minutes later, be transported back nearly 4,000 years? An Iráklion merchant, Minos Kalokairinós, discovered the site of ancient Knossos, the renowned city of the Minoans, in 1878 and, a quarter of a century later, Sir Arthur Evans purchased part of this site and began a systematic exploration.

Evans used his own fortune—sponsorship, government grants: what are they?—and, assisted by archaeologists and artists, excavated and then rebuilt Knossos in his own image rather than in that of King Minos—or so say his detractors. Still, without Evans' reinforced concrete and the brushwork of the Gilliérons, father and son, who copied and added to those frescoes (the originals are in the Iráklion Museum) the average uninitiated or unschooled visitor would be much less excited about the glories of Knossos.

What the visitor to Knossos sees are the remains of a magnificent palace and auxiliary buildings (Little Palace, royal villa, caravanserai) constructed during the so-called neopalatial period which extended from approximately 1700 B.C. to 1380 B.C. Exiguous remains of earlier periods (prepalatial from 2000 B.C. to 1700 B.C.) and later periods (postpalatial from 1300 B.C. to 1100 B.C.) can also be found.

The remains cover more than four acres (nearly two hectares) and the site is usually very crowded. The best time to visit is early in the morning or just before closing time, when there are fewer visitors. Alternatively, try exploring the site backwards—by beginning at the end and walking against the flow of traffic.

The city had a population of between 30,000 and 100,000. The Great Palace, an extraordinary complex of buildings divided by terraces, staircases and yards, had more than 1,300 rooms. It is easy to appreciate the legend that Knossos was a labyrinth built by Daedulos, on the orders of King Minos, to hide the half-man, half-bull minotaur conceived by his wife Pasiphaë, who had been infatuated with the white bull sent by Poseidon.

The east and west wings of the Great Palace are separated by a large central court. Was it here that the bull dancing took place? An exquisite ivory of the bull and the youthful acrobat can be viewed in the Iráklion Museum where, incidentally, most of the artefacts are from the neopalatial ruins.

The Grand Staircase, with its five flights in the centre of the palace, formed the official approach to the Royal Quarters and is one of the major architectural achievements of antiquity. Observe the imaginative manner in which the central light-well allowed natural light to illuminate and brighten the royal rooms.

Gaze upon the original alabaster throne of Minos, guarded by a pair of painted griffins. Sadly, until only 25 years ago, visitors could actually sit on this, the oldest throne in the world. Instead, in the northwest corner of Knossos, walk the Royal Road, the oldest road in Europe, which was flanked by houses and workshops.

Back in the palace, observe the Queen's clay bathtub—yes, Pasiphaë did bathe here—and her lavatory and appreciate that the Minoans were far ahead of their time in many aspects. Remains in the Queen's *toilette* suggest that there may have been running water from cisterns on a higher level and, at times, one wonders if the hydraulic technology in the eastern bastion is not more sophisticated than that found today in many hotels on Crete.

Knossos was not only a palace for the royal family and their attendant nobles and functionaries but was also a sacred precinct as testified to by the lustral baths which were used for bathing and anointing. The complex also had workshops and storerooms where enormous *pithoi* containing wine, oil and grain were stored. These large Ali Baba jars are still made in villages such as Margarítes and Thrapsano.

Although the names of the workmen who built Knossos are not known they are remembered, 3,000 years later, by the incisions of tridents and double-headed axes which can be seen on many ashlar blocks. How did it end? Theories abound, one of which claims that after a catastrophic explosion on the island of Santorini, a tidal wave swept away the wonder that was Knossos.

Human remains were found in this temple and it is suggested that when it was destroyed by an earthquake a priest was in the act of ritually sacrificing a youth. Such suggestions have outraged some scholars just as much as Nikos Kazantákis' books have outraged the established church.

A steep climb from Arhanes (allow 45 minutes) leads to the summit of **Mount Júktas** (2,703 feet/811 metres) from where you can admire the panorama while griffin vultures swoop overhead. On the summit are a Minoan peak sanctuary, a 14th-century chapel and caves in which Zeus is said to be buried. This proves the truth of the aphorism that "all Cretans are liars" because, in the opinion of other Greeks, Zeus is immortal.

Straight on from Varvará is a breathtaking view of the lush **Plain of Mesára**. Rich soil and a benign climate make this a cornucopia where the wild flowers are said to be taller and larger than anywhere else in Crete.

After 10 miles (16 km) **Gortyn** (Gortis) is reached. This was the capital of the Romans who came to Crete in the first century B.C. to settle feuds but who stayed to conquer—how familiar! Outstanding and upstanding are the Roman odeon and a Byzantine basilica. The latter is by far the best preserved early church in Crete and was built to house the tomb of Titus, Crete's first bishop, who died in A.D. 105.

However, the most renowned artefacts are some stone blocks incorporated into the odeon. About 2,500 years ago more than 17,000 characters were incised on these to produce the Code of Gortyn which consists of rules governing the behaviour of the people. The script is written in the ox-plough manner (reading left to right along one line and then right to left along the next).

Immediately before Gortyn is the almost sacred village of **Ayii Déka** (Holy Ten) with its heavily restored medieval church into which are incorporated fragments from Gortyn. Ayii Déka is renowned because, in A.D. 250, 10 men were executed who are not only

Sandy MacGillivray, director of the British School of Classical Studies on Crete.

among the most revered of Cretan saints but who are glorified as the first in a long line of Cretans willing to sacrifice themselves by opposing tyrannous occupiers of their beloved island.

Those in search of more classical ruins, of health and of good swimming might wish, before continuing to Phaistós, to drive south to **Lentas** over a mountainous road which provides magnificent vistas. Ancient Lebéna was the port for Gortyn and its therapeutic springs made it a renowned healing sanctuary with an Asklépieion (temple to Asklépios, the god of healing). Traces of this sanctuary with mosaic floors and large baths can be seen.

In an attempt to equal, if not emulate, the ancients, nude bathing is popular on Lentas' best beach, beyond the headland at the western end of the village.

Phaistós (also spelled Festos), Crete's second great Minoan site, occupies a magnificent location 10 miles (16 km) south of Gortyn. Most of the remains are from the neopalatial period although part of the floor plan of the protopalatial palace is discernible. Staterooms, religious quarters, workshops and storerooms can all be identified. Outstanding is the Grand Stairway. At Phaistós those purists who bristle at Knossos' reconstruction can let their imagination run riot.

Nearby, again on a glorious site with views of the Libyan Sea, are the charming Minoan ruins of **Ayia Triada** whose exact function still causes speculation—a palace, a villa, several villas?

And so to **Matala**, 75 miles (120 km) from Iráklion, and practically at the mid-point of the south coast. Matala first gained renown when the sandstone caves in the cliffs which rise above the small, excellent sandy beach became home of the world's hippies. Today, the small resort is busy, yet not frenetic. The scenic 30-minute walk to **Red Beach** is highly recommended.

Ayia Galíni, the other major south coast resort, also lies on the Gulf of Mesára but if Matala is too boisterous then Ayia Galíni may well be the same.

The harbour, with a short wide quay

Shepherds milking in the mountains. Right, Spyros Hrisofakes with a photo of the courtesan who inspired Kazantzákis.

ZORBA'S LEGACY

Seldom has a fictional character so engulfed its creator as did *Zorba the Greek* swallow Nikos Kazantzákis (1883-1957), the most renowned Greek writer of the modern era. (Incidentally, Odysseus Elytis, the Nobel prizewinner in literature in 1979, was also born in Crete.) Although Kazantzákis' output was large and varied, it is to the rugged, warm and happy-go-lucky Zorba, who can still be encountered on Crete, that Kazantzákis owed his international reputation.

At least, that was so until another of his books was also made into a film, *The Last Temptation of Christ*. When this book was first published, the Orthodox Church sought to prosecute Kazantzákis. When it was screened in 1988, many church leaders the world over sought to have it banned. In Athens, priests marched on the cinemas where the movie was playing and projection screens were slashed in anger.

Common to *Zorba* and *Last Temptation* is Kazantzákis' conflict between spirit and flesh, between Christ and Dionysos. Kazantzákis lost his faith while a teenager because he was unable to reconcile Darwin's teachings with Christianity's promise of an afterlife. But, he never lost his Christian convictions.

Although Kazantzákis left Crete when a youngster, it is here that he is

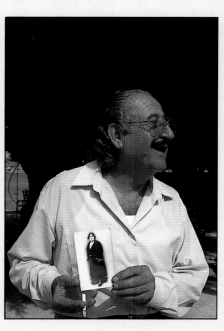

buried—for, once a Cretan, always a Cretan; indeed, no self-respecting Cretan refers to himself as a Greek. Such chauvinism is fully justified in Kazantzákis' case: when he was born in 1883, Crete had not yet become a part of the Greek nation but was still embroiled in attempts to free itself from the Turkish yoke, a struggle which caused the Kazantzákis family to move to the island of Naxos soon after Nikos was born.

Yet, because of his non-conformist views and writings, Kazantzákis was denied burial in a Christian cemetery with the full rites of the Greek Orthodox church. He was buried in the Martinengo bastion (fortunately, one of the better maintained sections) of the Iráklion walls and his tomb carries this inscription, a testimony to his life: "I hope for nothing. I fear nothing. I am free."

A statue in Eleftherias (Freedom) Square in Iráklion honours him more than does his grave on the battlements.

His admirers will make for the new Kazantzákis Museum in the village of Mirtía (15 miles/24 km) due south of Iráklion (when Kazantzákis was born here, it was called Varvári). Well arranged displays illustrate Kazantzákis' personal, literary and political life both in Greece and abroad, while one room is entirely devoted to *Zorba*. Also worth visiting is the Historical and Ethnographic Museum in Iráklion where a room represents a study of Kazantzákis. The Arkádi Monastery, shown on the 100-drachma note, features in *Freedom or Death*, Kazantzákis' most powerful novel.

Those who favour fiction rather than fact, frolics rather than philosophy, have much to see. Ierápetra was the home of Madame Hortense, the French courtesan who featured in *Zorba*. Visitors may be shown where her still body was washed and where, even before the body was cold, the old harpies rushed in and stripped Madame Hortense's apartment of all her possessions.

And, in Ierápetra, Spyros Hrisofakes, a sprightly 60-year-old with waxed moustache, still remembers the French courtesan who was the model for Kazantzákis' Madame Hortense and whose favours he, although a mere child, so desired. However, Spyros had to be content with gifts of candies from the beauty.

Much of *Zorba* was filmed in Pláka and, high above it, Kókkino Horió, which lie on the coast midway between Rethymnon and Haniá. Here *habitués* of the local tavernas may not recall the name of Kazantzákis but well remember that of Anthony Quinn. Then, in the northwest corner of the Akrotíri Peninsula, there is Stavrós with its pleasant beach, shallow waters and towering cliffs—known to the locals as "Zorba's Mountain"—where the film's climax was shot.

Although Kazantzákis roamed the world and lived in several countries, Crete stayed in his thoughts. Not only are *Zorba* and *Freedom or Death* set in Crete but the story of *The Odyssey Modern Sequel* becomes deeply interwoven with the island.

and a tiny main street jammed with tavernas and bars, is enclosed within a crescent of steep hills covered with modest small hotels. Nightlife goes on into the wee small hours. Not the place for those prone to heart attacks!

An almost mandatory pilgrimage from **Plakiás** is to the **Monastery of Préveli** (eight miles/13 km). En route, evocative ruins of the Monastery of Ayios Ioánnis are passed. Préveli has a superb position, an interesting museum with a piece of the True Cross and a courtyard fountain with the inscription, "Wash your sins, not only your face". Below the monastery is a beach from where Allied troops in World War II escaped to waiting submarines after being sheltered by the monks.

Hora Sphakíon, (Sfakia) the centre of Sphakiá and home of the Sphákians, who are the epitome of the brave, fiery, intrepid Cretans, is another of those tiny, cliff-hanging, picturesque ports. Its *raison d'être* today—but don't tell this to the Sphákians—is to transfer exhausted tourists returning by ferry from their Samaria Gorge excursions.

Other villages on the south coast which attract discerning visitors but which are not yet tourist towns are **Kali Limenes**, **Loutro**, **Finikas**, **Sougia** and **Lissos**. Explore diligently and it is possible that, in years to come, you can claim to have been there when!

Back in Iráklion, an oleander-lined expressway runs west to Rethymnon. Some however, might prefer to travel more leisurely on the old road. Leave the former at the 14-mile (22-km) mark and in a few minutes **Phodele** (Fodele), a small village rich in orange trees and locally made embroidery, is reached. A restored house here is said to be the birthplace of Doménikos Theotokópoulos, better known as **El Greco**. Phodele's fame may be fleeting for the latest word is that El Greco was probably born in Iráklion.Back on the expressway, turn seawards at the 27-mile (44-km) mark to reach the idyllic tiny resort of **Bali** which is clustered around three small bays at the foot of a hill.

At **Platanes**, just before Rethymnon,

The caves a▶
Matala.

turn southeast for the beautifully situated **Arkádi Monastery**, one of the most sacred shrines in Crete. You are not experiencing *déjà vu*; the elaborate 16th-century western façade of the double-nave church features on the 100 drachma note.

In 1886, the monastery, sheltering hundreds of women and children, was attacked by the Turks. Rather than surrender, the abbot ordered that the gunpowder stored in the now roofless room in the northwest corner of the courtyard be ignited thus killing both enemy and refugees (although one infant was blown into a tree and survived to become a nun). This act of defiance brought the plight of the Cretans to the public eye of and gained for them the sympathy and assistance of much of Europe.

Rethymnon,(Rethimno) which prides itself on being Crete's intellectual capital, scarcely qualifies as a town. A small, picturesque Venetian harbour, Rethymnon's major attraction is a quayside choc-a-bloc with colourful fish restaurants guarded by an elegant lighthouse. North of the harbour is the immense ruined **Fortétza**, said to be the largest Venetian castle, and from where excellent views may be enjoyed.

Rethymnon's other attractions—the **Rimondi Fountain**, the **museum** and the **Nerandzes Mosque**—all lie between the harbour and fortress. If open, then the ascent of the Nerandzes Mosque minaret is rewarding. Venetian houses with unexpected architectural delights can be found in the narrow streets linking these sights, while Turkish delights in the shape of minarets and overhanging wooden balconies give Rethymnon a Turkish, rather than a Greek, raffishness.

Besotted shoppers, especially those in search of leather and textiles, will find their nirvana in narrow, crowded **Paleologou Street**. Sun worshippers will make for Rethymnon's wide, flat beach with perfectly decent sands and backed by a palm-shaded promenade which starts immediately to the east of the harbour and stretches past the new

Close-up of the caves.

SAMARIA GORGE

The most exciting and spectacular adventure which Crete offers the average visitor is a walk through the Samaria Gorge, the longest ravine (11 miles/18 km) in Europe. The journey starts at Xylóskalou at the end of the vast Omalós Plain by descending a steep wooden stairway.

After a mile or so, sea level is reached. Five miles (eight km) further along and the abandoned village of Samaria and its church come into view. Stop and admire the church's lovely 14th-century frescoes: this provides the opportunity, without loss of face, to regain your breath.

The going now gets tough and involves criss-crossing the river-bed. Be warned: flash floods have been known to occur, so before going further check with the locals about weather conditions.

The gorge narrows and the walls soar straight upwards for 1,000 to 2,000 ft (300 to 600 metres). Soon after passing the Church of Aphendis Christos, the Sidheroportes (Iron Gates) are reached and the gorge, scarcely penetrated by sunlight, is little more then seven ft (two metres) wide. However, it is doubtful if any but a giant can, as is claimed, stretch out their arms to touch each side of the gorge.

If, overcome with exuberance, you feel the urge to burst into song—don't. The park is under the aegis of the Haniá Forest Service which specifically forbids, among other activities, singing.

All the while, the elusive Cretan wild goat, the *agrimi*, is watching your efforts, but it is unlikely that you will notice. On the other hand, even the most innocent of botanists will be delighted by the gorge, and ornithologists have been known to spot bearded vultures.

And so to Ayia Rouméli and the Church of the Panayía. However, all is not over: this is old, abandoned Ayia Rouméli and the goal is new Ayia Rouméli on the coast. This means a further two miles (three km) of anticlimactic and hot walking before celebrating with that longed-for swim.

Refreshed, the only exit from the gorge, other then retracing the same route, is by boat eastwards to Hóra Sphakíon or westwards to Paleohora. There are no roads.

The gorge is open from about the beginning of March until the end of October. Allow six hours for the stroll.

Samaria Gorge is the longest ravine in Europe.

part of town for several miles.

Rethymnon and Haniá to the west are joined by an expressway and an old road. Leave the former at the 14-mile (22-km) mark and in five minutes enter **Yeoryioupolis** (Georgeioupoli) at the mouth of the River Vrysanos. This delightful hideaway has a good long beach and eucalyptus-shaded square.

Aptéra, a large flat plateau above Kalyves, provides not only excellent views of the enormous **Gulf of Soúda** and the Akrotíri peninsula but also insights into Crete's history. Visit the recently restored **Ayios Ioánnis Theológos Monastery**, the massive ruined Turkish fort and the Greco-Roman remains. The name Aptéra ("wingless ones") is derived from the Sirens who, defeated in musical contest by the Muses, discarded their wings and threw themselves into the bay where they became the White Islands.

Haniá, (Khaniá, Chaniá), 37 miles (59 km) from Rethymnon, Crete's second city and its capital until 1971, is a larger version of Rethymnon and claims to be one of the oldest continuously inhabited cities in the world. Its jewel is the boat-free outer **Venetian harbour**. The quayside is wide and backed by charming, colourful old buildings whose reflections shimmer in the water. The ambience is of the Levant and this is *the* place for the *volta*.

The restored 17th-century **Mosque of Hassan Pasha**, the oldest mosque in Crete, stands at one end of the quay and is now the tourist office while the restored Firka Sea Fortress, which houses the **Naval Museum**, occupies the other end. Here the Greek flag was officially raised for the first time on Crete in 1913. The **Old Town** where artisans, especially leather workers, still occupy workshops, can be entered from this point by way of Angelou and Theotokopoulou Streets. Both have splendid examples of domestic Venetian architecture and will provide much pleasure to dedicated shoppers.

The **Archaeological Museum** occupies the Monastery of St Francis, one of the best preserved and the largest of a score of still-standing Venetian churches. The **Church of St Nicholas**, as a result of various architectural as well as religious conversions, boasts both a minaret and a campanile. Another example of ecumenicalism is the small, drab **Orthodox Cathedral** built by a grateful Turkish Muslim whose son's life was saved by the intervention of the Virgin Mary.

In the **New Town** visit the attractive, lofty glass-covered **cruciform market**; the less exciting **Historical Museum and Archives** and the family home of Eleftherios Venizélos, father of the modern Greek nation.

Those with a sense of history will visit Mournies and Theriso, villages immediately south of Haniá. The house in which Venizélos was born, now a museum, is in Mournies. From here, a delightful journey through the **Theriso Gorge** brings the visitor to the village of that name. Much revered by Cretans is the house of Venizélos' mother which served as a revolutionary headquarters and which is now a national shrine.

Akrotíri, a limestone peninsula stretching northwards, is full of interest. First visit the **Hill of Prophet Elias**, where revolutionary Cretans gathered in 1897 to demand union with Greece. Here are the simple graves of Venizélos and his son Sophoklís.

Other graves—1,527 of them—are found at the nearby immaculately maintained **Commonwealth Cemetery** where British and Commonwealth troops killed in the 1941 Battle of Crete are buried. (Equal honour is given to three times that number of Germans who are buried in the well-tended cemetery at **Máleme**, 10 miles (16 km) west of Haniá. And, on the western outskirts of Haniá stands a massive memorial topped by a diving eagle which honours those Germans who died attempting to oppress the Cretans: surely a rare example of tolerance.

Farther out on the peninsula is the important **Monastery of Ayia Triádha**. Further on, and reached by a deteriorating road, is **Gouvernéto Monastery**, a century older. Both have

Dusk over Haniá.

236

many treasures and shaded courtyards where the visitor can chat with monks.

From Gouvernéto a none-too-easy 20-minute downhill scramble leads to the abandoned, enchanting—and possibly enchanted—**Katholikó Monastery** hidden in a ravine and populated by goats. Dating from about 1200, this is, if not the oldest, certainly one of the first monastic settlements in Crete.

The road west from Haniá hugs the coast passing at first several busy small resorts which merge imperceptibly with each other and then arriving at the **Kolimbari** crossroads.

Proceed westwards through hilly country and emerge through a cleft to memorable views of the **Plain of Kastélli** and the **Bay of Kissamos** enclosed within the peninsulas of Rodopou and **Gramboúsa**. These are rather fancifully compared to a bull's horns. The road now makes a torturous descent to the plain and so to pleasant **Kastélli** with its wide, broad beach, some Roman ruins and a seldom open museum.

Turn left at Plátanos and a twisting road, reminiscent of a corniche, leads after 20 miles (32 km) to **Váthi** and several splendidly frescoed Byzantine churches. From Váthi a poor road through a ravine hits the coast at **Stómio** from where it is another couple of miles to the **Khrysoskalitissa Convent**. The name means "Golden Stairway" and refers to the fact that one of the 90 steps descending from the terrace to a cove is made of gold. Failure to observe that step is proof that you have sinned.

From Khrysoskalitissa a barely negotiable road terminates at the broad, flat sandy beach of **Elaphonísi**, bordering what is practically a lagoon. Wade across a sandbar to an islet which has excellent beaches and you are at the westernmost point of Crete. This is possibly the best spot in all Crete for beach lovers: not easy to reach yet quite busy with campers.

Around the corner lies **Paleohora** (Palaiokhora), a delightful resort with a ruined Venetian castle.

Back to Iráklion: Return to Iráklion and continue eastwards on the expressway

hadows in
he
fternoon.

A Cretan Custom

Travellers who take the road in western Crete from the town of Kastélli to the village of Ano Palaiókastro in search of the ruins of Polyrrhénia (also called Polirinía) are in for an unusual, yet typical Cretan surprise. The road climbs and twists past olive groves and, after five miles (eight km), terminates at Ano Palaiókastro. From here the ruins can be reached only by walking through the gardens of villagers.

The barking of an especially ferocious fenced-in dog serves not only to terrify the tourist but also to alert Mr Pirounakis to the approaching stranger. Mr Pirounakis welcomes you with *Elláte! Kathíste!* (Come! Sit down!). The greeting is timely for you are sure to be puffing and panting, completely un-nerved and uncertain as to which is the route to the ruins.

Within the house all is bare and white-washed. Mr Pirounakis immediately pours for you a glass of *tsikouthiá*, Cretan fire-water, but he abstains on account of a heart condition. Sweetmeats follow and then comes the interrogation. And, be sure, no matter what country you are from—Japan or Yugoslavia, England or the States—Mr Pirounakis will have hosted previous visitors from there. In evidence Mr Pirounakis produces his three large guest books and hundreds of picture postcards sent by those he has entertained and who now write to him. Simple arithmetic reveals that Mr Pirounakis entertains about 500 tourists annually and dispenses many litres of the lethal *tsikouthiá*.

Mrs Pirounakis soon appears and now that her husband is comfortably settled refills your glass. It is difficult to depart and continue on to Polyrrhénia, for the Pirounakis pair believe that it is a matter of pride and honour to offer comfort to strangers. Cretans pay more than lip service to Xenios Zeus, the patron god of hospitality.

Farewells are finally permitted and you can continue your sight-seeing. A stiff climb of a few more minutes and the scattered, inchoate ruins of Polyrrhénia are reached. However, it is not for the mute stones but rather for the superb views of the Gulf of Kissamos and, above all, for Cretan hospitality in the shape of Mr and Mrs Pirounakis that the traveller visits Ano Palaiókastro and Polyrrhénia.

Mr and Mrs Pirounakis welcome visitors from all over the world.

for 15 miles (24 km). Then forget about "highway". You have reached the Cretan Riviera—a stretch reminiscent of Blackpool or Coney Island—with the resorts of **Khersónisos, Stalís** and **Mállia**. Search not for elegance: bars and *pizzerias* abound: ethnic it ain't. However, the beaches are among the best even although much sand is occupied by resorts.

Khersónisos has scanty Greek and Roman remains while close to the beach near Mállia is a renowned Minoan site. Stalís has to settle for palm trees.

The Palace at Mállia, traditionally associated with King Sarpendon, brother of Minos, is contemporary with that at Knossos. The ruins are not so extensive as those at Knossos and Phaistós but, even without reconstruction, are more readily understood. Remarkable are the number of store rooms and workrooms which suggest more a country villa than a palace. Current excavations have uncovered the Chrysólakkos, the Golden Pit, from the protopalatial period (1900-1700 B.C.). The name is derived from the numerous gold artefacts found in this enormous mausoleum.

Soon after leaving Mállia, the main road passes the chapel of **Ayios Geórgios Selenáris**. Public transport stops here to permit passengers to give thanks for a journey completed and to pray for a safe continuation. If you had travelled in the days of the old road, you would have been eager to do just this. Such shrines are not too uncommon at the midpoint of dangerous roads.

And so to **Ayios Nikólaos**, invariably abbreviated to Agnik, 43 miles/69 km from Iráklion, which is *the* resort—the San Tropez of Crete. This picture postcard paradise, overlooked by the eastern mountains, is magnificently situated on the Gulf of Mirabello. Here, and at neighbouring **Eloúnda**, are the island's best hotels. Unfortunately, Agnik lacks a decent beach, although there are some passable sands a couple of miles to the east. Restaurants and hotels, discos and cafés clutter around Agnik's **Mandraki harbour** and the

Cretan countryside.

small so-called "bottomless" lagoon. These are joined by a narrow strip of water over which passes a short, narrow bridge. Hedonists have been known to tear themselves away from sybaritic life to visit the town's **archaeological and folk museums**.

The **Lasíthi Plain**, at an altitude of about 2,800 ft (840 metres) is, as far as the eye can see, a regular cornucopia. Impeccably cultivated land supports potatoes and grain crops, apples and pears. The visitor can well believe that Crete was the granary of Rome and will recall Pliny's statement that whatever is produced in Crete is incomparably better than that which is produced in other parts. However, rare is the day when you will see the unfurled sails of the 10,000 windmills which irrigate the rich alluvial soil.

Proceed counter-clockwise around the plateau. Psihro is the starting point for the descent to the giant **Diktaian Cave**, supposedly the birthplace of Zeus. Guides here can be irritating but how, without one, will you be able to distinguish the nipples upon which Zeus suckled from all the other stalactites and stalagmites? Before leaving the plain try to visit **Tzermiádo** and its **Kronioan** (Trapeza) **Cave** which is the mythical home of Kronos and Rhea, the parents of Zeus.

Clinging to the mountainside above Agnik is **Kritsá**—"the largest village in Crete". It is said to be the home of the best weavers on the island and their brilliantly coloured work hangs everywhere complementing the flowers and contrasting with the whitewashed homes which line the narrow passageways and alleys. Lovely frescoes adorn the church of Ayios Yeoryios.

Immediately below Kritsá is the church of **Panayía Kerá** which is Crete's greatest Byzantine treasure. The entire interior is a picture book bible consisting of 12th to 14th-century frescoes. Indicative of changing times, until a few years ago Panayía Kerá was a functioning church: it is now a museum and charges admission.

A couple of miles beyond and above

Pots in some of Crete's more remote areas are still made as in Minoan times.

Kritsá are the ruins of **Lató**. The pleasure here lies not so much in the fairly extensive remains of a Greco-Roman city but in superb views from the northern acropolis across plains covered with an infinite number of olive and almond trees to the coast and to Ayios Nikólaos (in ancient days the port for Lató) and beyond to the Gulf of Mirabello and the Sitia mountains. To sit here and to absorb the view with the background music provided by the bells of unseen sheep is to feel completely chaste.

The nearby island of **Spinalónga** with its ruined Venetian fortress is readily reached from Ayios Nikólaos. Poignant memories abound on this island which was a leper colony until 1957—the last in Europe. Onassis then considered building a casino here.

Leave Agnik and head eastwards for Sitia. After 12 miles (19 km) **Gourniá**, the poor man's Pompeii, is reached. Spread over a ridge, overlooking the sea, are remains, not of another palace, but of streets and houses of a Minoan town. Especially in spring, when the site is covered with a riot of flowers and perfume fills the air, even those bored with old stones will be delighted.

A further few miles and a poorly surfaced side-road drops to the unspoiled fishing village of **Móhlos**. The tiny island opposite which can be readily reached by strong swimmers bears the same name and has scanty Minoan ruins. Somewhat beyond is the larger island of **Pseíra** where a Minoan town and port are currently being excavated. (Both islands can, on occasions, be reached by boat from Ayios Nikólaos.)

Sitia, is a somewhat laid-back town which, to the delight of visitors and the chagrin of locals, has not yet made the big time. Here are the almost obligatory Venetian fort, archaeological museum and a disappointing beach. There is also a folklore museum.

Toploú Monastery, its tall 16th-century Italianate bell-tower beckoning like the minaret of a mosque, stands in splendid isolation in the middle of nowhere beyond Sitia. The monastery derives its name from a renowned can-

wo uses for
ots.

non (*toploú* is Turkish for cannon ball) which formerly protected it. The monks also had other methods of protecting themselves: observe the hole above the monastery gate through which they poured hot oil over their assailants.

Five miles (eight km) further on is **Vái** renowned for myriad palm trees and a large sandy beach which brings to Crete a taste of far-away tropics. Don't believe it. The palm trees are not the species associated with desert islands and the beach is usually crowded. Better make for quiet, palm-less **Itanos**, a couple of miles farther north.

Southwards from Itanos is **Paleokastro** which hit the headlines because of outstanding finds at the largest Minoan town yet uncovered. Beaches about a mile away, especially at the southern end of the bay, are worth visiting.

Further on is **Ano Zákros**, the starting point to Káto Zákros and the fourth great Minoan site. Hikers will prefer to make their way from Upper to Lower Zákros by walking through the spectacular **Ravine of the Dead**, so-called because of its caves which were used for Minoan burials.

Káto Zákros is a dig which you could fund. In the 1960s Dr Nikolas Pláton, director of the Archaeological Service, was asked by the Pomerances, a New York business couple, if any Minoan sites had still to be excavated. Yes, he told them. What then was the problem? Money. The Pomerances said that, with no strings attached, they would underwrite the dig. During vacations, they work as labourers.

The ruins at Káto Zákros are from the New Palace era, but there are intrusions from the Old Palace era. They are often waterlogged because Crete is tipping over longitudinally with its eastern end sinking below and its western end rising above the water table. Close to the main dig, with the customary central courtyard and royal, religious and domestic buildings and workshops radiating outwards, are remains of a Minoan town and of a sheltered Minoan harbour which was ideally situated for trade with the Levant and Egypt. As at most Minoan sites, the setting is everything.

Back at Gourniá, a flat road shoots across the island's isthmus to **Ierápetra**, the largest town on the south coast and the southernmost in all Europe. Over the past decade Ierápetra has enjoyed a boom, not only because of tourism but also because of market gardening and the uncovering of archaeological sites. The town, scarcely atmospheric, has a short promenade at the rear of a not-so-good beach, the inevitable archaeological museum and a small Venetian fort.

Eastwards, the new inchoate resort of **Makriyialos**, which has a fairly good beach, is reached. From here a side road leads to the small 14th-century **Kapsás Monastery**, built snugly into the cliffs at the entrance to a gorge. Monks will show you, encased in a silver casket, the body of Gerondoyíannis, a 19th-century eccentric, who is a kind of a cult figure. Káto Zákros is practically around the corner but cannot be reached without returning to Makriyialos and then travelling on twisting mountain roads to Sitia.

Left, a woman paints miniatures in her spare time. Right, a mischievous donkey

SAILING THE SEAS

While the package holidaymaker and the ubiquitous backpacker have to rely on ferries to travel among the islands, the yachtsman can enjoy a remarkable degree of independence without having to face too much bureaucracy. But some paperwork, unfortunately, is unavoidable.

For those sailing into Greek waters in their own yacht, customs clearance in one of 28 designated entry ports (the list may be obtained from tourist boards or a country's national sailing authority) is necessary to obtain a Transit Log (yachts over 12 metres long) or a Temporary Duty-Free Admission booklet for yachts under 12 metres long. Usually, both these documents are valid for six months and enable a crew to sail freely throughout the country.

A visiting yacht should be officially registered in its country of origin and its skipper should make sure that each member of the crew has a valid passport. It is worth writing out a crew list with passport numbers so that any official check can be made easier.

Those who choose to charter a yacht in Greece will find the system simplified because all charter vessels must be sailing under the Greek flag, even if you are hiring a yacht from, say, a British-based company. Nevertheless, crew lists must be completed on arrival and charterers should not leave their holiday base until this has been completed. Some of these regulations may eventually be relaxed as Greece implements the European Community's myriad rules.

Sailing in the Dodecanese has the added problem of negotiating the Turkish/Greek border which weaves its way through a string of islands. The Turks insist that anyone sailing in their waters should clear customs at one of their ports of entry. The border is policed at sea and it is therefore unwise to zig-zag across this imaginary line unless you intend to enter Turkey officially.

Chartering, now a fundamental part of the sailing scene in Greece, began throughout the islands in the mid-1970s, the idea of an enterprising group of British boat owners who decided that they had had enough of English summers and wanted to holiday in the sun. This type of sailing is increasingly prevalent and has done much to encourage the development of marinas and improved facilities like the extensive provision of fresh drinking water.

Today, chartering operates on a sophisticated basis. Gone are the days of worn-out, poorly equipped yachts with missing items of inventory and indifferent local agents.

Competition has enabled reputable charter companies to emerge, supplying yachts which are renewed every three years or so. They are designed for holidays in the sun and equipped to a luxurious standard with deep freezes, deck showers, snorkelling equipment and even a pair of gardening gloves to handle the anchor chain.

It's important to match experience with the correct type of charter. Inexperienced sailors should select a flotilla holiday where 12 yachts cruise in company under the instructive eye of a lead boat crew. For the more experienced who have a basic knowledge of navigation and can handle a boat in stronger winds, a "burbot", aboard which the charterer becomes the skipper, provides a really independent holiday.

Finally, those who can afford a crewed charter can simply relax on deck and leave all the sailing, boat handling and even the cooking to paid hands. But expect to pay around $2,000 a day.

Whether you are taking your own yacht to Greece or chartering, the choice of sailing areas is large and careful selection should take particular account of varying local wind characteristics.

The recognised sailing season is from April to October when skies are clear, and temperatures rise into the 80s and 90s Fahr-

the Cyclades, predominantly from the north. More recently, the strong midsummer northerlies which blow down the Turkish coast have led some charter companies to grade this area, the Dodecanese, as the most difficult in which to sail.

Weather forecasts for yachtsmen are broadcast by Athens Radio in Greek with special warnings in English. Don't rely on the advice of local port captains when it comes to the weather.

For those looking for less lively sailing conditions, the Saronic Gulf and the Ionian islands offer the best prospects. This is because both are well protected by islands in close proximity to each other and the *mel-*

enheit (25 to 35C) in July and August.

Winds throughout the Greek sea area tend to be from the north and the most talked-about weather phenomenon is the *meltemi*, which affects the whole of the Aegean and can reach Beaufort Force 7 to 8 in midsummer. It is an unpredictable wind, can arrive without warning and blow for as little as one hour or as long as one week.

Yachtsmen must take care not to be caught on a lee shore and they should be aware that the *meltemi* can cause an extremely uncomfortable steep, short sea.

In the northern Aegean the *meltemi* blows from the northeast and, further south towards

temi tends not to blow here.

The Ionian is blessed with a wind called the *maestros*, again from the north but nowhere near as strong as the *meltemi*. The *maestros* tends only to blow in the afternoon when the heat of mainland Greece accelerates the wind off the sea. Occasionally a hot, southerly *sirocco* wind, often carrying red dust from North Africa, will blow hard in the Peloponnese but it doesn't last long.

Despite all these descriptions of local winds, Greece is often quite windless and yachtsmen should sometimes be prepared to motor. Whatever the conditions, the sun and the increased glare off the water—which can produce momentary blindness—should be guarded against at all times, particularly when sailing.

The biggest concentration of marinas in Greece is on the coast of Attica near Athens and Piraeus; but because of the commercial shipping and general ship movements in and out of the capital—to say nothing of the conurbation's industrial waste—it is not an area of peace and beauty. Zea Marina, near Piraeus, is hot, noisy and smelly; Mikrolimano, the home of the Greek ocean racing fleet, is cleaner and prettier and Kalamaki, five miles from central Athens, is large, new but featureless.The other major marinas among or near the Greek islands are at Thes-

saloniki, where there is an excellent development at Kalamarias; Gouvia, near Corfu, still far from finished and polluted by a local sewer outfall; and the large Mandraki marina at Rhodes, more suited to larger yachts. All these marinas make excellent "staging posts" for yachts which need to re-stock with food and water. There are, of course, charter bases in all these locations which normally means there are repair and chandlery facilities on hand.

But the greatest appeal of the Greek is-

Left, sailing the seas. Above, a girl savours the sea breeze.

lands is the beauty and solitude offered by their remoteness. The green islands of the Ionian are, perhaps, the yachtsman's first choice for a number of reasons. As already explained, the Ionian offers safe cruising because of the shelter to the east of the islands, but if yachtsmen want more lively conditions, a sail to the west of the islands of Lefkas and Cephalonia will provide marvellous sailing. Easy anchorages and safe village moorings are within a few hours' sail of each other throughout the chain.

Spring sailing: Anyone cruising the area is likely to traverse the ancient and recently improved Lefkas (Lefkada) Canal and beat north for 30 miles (48 km) to Corfu. Apart from the already mentioned Gouvia marina (about an hour's sail from the city), Corfu boasts its own, more convenient marina, ideal for a city tour and for bunkering water and fuel but appallingly dirty, full of the city's rubbish and sewage. The time to sail the Ionian is definitely during spring and autumn months—mid-summer sees Italian yachtsmen pouring over from the heel of Italy, clogging up the numerous but small harbours.

The Saronic Gulf is a favourite haunt of cruising yachts because of the attractive towns which offer shelter on islands like Hydra, Spetsai and the much underrated coast of the mainland Peloponnese. In midseason it might be difficult to find a berth close to one of the quayside tavernas where restaurateurs have developed their entrepreneurial skills to tempt crews to their quayside tables. Almost without exception, mooring is stern or bows to town quays close to the best tavernas.

Moving east from the Saronic, the influence of the *meltemi* becomes stronger and it is not until one travels north of the Sporades, still affected by the northeast *meltemi*, that one finds more virgin cruising grounds among the great inlets and peninsulas to the east of the deep bay which has Thessaloniki at its head. There are fewer villages and towns along this coast and yachtsmen should be prepared to anchor, sometimes in water more than 100ft (30 metres) deep.

Sailing a yacht is a rewarding way of exploring this country of islands. In many cases, it is the only way of reaching some remote corners. (For more information and useful addresses see *Travel Tips* section).

SEA, SUN, SAND AND SEX

"Where else," Air Chief Marshall Sir Christopher Foxley-Norris, GCB, DSO, RAF wanted to know, "would your bank manager offer to toss you double or quits when you want to cash a cheque?" He was also intrigued by the mice on the island, which on two successive nights robbed a trap and got away. On the third, he set the trap but forgot to bait it—and caught two mice at once. Sir Christopher was explaining what had persuaded him to buy a house on Skiathos. The question always being put to people like him is whether in the first instance the appeal lay in island life generally, the Greek islands specifically, or in Skiathos in particular. The answer is invariably "yes" to all parts of the question, but as the islands have changed greatly in recent years so, too, have the attractions which lure visitors.

An airport was built on Skiathos in the mid-1970s and put the island within three or four hours of direct flight from northern Europe. The number of visitors multiplied many times over, and the queues waiting to cash cheques and change money at the bank would quickly have put an end to leisurely games of chance between Sir Christopher and his bank manager.

Skiathos retains, against the odds, much of the charm that appealed to Sir Christopher, but it had to adapt to the mass market. The lexicon of modern tourism is four "Ss", the belief or hope that a beach in a hot country will produce the desired result: Sea plus Sun plus Sand equals Sex.

With probably the best beaches in Greece, 70 in all, Skiathos was inevitably going to be the setting for many such expectations. The tourist industry boomed and gave the island a reputation as "the straight Mykonos".

Until the construction of the airport, Skiathos was typical of small, relatively inaccessible Aegean islands. The unmarried men on the island might have assumed that unattached women were old dears who shrouded themselves in black and hobbled about on sticks. If other types existed, they were with-

out exception under lock and key.

The Northerners disgorged from charter flights seemed to arrange matters differently. Many travelled as couples—but not enough, it was observed, to preclude a surprisingly healthy surplus of single women who, moreover, welcomed male company, not least local fishermen with time on their hands because of the summer ban on commercial operations in the national interest of conservation.

One of those early arrivals was a woman,

now respectably middle-aged, who was to return year after year. Her annual pilgrimage began in Australia. What was it that made the immense journey worthwhile? "At home," she said, "I worked in an office and was one in a million. Here, everyone got to know me. I walked down the street and waved back to them, like a queen."

The *only* reason? Australians are commendably candid: "No, I used to come for what all the single women were after: sex."

Traditional word, new meaning: The local response to this interesting turn of events was, if not a lexicon of their own, a password: "*kamaki*". To the older fishermen, it

Preceding pages: foreign girl meets island boys.. Left, the street of Mykonos. Above, the word *kamaki* has taken on a new meaning.

was simply what they called the trident used for spearing octopus. To the younger ones, the word retained some of the old meaning in referring instead to the pursuit and conquest of foreign females.

Fumbling island novices couldn't believe their luck and probably interpreted it as a belated blessing from the notably randy deity on Mount Olympus. *Kamaki*, some decided, could be played as a divine game, in the way gods clocked up merit by doing good works. In the modern idiom, they played for points, as in bridge or billiards.

The rules of the game, with local variations, are supposed to be secret, and a request for details would normally be as pro-

At the time of this exclusive interview, the highest score possible on the island ("six, maybe seven") was invested in an 18-year-old Canadian girl who, the *kamaki* set were fascinated to learn, was a serving member of the Royal Canadian Mounted Police. The theoretical maximum of 10 points, which few expected ever to achieve, lay in the rarified realm of "North Korean and Eskimo" women.

Reversing the roles: While male-orientated hedonism in Thailand or the Philippines attracts criticism from certain quarters, *kamaki* reverses the roles and the female victims, if any, are willing. There are occasional casualties among the men, however, the result of

ductive as asking the mafia for their end-of-year profit and loss accounts. Lips can be loosened, however, by vanity (or perhaps a mischievous sense of humour), so it is possible to reveal here that on Skiathos points are awarded on a scale of one to ten.

An Englishwoman is worth just one point, while Germans and Norwegians are joint second-to-last and worth two. The criteria, *kamaki* contestants take pains to emphasise, are not concerned with individual or national performance. They reflect availability. The English are the single largest group of visitors to Skiathos; Germans and Norwegians are roughly equal next in line.

hectic preparations for the opening of the *kamaki* season. Serious contestants will spend the spring energetically working on their physiques by lifting weights. The modern idea of Adonis, on the evidence of the past few years, is not only muscular but blond. Very blond.

The climax of spring training is the ritual anointing of heads with peroxide bleach, but stubbornly swarthy scalps may end up with an identity crisis which results in that sad *kamaki* casualty, the Greek piebald.

Frantic, untutored weight-lifting can also go horribly wrong. Like rabbits out of a hat, muscles can pop up where least expected, useless for all practical purposes and aesthetically very absurd.

On the whole, though, the results would seem to be satisfactory. "The boys are beautiful," said an American woman reminiscing about happy times on a number of islands. "Personally, I've only been to bed with a couple of them, but I love looking at them. Women feel they're a long way from home, nobody would know, so… It helps if the boy can speak English but, if he can't that's okay too." In response to a question based on inside information, she recalled that on the morning after the two occasions she remembered best, she was indeed asked for a photograph of herself.

points may feel slightly squeamish on being asked to read out loud, and conceivably then write a reply to, missives from their predecessors. The pressure was too great for one young woman who arrived on Skiathos late in the summer with the intention of remaining over the winter. She wrote: "I arrived here carefree, honest and innocently trusting. It broke my heart when I had to acknowledge that you cannot trust 90 per cent of what a Greek boy says to you, and that, however genuinely sensitive and warm he sounds, there are always ulterior motives behind the eulogy. It's sad, it's true, but then this is a Greek island."

A proposal of marriage: What the letter

If the nomination of the *Kamaki* King at the end of the summer season is at all contentious, the collection of photographs could be introduced as evidence and influence the island jury. Failing photographs, letters (written on flights home with time to kill?) do almost as well.

While the majority of *kamaki* contestants have picked up basic conversational English over the years, their proficiency may not extend to reading or writing letters in return. Even the most stoical providers of *kamaki*

Left, a girl with a view. Above, the beginning of a brief encounter?

omitted was that she had received, and given consideration to, a marriage proposal from a young fisherman who was the unchallenged *kamaki* champion of the season just then drawing to a close. He had made it known, although not directly to her, that the intended marriage would last only until the following spring, when he would have to shed his conjugal entanglement in order to prepare for the defence of his title. If that were not enough to demoralise the girl, she also discovered that at the end of the previous summer and on exactly the same principles, he had married—and subsequently divorced—someone else.

MAN, MYTH AND MUSIC

The visitor is ambling along some majestic harbour at sunset, with the sea breeze between the masts of the yachts and caiques, and looking forward to a meal of fried octopus, washed down perhaps with a little diluted *ouzo*. What better way to top the evening than with some tinkling *bouzouki* music? After all, isn't *bouzouki* music the quintessence of all things Greek?

No. What most of the world believes is Greek music—urged on by record companies out to make big drachmas out of foreigners' ignorance—is really a Slavic-Turkish amalgam of insipid musical styles dressed up to become acceptable to the western ear and played on an instrument that itself has a Turkish name. The pear-shaped stringed instrument known as the *bouzouki* takes its name from the Turkish word for "head". Its tinny tone suggests more the steppes of Asia or the deserts of the Middle East than the bracing air and clear mountains of Greece.

Debunking the *bouzouki*: The great *bouzouki* myth was fanned to a flame by the *Zorba the Greek* fad in the mid-1960s, and has overshadowed the *real* Aegean music hidden away behind the false tavernas and blaring speakers. It has an altogether cleaner sound—gentler, nobler than the commercial pap being sold in Athens record shops and souvenir dens. The rhythms, often in unconventional time-signatures, are lilting and hypnotic. The melodies are exquisite, and the lyrics grapple with eternal human themes—the sea that took a loved one, the island mother who wonders if her sons will ever return from foreign lands, the precious days when the endless fishing can be laid aside and clean clothes can be donned for the festival of the Virgin Mary.

In the Ionian islands—Corfu, Zakynthos and Lefkas, for example—the Italian sound reigns. Its emphasis is on guitar and violin and western harmonic progressions, with somewhat Italianate orchestrating.

And then there's the music of the mountains—prouder and more heroic than the

island variety. Again, this has nothing to do with commercialism. In mainland Greek folk music, clear notes of the clarinet dominate, its melody line whirling in incredible improvisation to the accompaniment of a plain guitar and a rudimentary drum.

As the catalogue continues, the great variety of Greek music becomes more apparent. Composers such as Yannis Markopoulos have successfully developed Greek folk themes into modern, orchestrated works of great emotional power. Mikis Theodorakis is a name known to Europeans and Americans for more than 20 years, though his political activism has often let his artistic labours suffer. Manos Hadjidakis, the greatest modern Greek composer, has forged an orchestral Greek sound that sells worldwide.

Greek music, of course, is as old as Greek history. The ancient music was monophonic—without harmonies—and its scales were apparently simple, probably much like an ecclesiastical chant line today. The scale of traditional Greek music is still five-tone, a system passed on to all the later peoples of the Middle East. The musician places notes not in the *do-re-mi* (C-D-E) order as western

Preceding pages: musicians on Karpathos playing lyra and lute. Left, a music shop. Right, an island-hopping *bouzouki*.

people do, but *do-do sharp-mi* (C-C sharp-E). It can be argued from this that Middle Eastern music, through the Byzantine Empire, is based on Greek models.

Over the centuries Greek became a crucible of musical influences. The wind of Africa blows in the relentless throb of the Cretan lyra. The gentle Aegean island songs have some of the tinkling Turkish *santdouri* (a zither-like instrument played with felt sticks) that brings out the echoing stretches of blue sea between the island mountains. Slavic ditties have long been the staple of the northern Greeks, while the Italian *cantate* brought the seven-tone scale into use.

Greece's lyrics were never divorced from

9/8 and even 11/8 beats of Greek folk music today are the natural continuation—something western jazz musicians are only just starting to appreciate.

The Greek has always written music easily—although the term "written" hardly applies. He never had to sit down with pen and paper and worry about whether he wanted a 3/4 or 4/4, a major or a minor key, or whether he should drop a word because the bar could not hold another eighth note. He had it all ready in his soul, where there were no "bars" to confine what he felt. He was restless, so he pounded his feet on the floor, flung out his arms, tossed back his head. Thus were born the laments out of which modern Greek folk

the music, as they were in the West. From Homer onwards, both have been inseparable; instrumental music remains a relative rarity. While western theoreticians coldly dissected melody, harmony and rhythm and promulgated strict laws governing them, the untaught Greek felt no such restraint.

Western rhythm, for example, was boxed into a space measuring 3 by 4, out of which not even a Beethoven dared venture. The Greeks, on the other hand, adapted their music rhythms to the cadences of their speech. Homer's hexameter is the clearest indication of how ancient Greeks spoke in their inspired moments. The catchy 5/8, 7/8,

music springs. If this primitive dance-feeling came out a regular 2/4 or 4/4, fine. If not, better still. The only rules were no rules.

The composer Mimis Plessas, a former jazzman who now accounts for a good portion of Greek movie soundtrack music says: "Imagine the field cry of the black man transported to Greece—that's what Greek music is." Plessas relates an interesting account of a jam session with American jazz trumpeter Dizzy Gillespie in 1953. Being Greek, Plessas had no trouble fingering a nimble 7/8 folk rhythm on the piano—and promptly lost Dizzy. "I can't do it—something's missing," said the great jazzman.

Rembétiko, rembétika: It is these odd rhythms that can be found even in *bouzouki* music—the kind that is not too commercial and that accurately expresses the proletariat yearnings of the workers of Piraeus in the 1920s. This was the time of the *rembétika*, played in dead serious demeanour in smoke-filled basements where hashish and fast women were an evening's delights. The soundtrack of Costas Ferris' movie *Rembétiko* provides the clearest picture of *rembétika*, to be appreciated only by keeping in mind that it expresses the soul of just one small corner of Athens, and not Greece as a whole. One record album that made Greek musical history is Manos Hadjidakis's *Gi-*

cendo of pride, and one comes away purified as from an ancient Greek tragedy.

The Cretan Yannis Markopoulos brings an earthier tone into his themes. But, a dominant melodic line and pungent harmonies in just the right places give a power quite out of proportion to its component part.

Markopoulos's most celebrated work, *Periodia Proti*, is an album of instrumental music issued in 1978. Here, the magic of the Cretan lyra mixes with nostalgic melodies from the Asia Minor coast, an ancient homeland that the Greeks lost in 1922 and have never forgotten. Nostalgia, in fact, permeates the record. Markopoulos takes us to a purer, nobler Greece before the deafening

oconda's Smile recorded in New York in 1964, a work that has not been equalled for sheer emotive power. While listening to it, one feel that this is indeed Greece: the Parthenon shining in the moonlight, the white sails in the breezy Saronic Gulf, the geraniums on the poor verandas, and a happy, hospitable people. No trace of Asiatic pessimism here, no tremulous half-notes; but plenty of uniquely Greek time-signatures that clear the soul of its cobwebs. A breath of fresh air here, a tear there, a cres-

Left and above, a musical interlude on Zakynthos.

bouzouki carried all before it.

But for a proper first contact with the roots of Greek music, one cannot do better than visit Athens' Dora Stratou folk dance theatre just behind the Acropolis. On warm summer evenings, as the cicadas buzz softly in the surrounding pine wood and the bustling city is out of sight and sound, the folk musicians appear to stroll out of another time. As the dancers whirl and leap, the traditional clarinet, guitars, lyra, *santdouri*, Thracian bagpipe and drum echo off the slopes. It is in such a place, rather than in the expensive *bouzouki* tavernas and nightclubs, that one hears the authentic sound of Greece.

CRAFTS AND CUSTOMS

What *is* craft work and what isn't? Strictly speaking, it is something which is made individually or in small quantities out of local materials to serve some useful purpose, and so the definition covers textiles (including embroidery and weaving), lacemaking, pottery, wood work, basketry and some forms of stonemasonry and metal work. If the article is embellished so that the function of which it is technically capable becomes secondary, it becomes "folk art".

What neither definition covers is tacky souvenirs which materialise wherever tourists congregate in any numbers. As these are usually mass-produced, probably imported, completely impractical and only dubiously decorative, they fail on all counts.

Many of the craft pieces on display in Greek island homes are between 50 and 150 years old. Anything older would have required extraordinary care in order to survive under the rather spartan and at times extremely damp conditions which frequently exist in small stone-built island houses. A particularly fine piece of silk embroidery may have been handed down over several generations, but the same degree of attention is unlikely to have been extended to, say, a wooden utensil or basket. Really old objects of value are generally of a religious—rather than a secular—nature.

Vital clues: Greek island crafts are normally associated with, and identifiable as the work of, one or other of the island chains. A certain form of design and motif would be recognisably from the Cyclades, for example, and not elsewhere.

There are interesting exceptions to the rule, however: Paros, although geographically one of the Cyclades, has a dialect and crafts more closely related to the Sporades; while Skyros, which *is* one of the Sporades, has gone off on its own to become the odd man out in that chain.

Bed curtains, door lintels and wooden panels of the Cyclades use a standardised and repeated pattern of geometric motifs;

Skyros, on the other hand, prefers large birds, flowers and ships on wide-open, white backgrounds.

To enter a house in Skyros even today is to be taken aback by entire walls dripping in pottery, vases, plates, dishes—household articles in such numbers that there could not conceivably be a use for all or even half of them. It has always been so. As these collections represented a large measure of a family's wealth, security in troubled times in the form of pirates could be a problem. The so-

lution was to have a second home within the protective walls of the city fortress used exclusively for personal belongings.

It doesn't necessarily follow that these compulsive hoarders kept a large force of local craftsmen in full employment. Much of it might have come from abroad, or even from the pirates themselves. Nevertheless, Skyros did have its own craft industry, and an important one.

In the last century Greece tended to be a backwater. The islands were often cut off from one another by being subject to different political masters, isolated, and of necessity self-sufficient at a desperately low level

Preceding pages: a summer evening in Corfu. Left, an 18th-century bed-curtain from Kos. Right, a carpet school in Santorini.

of subsistence. The crafts flourished because what the islanders couldn't make for themselves they had to do without.

The economic changes of the present century, including the gradual move away from subsistence to a cash economy, made the islands more outward-looking, and there was a natural desire to acquire "prestigious" and costly foreign goods which made daily life less arduous.

As a result, fewer traditional objects were produced and those which already existed attained the value of relatively rare objects. A mother might therefore take embroidery which had been part of her dowry and cut it into pieces for daughters unable or not in-

clined to invest a similar amount of time and attention in their own marriage endowments.

The craft items most likely to be supplanted were things like embroideries and small wooden items for which there were cheap and more modern substitutes. Local production of large pots, for example, was prolonged because they were awkward to import and were needed in large numbers for carrying and storing water, cooking and a dozen other purposes. Eventually, however, even these considerations became immaterial, and within the past 50 years there has been little in the way of craft work which has not been overtaken by development.

There was always a very pronounced division of Greek crafts between those produced by men and by women. The latter went in for weaving, embroidery, lace and basket-making; the former for potting, wood and stone work. That in itself is not surprising, but some of the pragmatic implications may be less obvious.

The crafts practised by women tended to be more suited to being taken up for short periods and then laid aside at a moment's notice in order to attend to other pressing domestic duties.

On the whole, these crafts required no special equipment and could thus be carried out in or near the home. This fitted in well with the social conventions of traditional island society in which women were not as visible as men and, in particular, young girls of marriageable age were restricted in their contacts even within their own village.

In contrast, the men on the islands treated their work as a full-time job, performed it in premises reserved for the purpose, and relied on being able to call on colleagues to lend a hand whenever it was necessary.

Pride of place: Both men and women in their respective ways worked with local raw materials such as wool, clay and wood. If small quantities of silk, for example, had to be imported, it would be given pride of place in the finished article. They were producing goods only for themselves, or at most to fulfil a need within the immediate community.

The notion of producing a surplus for sale to other people was virtually unknown, although there were some famous exceptions to the rule: the itinerant Thrapsano potters of Crete, for instance, took just their skills from one island to another and worked with local clays. They were paid for their services in cash or goods.

It would be premature, however, to compose the final obituary for traditional island crafts; one needs only to travel to Skyros to see a thriving, albeit small industry. The dire necessity that put such a premium on the skills may have passed, but they are not yet dead. Production may be down to a trickle but the results, when the souvenirs are brushed aside, are still there to be seen.

Left, many tourists choose textiles as souvenirs. Right, women's crafts are done in short periods to allow for domestic duties.

SHIPS IN THE NIGHT

Having more than 50 inhabited islands, means having transport to serve them, and in shipping Greece has made its mark on the world business scene. Anyone who has experienced the airy ride over the blue Aegean waves, with the prows of the white ships rivalling the dazzling sun itself, knows the Greeks' affinity for their boats.

The golden days of the Onassis and Niarchos magnates, however, are over. With the death of Aristotle Onassis and, later, his daughter Christina, the dynasty which thrived on oil and the dubious utterances of gossip columnists has elected for a low profile. So, too, has Stavros Niarchos and his like. Greek shipping, in fact, is run from about one square kilometre of office blocks untidily clustered together in the port city of Piraeus, centring on the seafront Akti Miaouli, where international bankers in pinstriped suits rub shoulders with burly crewmen and dusky banana vendors.

There are fewer ships than before around Piraeus and the islands, too. It was in 1981 that the number of ships flying the blue and white Greek flag hit the 4,000 mark. But decline was swift and sudden. World trade slumped, the election of a socialist government in Athens frightened many business people, and Far Eastern countries grabbed a lot of business with their cut prices. By 1985 Greece's ships fell to about half the 1981 peak figures. Only recently has a slight rise been noted again.

Through it all, Greece's shipowners have shown themselves to be a resilient breed. Despite the frightening drop in the Greek-flag merchant fleet, very few of the 600-plus shipping firms jostling cheek-by-jowl in Piraeus actually went out of business. The reason was simple: they simply switched the flag on their ships. It takes just six hours of red tape to do this. Owners run down the blue and white and run up what are known as "flags of convenience". Countries such as Panama and Liberia, eager for new business, offer their flags plus minimal taxes.

Shipowners in financial trouble grab this opportunity, thus saving thousands of dollars a day in operating costs.

The owners, too, remain emotionally, even mystically, committed to their businesses. Indeed, few satisfactions can equal that of gazing out of one's air-conditioned headquarters seven floors over the Akti Miaouli and watching one's ship come in, plying the waves among the myriad coastal and cruise vessels. It is this feeling of ranging, ocean-going freedom that has made Greek shipowners cling to their profession like barnacles.

"We sat here day and night watching the shipping crisis going from bad to worse," said shipowner Nikos Efthymiou. "We could do it because shipping is in our blood."

Shipwrecked: The same love affair has lasted a long time. When the first Greek tribes pushed down from the Balkan peninsula after 1900 B.C., they found a highly-developed shipping civilisation on the coasts and around the islands. Archaeologists believe thousands of ancient wrecks litter the Aegean floor.

Two of the oldest wrecks in the Mediterranean have been located, dating back to perhaps 2500 B.C., hundreds of years before the Greeks appeared on the scene and far too deep to be retrieved by present methods. Later wrecks are more common—and accessible. In the Roman era, between 150 B.C. and A.D. 300, hundreds of wooden ships crisscrossed the Aegean carrying Greece's chief exports: wine, olive oil and art. One work of art salvaged from a Roman wreck is a bronze likeness of Augustus Caesar, now in an Athens museum.

Ancient traditions credited the ruler of the Minoan kingdom of Crete, usually termed King Minos, with building up the first real navy in the Aegean. Thucydides, Greece's greatest historian wrote: "He conquered the Cyclades, and was the first coloniser of most of them." Minos also cleared the sea of pirates, a recurring scourge.

Interestingly, when the Romans conquered Greece they remained quite fearful of the open sea and used Greek crews for their ships. The remains of the villas of Roman shipowners (*navicularii*) have been found on the once-sacred island of Delos, just off Mykonos. At the time of Christ, Delos had become a busy shipping centre, boasting colonies of rich shippers from as far away as Sicily and Palestine.

When the Roman Empire became the Byzantine, the powerful state required a powerful merchant fleet, which was why the Greeks, when they decided to throw off the Ottoman yoke in the 19th century, had redoubtable ships and seaman who effectively harassed the Turkish men of war.

After independence, the island of Syros became young Greece's shipping and trading centre. Greece's oldest operating ship-change: in 1833, four years after independence, it had a single church and a handful of houses, and all of 22 inhabitants. By the turn of the century, the once-bare rocks and pebble strands had been transformed into a densely-packed city of 50,000 people, with belching smokestacks on the horizon and quaint Dreadnought battleships darting among the merchantmen with their masts swaying in the wind.

Piraeus had another, obvious advantage: it was far closer to the administrative and government centre of Athens, which wanted to control as much as possible the young nation's economic growth.

Cruising the waves: As far as the Greek

yard, Neórion, was founded on Syros in 1861. At the time it was a revolutionary development, attracting British know-how and capital. The first Greek shipping bank, Archangelos, in 1879 published the first national shipping statistics: 3,025 sailing ships and 49 new steamships—about the same as in the year 1983.

Syros didn't have much of a heyday, because Piraeus, the ancient shipping port of Athens, was being rebuilt. It had been a tiny backwater after the Roman general Sulla had razed it in 86 B.C. But two illustrations of 1900, preserved in the Aegean Maritime Museum on Mykonos, show the startling

islands are concerned, it is passenger—rather than cargo—shipping that is the big foreign-exchange earner. The jewels in the crown of Greek passenger shipping are the cruise liners, some with floating hotels, complete with swimming pools, boutiques, and a choice of restaurants which ply world routes from the Aegean and Turkey to Alaska and the Caribbean.

Ironically, tremors of the old pirate problems have cropped up to give the cruise industry a blow. On 11 June 1988 Palestinian extremists brought death and destruction on board the cruise ship *City of Poros* as it was heading back to Piraeus after a one-day cruise. The incident, in which nine French tourists were killed, highlighted the need for security—a concern which, until then, was blissfully absent from Greek holiday ports.

As holiday makers cancelled their trips in response to terrorism stories in the newspapers, the cruise ship industry lost money and slashed its fares—providing an incentive for more travelling. Passengers who took up the offer found that the traditional island hospitality—and excellent on-board service facilities—had survived the terrorist incident intact.

Cruise liners and other passenger craft also touch at Turkish ports, mainly Kusadasi, contributing to a bridging of the pean Community partners have been asking that Greece opens up its domestic ship routes to competition from other maritime nations—a demand that Greece is strenuously resisting.

The argument in Athens is that, if the sealanes are opened up to ships of other countries, what will stop Turkish ships from grabbing the Aegean routes—possibly as a first step towards claiming some sovereignty over the eastern Aegean Greek islands?

Conflict on the seas: This argument isn't as far-fetched as it might at first appear. Greece and Turkey have been glaring at, and occasionally fighting, each other over the Aegean for decades. The brink-of-war tension of

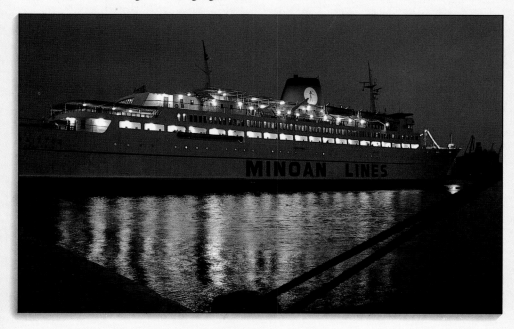

eternal political and ethnic tension between the Greeks and the Turks. But here the Greeks plan to keep competing nations out of their lucrative Aegean trade.

The magic word is *cabotage*, an international law term meaning that any nation has a right to exclude others from carrying goods and passengers between its own ports. So far, Greece's passenger ships have served their own island routes, connecting them with Piraeus. But now that Greece is a member of the European Community, the other Euro-

Left and right: shipping and cruise liners are major foreign-exchange earners.

March 1987 was simply one more flare-up.

Politicians in Athens are convinced that Turkey is eyeing some of the easternmost Greek islands; Samos, for example, is a shotgun-blast away from the Turkish coast. Turkey is the only major country that has not signed the 1958 Geneva Convention on the Law of the Sea giving islands their own sovereign rights, even when off the coast of bigger countries. Why the refusal? The Greeks answer that obviously, Turkey is "expansionist". And, regardless of how much pressure is exercised from the European Community or other maritime nations, Greece intends to keep hold of its Aegean.

ZORBAS

PIZZA ZORBAS   390
SPAGHETTI BOLOGNESE   178
SPAGHETTI GARBONALA   250
SAGANAKIA   155
FRESH FISH (κιλό ρωτήστε) 1600
VILLAGE SALAD   146
POTATOE SALAD   77

CATERING FOR ALL TASTES

The British popular press revelled in the case of a London grandmother who invested her £30,000 life savings in a restaurant on Rhodes and looked forward to a happy and prosperous retirement. Instead, she found herself locked up in a cell with the prospect of spending the next five months there unless she bought off the sentence for the equivalent of £1,000.

The first lesson for any foreigner wishing to follow Mrs Molly Huddleston's example by starting a business on a Greek island is that the Greek legal process can all too easily begin rather than end with a spell in prison. Detailed prosecution, defence, litigation and so forth take place later, often much later. A knowledge of the law and the resolve to remain meticulously on the right side of it are therefore desirable starting points—although developing the knack of shadow boxing with an opponent of stupefying complexity is the ultimate triumph.

So where had Mrs Huddleston, 55, gone wrong? It was her belief that visitors to the island might occasionally enjoy "traditional British food" after so much Greek, and that is what she provided. Cucumbers and tomatoes are optional ingredients in a British salad, but she had forgotten (or perhaps had never known) that she was in Greece and that the contents of a salad are defined by law. Mrs Huddleston's salads were either light on the cucumbers and tomatoes or omitted them altogether, a serious matter.

Furthermore, while Mrs Huddleston was aware of the fixed price for a potato, she rashly assumed that she could charge a little more if she filled them with chilli sauce, a dish popular with her more discerning customers. That, too, went into the policeman's notebook.

Mrs Huddleston's misfortune was not a flash in the pan—the work, say, of a bad-tempered policeman with a grudge or a hangover. At the same time, at the other end of the Aegean, a young American chef had given up his job at a prestigious New York

hotel to pursue the ambition of opening his own restaurant. He had never seen a Greek island, but the enthusiastic description by a Greek friend who knew the islands and of a restaurant that happened to be for sale made up his mind.

The friend was a lawyer, so Fat Ronnie, by nature a cautious fellow, avoided some of the pitfalls into which naïve foreign investors might plunge. The sale of bars and discos, in particular, is seldom cut and dried. The owner will probably open negotiations asking for a large lump sum for "goodwill", a percentage of turnover in perpetuity, and "rent". Buyers anxious to secure next year's place in paradise before this year's charter flight goes back should not be too eager to accept that all property transactions are concluded along such lines.

Legal advice may not be cut and dried either, however. On the smaller islands, there are probably no more than a couple of local lawyers (if any lawyers at all) and they will each act for one half of the population against the other. Being lawyers, they will respectively be at or near the top of ferociously polarised municipal politics and the make-or-break powers of patronage flowing from them. The foreign buyer ought to find out who the vendor's lawyer is (anyone would know!) and proceed forthwith to the other one.

Lobster tale: Fat Ronnie had astutely, if unknowingly, overcome potential difficulties in that direction, but he was nevertheless faring no better, (and possibly rather worse) than Mrs Huddleston in Rhodes. Within a fortnight of opening, he had logged no fewer than 107 separate offences which, in addition to violation of the notoriously demanding cucumber legislation, included the extraordinary business of a consignment of lobsters which, although still alive and still kicking, were deemed by the inspectors to be "not fresh".

A bemused Ronnie tried to find out what it all meant. The 107 offences? Prison, undoubtedly, until and unless he bought off the sentence or, as Mrs Huddleston was proposing, appealed quickly to the European Court of Human Rights. The "not fresh" lobsters?

If he couldn't produce a suitable receipt showing the precise date when he bought the lobsters, it was assumed that he had not bought them within the prescribed definition of "fresh" and therefore—presto!—his were not and the menu lied when it said they were. This was a compound offence, including a failure to meet the Greek equivalent of "truth in advertising".

The wisdom of business: The condemned lobsters were still alive when Ronnie had to destroy them under official supervision. At that point, Ronnie was seriously reconsidering the wisdom of starting his own business in Greece.

Foreigners who wish to pursue a career on

of legislation. Before catatonic paranoia sets in they ought to remind themselves that the laws were drawn up by Greeks for Greeks. The fact that foreigners become entangled is incidental.

The cucumber, tomato, fresh lobster regulations were designed specifically to give visitors a fair deal and to prevent profiteering. "The Greek government thinks all Greeks are crooks," a restaurateur—a Greek himself—explained. One of his colleagues, another Greek, had been in court the previous year because he had charged more than the stipulated price of a fixed portion of chicken for what was a lovingly created chicken curry with, in Greece, expensive

an island writing books or poetry or painting—anything, in fact, which the islanders themselves would not normally be doing—will be made to feel tremendously welcome, and the island economies depend on the annual influx of foreign waitresses and barmaids. Greek men are fiercely protective of their own interests when it comes to filling well-paid summer jobs, but they will concede that it is sometimes necessary to employ women, and they would rather have foreign women in those menial positions than their own.

Potential competitors, however, are likely to feel the full weight of the Greek mountain

extra ingredients.

The man in question was prominent in local politics, and even the fact that his party was in power could not prevent the charges being taken through the courts.

Fat Ronnie had originally planned to serve French and Italian food, but the inspectors rejected his draft menu because, without special dispensation, restaurants must have a preponderance of Greek dishes on the menu in the interest of cultural integrity. The law was brought in commendably to inhibit the fast-food, sausages and chips blight that has ruined so many places pandering to the tastes of mass tourism.

A shrewd restaurateur might get round that problem by putting on the menu as much *moussaka* and other staple Greek food as the inspectors require and even keep a token supply in stock. The waiters, however, would delicately—and with great stealth—steer customers towards the specialties of the house. The government's good intentions in both respects, making sure that visitors are not overcharged and that the tourist areas are not reduced to anonymous cultural slag heaps, unfortunately have a tendency to backfire badly.

Learning the rules: In the wrong hands, moreover, the rules become lethal ammunition. Prospective foreign businessmen

bus owners and water-sport concessionaires is impregnable. Islanders have been warned by taxi drivers not to allow any passengers other than close members of family into their cars; bus drivers will remonstrate violently with anyone who offers a lift to a hitch-hiker; and it is not worth speculating about the continuing seaworthiness of an unauthorised boat accepting payment for sightseeing or waterskiing.

If this prospectus for foreign business on the islands is less than flattering, it could not truthfully be otherwise. The smaller islands have only a short period in which to earn the money that will sustain the population over the closed and unlucrative winter months, so

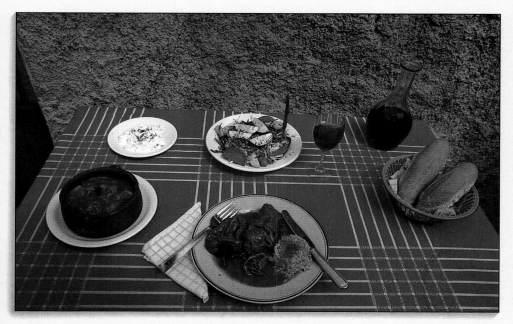

should divide their time between learning the rules and discovering acceptable ways of evading them. Their Greek neighbours would approve!

The emphasis so far has been on restaurants, bars and discos because those are the businesses to which foreign investors gravitate. The action in other spheres is even rougher than in the entertainment field because it is not so much the law of the land which rules but that of the jungle.

The protective self-interest of taxi drivers,

Left, catering island-style. Above, Greek meals tend to be simply presented.

the competitive element to be found among entrepreneurs anywhere is telescoped accordingly. Mrs Huddleston chose Rhodes because she knew the island well, having thoroughly enjoyed many holidays there in the past.

There have been too many histories like Mrs Huddleston's sad case to pretend that they didn't happen. All the more merit, then, to the minority of foreigners who have had the dream of countless visitors lazing on a beach and been equal to pulling it off. Eventually, and in a curious, quintessentially Greek way, the islanders probably admire them too.

ISLAND ELECTIONS

The time was clearly ripe when an island shopkeeper, an amiable old soul who liked poetry and had spoken warmly of his son's help in running the business, had the son by the throat and was spluttering with rage. The son, roughly twice his size, managed to break away and retreated into the road, howling. "The election," the old man explained, staring after him, "he just told me who he's voting for."

The candidates' posters had been going up for several days—as soon as the last of the season's charter flights had left. They showed the incumbent mayor wearing a benign and statesmanlike expression. The potential usurper was younger, had a large moustache, and affected the pose of a visionary. Gossip in the *ouzerie* revealed that "hate" would not cover what they thought of one another. The younger had once been hounded off the island—a suitcase literally thrown after him into a departing boat—for reasons that were never clear. He was back, they said in the *ouzerie*, for his revenge.

It would be difficult to exaggerate the passions aroused by island municipal elections. They are run on national party political lines, a passionate matter in its own right in Greece, but are wonderfully exacerbated by real as well as somewhat enigmatic local issues, the power of future patronage, and private feuds. Almost anything is capable of convulsing small, compressed communities of people who, at the time of the year when elections come round, have nothing else to do, are irascible after the strain of the tourist season, and are looking forward to a state-sanctioned opportunity to get cross.

The elections cannot be totally avoided, even if some islanders did wish to distance themselves from the flying fur. Voting is compulsory unless a voter can prove to have been more than 112 miles (180 km) from home on polling day. Failure to vote may lead to difficulties, for example, in acquiring a passport or having an old one renewed.

A previous election on a neighbouring island gave a foretaste of what might be in

A message for the people: Communist Party posters stuck to a decorative wall.

store. It had been predicted that the result of that previous election would be extremely close, and one of the candidates had arranged a secret weapon—30 registered voters who were living on the mainland but were willing to come back and vote for him. His opponent uncovered the plot and, in collusion with supporters at the mainland port where the returning voters had assembled, managed to have the ferry services to the island cancelled until after voting.

The Englishman telling this tale had been persuaded to fetch the stranded voters, an operation which involved sneaking away in his boat and collecting the voters under cover of darkness. After numerous complications of

particular, the mayor's failure to live up to his promises about new ones.

The interpreter became restless, and if her translations were to be taken literally, all the committee's replies ended with statements like "…and if you believe that, sir, you are an idiot." When the interpreter stormed out, saying that she could stand no more of their lies, she confirmed the suspicion that she might support the other candidate.

Down the road, the opposition was asked what they thought the election was about. Their spokesman reeled off a list which concerned democracy, a caring society, organised crime, human rights. "But what about drains?" he was prompted.

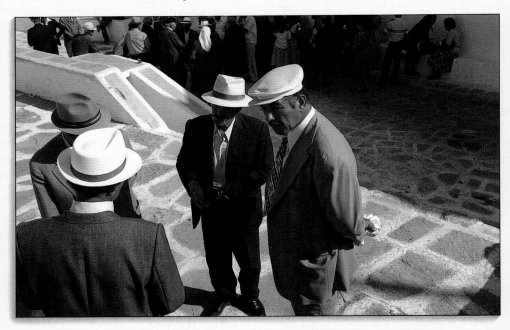

an appropriately Byzantine nature, the small boat returned to the island top-heavy with voters and their baggage with minutes to spare. It tottered into the fishing port to the cheers of supporters and the speechless fury of the opposition. The election result was tipped by the secret voters, with only one vote to spare.

With this incident to draw on, the election committee of the present challenger was approached. "What are the issues?" they were asked through an interpreter, a girl who worked in the shop next door. They went into conference and emerged with a verdict: "Drains." So drains were discussed and, in

"What about drains?" he echoed.

"Well, the other party says…"

"No!" The opposition candidate held up an admonishing finger. A lorry had come to a halt outside the campaign office. A gang of workmen climbed down and attacked the cobbles with pick-axes under the noses of the committee. "You see, no problem with drains. New ones."

Two days before voting, the candidates made their speeches—the challenger down on the quay, the incumbent afterwards outside the church. The general idea was that the audience would move on from one to hear the other. A hugely amplified fanfare announced the start. "Ladies and gentlemen," a voice boomed from behind the as yet empty balcony, "I give you…Dimitris Prevezanos!" Four small boys let off compressed-air hooters to herald the grand entrance.

Dimitris Prevezanos, however, failed to materialise. Another fanfare, another introduction, more hooting—and still no Dimitris Prevezanos. Instead, a water pipe chose that moment to detach itself from a tank above the balcony. Prevezanos supporters, wearing Sunday suits, leapt out of the way.

"The drains," was the reply when asked what's wrong. "His speech was about drains. Now he must talk about something else. Maybe he can't think of something else."

The mayor did not mention drains, presumably because by then most of the main street and the quay had been dug up, as no one on the island could have failed to notice. He concentrated on broader issues like the new airport building and was prepared to stand on his record.

An army contingent arrived on the island for polling day. A man was running a book on the results, with a plastic bag stuffed with bank notes to cover all bets. When asked how much, he winked: four million drachmas. It says something about the island that he felt able to wander off from time to time and leave the bag unattended on a table.

The bets were settled at 8 p.m. when red

It was a partisan opinion although when, third time lucky, the candidate did appear, he *did* have something to say about drains. He may have had other topics but the time taken to repair the pipe had to be subtracted from the time available before the incumbent went into action. When he finished speaking, the audience duly filed up the hill to listen to Kostas Papadoulis, the incumbent. The small boys passed their hooters to another set of small boys who would apply them to the task of getting Papadoulis re-elected.

Left, a political pow-wow. Above, two women discuss Greece's economic situation.

flares announced that the result was known: Papadoulis was back in office for four years. He was carried shoulder high around the village while a disappointed Dimitris Prevezanos was said to be packing for a further spell of exile, this time self-imposed, on the mainland.

The following morning, father and son resumed normal relations and—to almost nobody's surprise—the work on the drains ran into "technical difficulties" and ceased. They were not completed for the next big event on the calendar, Easter, and only just in time for the second, the charter flights which signalled the beginning of the tourist season.

WRITING THE GREAT NOVEL

Bring a woman, Lawrence Durrell advised Henry Miller in 1938, promising that in other respects his Greek island was the perfect place to get a novel written. "We could sail and bathe in mornings, have a fine sunny lunch with wine, then a long afternoon siesta, bathe before tea and then four hours' work in a slow rich evening." At the time, Miller was keen to finish a book and might have wondered about the efficacy of Durrell's idea of a hard day at the office.

Miller did finish the book—it was *Tropic of Capricorn*—and, although the extent to which it materialised on Corfu is unknown, the achievement ought to stand as a benchmark for the permanent presence that has since imposed itself on nearly every Greek island: writers wrestling with great works. Most of them would have thrown a beach towel in with a typewriter and decamped to their island expressly to write a book; others might have arrived for other reasons but been inspired by the amount of writing going on around them.

One such, a taxi driver from the Channel Islands, had taken a year's sabbatical on a small, green island, intending to devote himself to nudism. Suddenly inspired, he would take willing listeners aside to reveal the names of the main characters in the novel he was going to write. There was a Greek named Dimitris and an Italian, Giovanni, although he had not yet decided on surnames. The novel would be set in Greece and Italy, which were the two foreign countries he had visited. He had run into a problem, however, and would be grateful for help. He had been unable, he said, to think up a plot.

Of the ideas tossed at him, a weave of sex and murder most appealed. Every morning thereafter, he would set off for the nudist beach with his new notebook in hand.

He reported back to say that the novel was progressing well and had reached the murder scene. He admired the Len Deighton school of writing and was determined to get exactly right the technical details of the weapon used, in this case a hand gun. He had heard a name which he felt had the authentic ring of menace. He would call the gun "a Howitzer".

It was one of at least four books actually being written by expatriates on that particular island that year—as opposed to those under discussion over long lunches. One of them, a local history, had been in production for more than 20 years. It was by a clever Englishwoman who led a semi-reclusive existence in a primitive cottage high on a mountain. She would descend to the village once a week on a moped to do her shopping; otherwise nobody saw much of her. It was said that she'd come to the island to forget an unhappy love affair at Oxford.

The expatriate colony once published a little book about the island and in it was an article by her which demonstrated convincingly the rigour of a trained historian. The article is probably as much as anyone will ever know about a project which had occupied most of her adult life. That year, she destroyed the manuscript. Asked why, she shrugged and said nothing.

Conspiracy of distraction: During the tourist season, a conspiracy of distraction forever drives a wedge between writer and great work. Durrell's invitation to Miller sets out some of them: the weather is magnificent and the sea so congenial that there is always a plausible excuse to dive in and remain there for some time.

The temptation is to go swimming more and more as summer approaches, starting on one beach and coming ashore at another. Ostensibly, the goal is "to keep fit"; the parallel purpose is to keep an eye on the deliveries from heaven, manna arriving daily by chartered jet and, from the moment they stretch their long, lovely legs to apply sun tan oil, totally committed to the proverbial good time. Durrell's advice to Miller contains one anachronism: the women are here already.

Durrell's "fine sunny lunch with wine" is another of the yawning man-traps set for the island writer, especially the "with wine". By any criterion, expatriates who settle on islands are slightly odd. That makes them excellent company; it also means that, on the whole, they drink a bit.

Nobody ever resolves to drink less on a Greek island for the sake of saving money. Somewhere on the island there will be a wholesaler or a grocer who sells *ouzo* and brandy from the barrel—bring your own bottle. Short-term visitors are unlikely to have the time to find out who or where they are; expatriates, on the other hand, can find them blindfolded.

Credit is extended everywhere to resident writers. The trusting and hospitable Greeks revere Homer and are willing to regard anyone who can type with two fingers as a potential heir. The less flattering explanation is that in winter there is no way off most

Wine sold in huge bottles is commensurately cheap, and etiquette seems to require that once opened the bottle must be finished at one sitting.

One writer on the island discovered that, by reversing Durrell's timetable and applying himself in the mornings, he could turn out a slim volume of poetry per decade. Over lunch at his special table in a taverna below his house, he would discuss with another writer their respective great works. He was working on his third volume and was fairly confident that it would be ready by the turn of the millennium.

Lunches "with wine": These were definitely lunches "with wine", and he would mysteri-

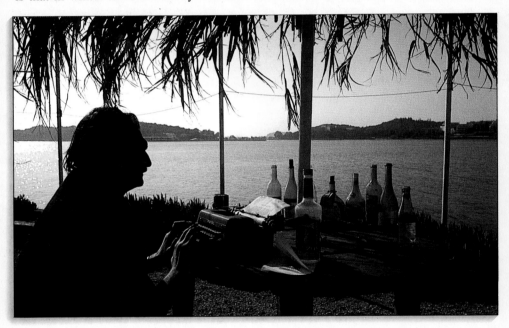

islands except by boat, and creditors are more than likely to be lining the quay.

Either way, their generosity can be a lifesaver because even writers who are in a position to have their banks at home send them money are often caught short. The rumour, never proven, is that banks in Athens will not forward foreign currency transfers to their branches while there is still hope that, unnoticed, they can play the markets with it.

Anguished telexes to Athens will eventually achieve a sheepish surrender and the means to go out and pay a trifling sum for a litre of the strong stuff.

ously arrange the bottles in a straight line on what seemed to be a constant compass bearing. Greek waiters don't clear empty bottles; it is their way of keeping track of the ever-increasing numbers.

A visit to the poet's house revealed that the view from the terrace bore down directly on the taverna and, in particular, on to "his" table. Concerned that too grand a lunch on the Durell model might, the following morning, jeopardise work on volume three, the poet's wife had acquired a powerful pair of binoculars and turned the terrace into an observation post. His favourite retsina was sold only in small bottles which, together with the tendency of a great many friends and acquaintances to drop by for a chat, meant the number of bottles could proliferate at impressive speed. All of this was monitored through the binoculars, and if the situation appeared to be getting out of hand, the loyal wife would descend imperially either to speak on the virtues of moderation or, *in extremis*, to march him off by the ear.

The studied arrangement of the bottles, then, was a smokescreen. "He thinks that I can only see one," his wife admitted when he went off to fish a bottle out of the fridge. "In that belief he is mistaken."

Whatever cloud may have been hanging over the third volume of poems, the first two

nothing for the expatriate colony to do. It would be inconceivable, for example, to squander the need to call at the post office and at the bank by allowing both errands to occur on a single outing, even if post office and bank happened to be close neighbours. Shopping is sensibly stretched over a whole day: a loaf of bread and eggs in the morning, say, and the balance after lunch—a lunch with friends and, of course, "with wine".

Corfu cannot have had many visitors when Miller dropped in on Durrell in 1938, but Durrell's own literary output from his island base proves that it can be done, if only by observing the sanctity of those four hours, either in the slow rich evening or, for a

were accomplished facts. Moreover, they were on sale in the local bookshop, a vindication for any writer whose credentials are called into question. Very few island writers are in a position to dispel doubt so triumphantly. Very few, indeed, are on sale anywhere or, deep in their hearts, expect to be. It is enough merely to be writing a book, regardless of the outcome.

In the winter months, when all but one or two of the bars and tavernas are closed and the sea is too cold for swimming, there is

Left, creating takes enormous concentration. Above, nourishment for would-be writers.

certain kind of poet, in the morning.

Less dedicated writers are more inclined to use the great novel as a filling for the vacuum, a cushion over atavistic Puritan misgivings about months of bone-idleness. It soothes the conscience and enhances the fun: after all, 150,000 completed words on paper are a better memento of an island visit than the stamps in one's passport before and afterwards.

All too often, of course, the great novel is never actually published—or indeed finished. But the possibility of its being completed provides the perfect excuse to return to the island for one more try.

ISLANDS OUT OF SEASON

It is only when the charter flights have finally returned to base that the real character of a small island, such as Serifos or Patmos, staggers out of its unseasonal hibernation. The larger islands are capable of absorbing a deluge of visitors without having to adopt when they arrive (and discard when they leave) a totally different identity. A visitor arriving in Crete in October would not discover, as could happen on a smaller island, that the police station had just closed and would not re-open until needed again late in the spring.

It is difficult to exaggerate the disfiguring impact when an island with a population measured in hundreds or the low thousands is swamped by 10 times the normal number all at the same time. How would Britain, say, with a population of 60 million, cope with 600 million visitors in one go? Residents of the United States wishing to imagine something on the same scale might like to consider the simultaneous arrival on their doorstep of the combined populations of China, India and the Soviet Union, plus a couple of European countries.

Quick change: Understandably dazed by the whole thing, the islanders have to find their feet again when everyone goes away. Superficially, the change into winter uniform is swift. Migrant waiters and kitchen staff pile on to departing ferries to look for winter jobs on the mainland. Awnings over pavement cafés are rolled up and stowed; the chairs and tables stacked and dragged away. Most of the shops are closed and padlocked.

Stray puppies sniff about, disconcerted by the interruption in the supply of unfinished moussaka handed down on visitors' plates. They learn cunning fast enough—both to eat and to escape the furtive culling necessary to keep their numbers down. Surplus cats are treated more leniently—except, perhaps, by fugitive dogs.

A good sign that the islanders are feeling themselves again after the grinding hours they have put in during the season is the resumption of the evening promenade, an almost formal ritual in which small groups file from one end of the locally prescribed route to the other and back again. Overtaking is apparently not allowed. Among them are the elderly and handicapped who are seldom seen in public places during the season. Winter visitors who join the throng are bound to attract curious glances from the traffic going in the opposite direction. The process of recognition and acceptance as an honorary member of the community is a ritual in itself. First, perhaps, a half-cocked eyebrow; later, a nod; ultimately, triumphantly, a stop for a chat.

The promenade is a chance to observe all kinds of island machinery in motion: frocked and hatted Orthodox priests, symbols of a former propriety that doesn't stand a chance against the summer heathens, reassert their magisterial presence among the faithful. Office-bearers and petitioners in the schismatic world of island politics fall into step with the mayor for a mobile conference.

A winter's tale: If the municipal elections are in sight, the plotting that goes on during the promenade will explode into campaigns which sound like the rumble of impending civil war. The party manifestos may commend or deplore, as the case may be, the state of the village drains, but the winner's powers of patronage are such that the outcome is regarded, not unrealistically, as a matter of economic life or death.

Visitors can skip politics, however, and still feel that they are part of local life. There are any number of processions through the streets, the mayor and priests conspicuously linked in secular-clerical solidarity at the head of an enthusiastic brass band. The religious festivals, notably Easter, usually include a pilgrimage to a monastery where—and this is not a literary invention—the fellow who falls over three times a week in the *ouzerie* may materialise as a solemn acolyte with a good voice for ceremonial chant. When the service is over, the grounds are turned into a picnic area for a party which may last until dawn.

Ouzeries, basic drinking establishments where a request for a cocktail would draw a blank stare, stay open through the winter.

Some of the tavernas and posher bars may too, although probably on an informal rota as if the owners were sharing the workload. Even a disco may re-open, but that could last for only a night or two and on the next it may just as inexplicably close down again.

The locals have to buy food and other supplies, so there is never any difficulty getting hold of provisions. The smaller islands are seldom self-sufficient, however, and if they rely on ferries which are not nearly so frequent in winter—and are liable to be cancelled in bad weather (travellers with deadlines please note)—there may be temporary shortages of most fresh produce.

Power failures which last more than a day

cause a commotion because the bakeries can't function. The lesser kind go unnoticed, although not by wintering writers with electric typewriters or word processors. The latter may be found crying in the *ouzerie* after losing the contents of an electronic memory.

Commercial fishermen, who turn their hands to other jobs in summer when fishing is not allowed, go back to work. Their catch, though, looks expensive next to frozen meat mostly imported from Italy. The fishermen sail at dusk and return at dawn but, for the rest of the male population, the longer nights are the cue to bring out packs of playing cards. Officially, no money changes hands, but

passers-by could not fail to notice scraps of paper and meticulous accounting. In reality, there is a massive and endless redistribution of the summer takings, although by the following spring most of the money is supposedly back where it started.

Landlords don't expect to earn any rent in winter, so when a visitor comes along the negotiations are friendly and flexible. Prime accommodation on the sea may be worth a slight premium while the water is still at a tolerable temperature, although after September and before May there is hardly a beach in Greece which couldn't be annexed and occupied as private property.

If outdoor conditions are an important criterion, the southern islands are generally warmer. All over the Aegean, however, the winter wind will sometimes cut through to the bone, and houses that were not built specifically for the summer trade are more likely to have some form of heating. Tenants would be expected to pay for the fuel they use. It is worth asking about vacant farmhouses; these have the added advantage that neighbours are always popping around with eggs, a bottle and an extra glass. In the 1990s, this wholly agreeable way of life could be had for about 80,000 drachmas per month, not excluding fairly lavish consumption of local drink and cigarettes.

The English novelist Simon Raven spent the winter of 1960 on Hydra looking into "what goes on when winter comes, when the last epicene giggle has hovered and died in the October air". He decided he was among a bunch of atavistic pirates who, happily preoccupied by making money during the summer, reverted in winter to the old distrust of strangers who used to come only to spy on their illicit booty.

Hydra, like other islands, has since become accustomed to having a few foreigners stay on after the rest leave and, on the assumption the islanders never saw what Raven wrote about them, he would probably feel more comfortable among them now. The one impression formed then which he most definitely would not wish to change now is that only in winter could his eye make out what the island was really like.

Left, a heater on Ikaria. Right, January on Hydra. Following pages, sailing away; back(s) to the future.

TRAVEL TIPS

Getting There
306 By Air
306 By Sea
306 By Road

Travel Essentials
307 Visas & Passports
307 Money Matters
307 Health
308 What to Wear
308 What to Bring
309 Animal Quarantine
309 Customs
309 Reservations
309 Extension of Stay
309 On Departure

Getting Acquainted
309 Government & Economy
310 Geography & Population
310 Time Zone
310 Climate
310 Culture & Customs
311 Electricity
311 Business & Banking Hours
312 Public Holidays
312 Seasonal Festivals
313 Religious Festivals

Communications
313 Media
315 Postal Services
315 Telephone/Telegrams

Emergencies
315 Security & Crime
316 Loss/Theft
316 Pharmacies/Dental
316 Left Luggage

Getting Around
316 From the Airport
317 Domestic Travel
317 Water Transport
318 Public Transport
319 Private Transport

Where to Stay
319 Hotels
321 Private Rooms
321 Pensions
321 Villas & Apartments
322 Camping
322 Youth Hostels
322 Monasteries/Settlements

Food Digest
322 What to Eat
324 Where to Eat
324 Drinking Notes

Things to Do
325 Cruises
326 Excursions
326 Tour Guides

Culture Plus
326 Museums
329 Outdoor Movies

329 Nightlife

Shopping
330 What to Buy

330 Sports

331 Language

333 Further Reading

Useful Addresses
334 Tourist Information
335 Embassies & Consulates

336 Art/Photo Credits

337 Index

GETTING THERE

BY AIR

Quite a few of the more popular islands have international airports. These include Crete, Rhodes, Corfu, Kos, Skiathos, Mykonos, Lesvos, and Zakynthos and new channels for international travel open each season. Most people, however, fly to Athens first; then take a ferryboat or a domestic airplane to the island of their choice.

Greece has good air connections with all five continents and is serviced by numerous international airlines. There are different ways of flying at a much lower cost than the standard airline ticket (APEX, stand-by, last-minute seats, "bucket shops"), and you may want to inform yourself of the different possibilities and of their related advantages and disadvantages, before buying a ticket. By far the cheapest way to travel to Greece is by buying a charter flight, which can cost as little as £100 return from London. These usually arrive in the middle of the night (and depart in the middle of the night), are uncomfortable and can be chaotic. But they are very cheap nonetheless.

Athens has two air terminals. The East air terminal is for International and charter flights; the West terminal is for Olympic Airways flights and flights to the islands. Taxis or buses connect the two.

During the peak summer season it is impossible to walk through the East Terminal hangar which services charter flights without tripping over sleeping forms and rucksacks. All part of the fun.

BY SEA

The majority of visitors entering Greece by sea do so from the west, that is, from Italy. You can catch a boat to Greece from Venice, Ancona, and Bari, but the most regular service is from Brindisi. Daily ferry lines (somewhat less frequent in the low-season) connect Brindisi with the three main western Greek ports: Corfu, Igumenitsa and Patras. Corfu is a 9-hour trip, Igumenitsa 11 hours; and Patras 16 hours to 18 hours, depending on whether it is a direct boat or one making stops in Corfu and Igumenitsa. From Corfu it is possible to get a ferry, then a bus directly to Athens (about 11 hours), but Patras is best for travelling to Athens as regular buses and trains connect the two (about 4 hours by bus). If you plan to take your car with you on the boat, you should make a reservation well in advance. Otherwise, arriving a few hours before the departure time should suffice, except during peak seasons when booking in advance is advisable.

Italy and the west, however, are by no means the only provenance for Greece-bound sea travellers. Southward, boats connect Alexandria and Piraeus once every 10 to 15 days: eastward, boats run weekly between Haifa, Limassol and Piraeus, and once every five days between Volos, Cyprus and Syria, not to mention the numerous crossing-points between the East Aegean islands and the Turkish coast. Northward, frequent boats connect Piraeus and Istanbul, and in the summer boats run twice a month between Odessa (USSR) and Piraeus.

BY ROAD

The overland route from northwestern Europe to Greece is a long one – some 1,900 miles from London to Athens. It is an arduous and impractical travel option if you're just trying to get to Athens for a brief vacation, but it can be an interesting trip if you make the journey a part of your vacation. By car there is an E route that runs through the interior of Yugoslavia, entering Greece just above Thessaloniki. There are also inexpensive bus services, along the lines of the famous Magic Bus, which connect Athens and Thessaloniki with many European cities – a three and a half day trip from London. The various trains that you can take from northwest Europe will take about as long as the bus, will cost considerably more, but may get you to Greece feeling more intact. Hitching to Greece is also a possibility, though hitching through Yugoslavia is reported to be difficult.

If you're travelling to Greece from Asia you'll pass through Istanbul and cross into Greece at the Evros River. The recommended route is by car or bus. The road is good and the journey from Istanbul to Thessaloniki takes approximately 15 hours; various bus companies run the route. The train has the mythic appeal of running the route of the old Orient Express, but unless you're a great train fan, the travel may be prohibitive: some 25 hours from Thessaloniki to Istanbul. This trip crosses the fascinating region of Thrace; a fine adventure if you have the time and the spirit for it.

TRAVEL ESSENTIALS

VISAS & PASSPORTS

A valid passport is required for all travellers except the following:

1. Holders of a United Kingdom "British Visitor's" passport.
2. Holders of National Identity Card nationals of Austria, Belgium, France, West Germany, Italy, Luxembourg, Netherlands and Switzerland.
3. Holders of either a Military Identity Card (issued by NATO) or of Laissez Passer (issued by the United Nations).
4. Seamen, travelling on duty, who hold a Seaman's book.

No visa is required for citizens of the following countries:

For a stay of three months: United Kingdom, United States of America, Australia, New Zealand, Canada, Andorra, Argentina, Austria, Bahamas, Barbados, Belgium, Brazil, Cyprus, Denmark, Finland, France, Gambia, West Germany, Granada, Ireland, Iceland, Israel, Italy, Japan, Luxembourg, Liechtenstein, Malta, Mexico, Monaco, Morocco, the Netherlands, Norway, South Korea, Spain, Sweden, Switzerland.

For a stay of two months: Portugal, Republic of South Africa, Venezuela, Chile, Colombia, Dominican Republic, El Salvador, Haiti, Honduras, Guatemala, Ecuador, Kenya, Mozambique, Nicaragua, Panama, Paraguay, Peru, Uruguay, Zambia.

For a stay of one month: Tunisia and Hong Kong.

MONEY MATTERS

The Greek unit of money is the drachma. The Bank of Greece issues bank notes of 50, 100, 500, 1000, and 5000 drachmas, and coins of 50, 20, 10, 5, 2, and 1 drachmas.

EXCHANGE RATE

Rates of exchange go up or down daily. In Athens, to find out the current rate of exchange, call the National Bank of Greece, tel: 323 1802-9.

CREDIT CARDS

The plusher hotels, shops and restaurants of Athens and other larger islands all recognise the major international credit cards, but many tavernas will not. Stickers in the front windows will advise on which cards are acceptable, but be sure to check *before ordering* or buying that the arrangement is still valid. Generally, visitors to small islands are likely to encounter problems with credit cards.

TRAVELLERS' CHEQUES

As with credit cards, only the more popular islands will have facilities to cash travellers' cheques. This can be done in banks and in larger hotels by submitting proof of identity. A passport is the most accepted form of proof; be sure to retrieve it from your hotel reception desk before going to the bank.

CASH

Every island, no matter how remote, will have some form of banking system, but this could be as casual as the village mayor setting up a table under the only tree and doling out money. Other islands set up temporary banking facilities in tourist shops, post offices and OTE (telephone) offices and hours are irregular, never over weekends. Cash is often the only currency which is guaranteed legal tender on these far-flung islands, even at the "bank". If you plan to island-hop, jump ship or follow up on any itinerant whims, carry quantities of both drachmas and your native currency. Islanders are wonderfully honest and your cash will almost certainly be safe.

HEALTH

Residents of EEC countries are eligible to receive free emergency medical care. In Britain, it is necessary to obtain a form from the DHSS before leaving home, so check this out beforehand. Medical insurance is always a good idea for additional coverage. Be sure your policy covers the cost of an air taxi as this is the quickest way, in an emergency, off the smaller islands to the nearest hospital. If you plan to hire a car, a motorcycle or a moped, ensure that your policy covers all motoring accidents. The number of accidents, especially on mopeds, mounts annually.

DRINKING WATER

Carrying a large plastic bottle of mineral water is as common a sight on Greek islands as is carrying a *baguette* around Paris. Although tap water is essentially safe to drink, having a private water supply is much handier, as drinking fountains are few and the sun is fierce. Bottled water can be bought almost anywhere that sells food, even in beach cafés and tavernas.

INSECTS & PESTS

Snakes and scorpions can be found in rocky areas. They tend not to attack unless disturbed, but always dress in long trousers and socks when hill walking. Jellyfish (*medusas*) are less common these days but can still occasionally be seen (and should be avoided) near the shores of some beaches. Spiny sea urchins can give painful stings if stepped on in the water; a local Greek remedy is to rub the wound with olive oil and then gently massage the foot until the spines pop out. This rarely works, so wear plastic shoes when swimming.

The most common pest is the mosquito, which loves virgin white skin. Avoid perfumes and deodorants (it attracts them even more) and invest instead . in either of two items. The first is a coil, which, when lit and placed by the window, acts as an effective means of combat by smothering the mosquito in foul-smelling smoke. Even the smaller islands sell these coils in chemists or grocers. The second method is more modern: a plug-in electric coil which burns smokeless tablets called *Spira*. Practically odourless, it's worth seeking out in chemists or hardware shops on the larger islands.

SUNBURN

Each year hundreds of tourists are badly burnt by avoiding the obvious rule: take your tan slowly. For the first few days wear a sunhat and a sunblock. Observe, like sensible Greeks, the afternoon siesta when the sun is at its hottest, and stay on the beach for just a couple of hours in the mornings and the early evenings. Gradually work up to staying out longer, and remember to reapply suntan lotion whenever you come out of the sea. It's possible to get burned while swimming or sightseeing too. Wearing a tee-shirt over your swimsuit the first couple of days or when touring the island, and dressing in dark colours and long sleeves, avoids senseless burning.

DRUGS

All prescribed drugs should be packed in their original bottles, carefully labelled and marked. Failure to do so could result in an arrest for the possession of dangerous drugs. Greek authorities take the unauthorised use of drugs very seriously indeed; this is not the country in which to store cannabis, no matter how small the quantity. Err on the side of caution at all times.

WHAT TO WEAR

Island life is casual. It's possible to get by without offending anyone by dressing simply, in a tee-shirt dress and sandals (if a woman) or long trousers and a tee-shirt (if a man). Bathing costumes can be slipped on underneath. Disco clothes or wash-and-wear cottons are sold on most larger islands.

FOOTWEAR

Sandals are appropriate day or night. Plastic shoes are invaluable for swimming in water containing rocks, garbage or sea urchins; also for walking on the red-hot volcanic beaches of Santorini and Nissiros. Plastic shoes can usually be bought on the islands themselves. Sturdy walking shoes are required for mountain climbing or uphill strolls to monasteries as snakes are common in the hills. Three pairs of socks should suffice; one pair to wear while walking, one pair to dry in the hot sun, and one pair to wear at night; temperatures in the evenings can be surprisingly chilly.

WHAT TO BRING

These items should appear on every dedicated island-hopper's check-list, but again, most can be bought in Athens or the larger island cities: binoculars (invaluable, entertaining and often overlooked), tin opener, corkscrew, sharp knife, plastic fork and spoon (a good Swiss army knife includes most of these domestic items), folding drinking cup, torch (very important for steep island paths late at night), thermos flask, facecloth (unavailable in Greece), towel, beach towel, soap, little bags of soap powder, sticking plasters, antiseptic cream, sink plug, portable clothes line and pegs, insect repellent, aspirin, indigestion tablets, earplugs, an alarm clock and/or a watch. These last items are for catching ferries, caiques and island buses; no two island clocks tell the same time and ferries wait for no man.

BAGGAGE

The old saying which applies to travellers everywhere applies especially to those travelling on Greek islands: pack your suitcase, then unpack it and leave half the contents behind. Nothing ruins a holiday more than having to heave a heavy suitcase around unsuitable terrain, i.e. hills and ferryboat decks. Only the poshest hotels have mini-bus services to/ from the harbour or airport; if you plan to find accommodation on the spot, plan to carry your suitcase or stash it somewhere while you look around. (A few of the more popular islands offer temporary luggage storage facilities near the harbour.) If your suitcase is still too heavy for prolonged island-hopping, consider investing in a suitcase trolley which can be bought in the shopping arcades around Syntagma Square in Athens, or from a department store on Rhodes, Kos, Crete or Corfu.

A handy tip: carrying a basket or packing a smaller suitcase inside a larger one can be useful. The smaller one can be brought out for the beach or for short trips to other islands, while the larger one and its contents stay safely stored in the hotel.

ANIMAL QUARANTINE

Dogs and cats require health and rabies inoculation certificates issued by a vet in the country of origin before being allowed to enter Greece. The certificate must be issued not more than 12 months in the case of dogs and 6 months in the case of cats (and not less than 6 days prior to) arrival. Parrots and other birds must have a health certificate stating they are free from psittacosis.

CUSTOMS

If arriving from EEC countries: You are allowed to import free of duty the following items: 300 cigarettes or 75 cigars or 150 cigarillos or 400 grams of tobacco; 1.5 litres of alcoholic drink or 5 litres of wine; 75 grams of perfume, and gift items to a total value of 55,500 drachmas.

If arriving from non-EEC countries: You are allowed to import free of duty: 200 cigarettes or 50 cigars or 100 cigarillos or 250 grams of tobacco; 1 litre of alcoholic beverage or 2 litres of wine; 50 grams of perfume and gift items to a total value of 7,000 drachmas.

You may also bring one of each of the following: a camera and film; a movie camera and film; a projector; a pair of binoculars; a portable musical instrument; a portable radio, phonograph or tape recorder, a bicycle, and sports gear (tennis racquet, etc).

It is prohibited to import narcotics, medicine (except limited quantities prescribed by a licensed physician for your own use); explosives, weapons and (yes, that's right) computers or windsurfers – unless a Greek national residing in Greece guarantees the goods will be re-exported.

For other specific restrictions regarding the importation and exportation of such things as animals, plants, shotguns, pleasure craft and antiquities, contact the nearest Greek embassy, consulate or tourist organisation.

RESERVATIONS

The dual perils of Greek Civil Aviation strikes and package tour operators' double-booking practices means nothing should be left to chance. Confirm travel arrangements and hotel accommodation with your tour operator or travel agent approximately three days before leaving for Greece. When returning home, call the airline or the appropriate authority before setting off for Athens to catch a flight home. Inexpensive charter flights are often subject to several hours' delay, so be sure to slip a good novel or a pack of cards into your hand luggage and be prepared to sit it out, probably on the floor of the airport. Transfer to the Islands: For information on domestic airlines, or of how to reach Athens or Piraeus from the airports, see the section called "Getting Around".

EXTENSION OF STAY

Aliens with no visible means of support and/or without return tickets home may be refused an extension of stay. Otherwise, apply to have your visa extended from the Aliens Bureau at 9 Halkokondili Street, Athens, tel: 362 8301. If applying from one of the islands, contact the nearest police station for details of how to apply.

ON DEPARTURE

Leave plenty of time to reach Athens for your international flight home, especially if you are visiting a remote island. Any situation involving more than one Greek vehicle (plane, boat, taxi) is courting disaster, so leave nothing to chance. If the distance is far, or merely complicated, it might be an idea to break the journey into "laps" to prevent calamities along the way. On Halki or Symi, for instance, it would be wise to arrive on Rhodes the day before your flight departs; two days before if flying back from Athens via Rhodes.

GETTING ACQUAINTED

GOVERNMENT & ECONOMY

Strikes are a way of life in Greece. Should there not be one of the following, consider yourself lucky: a postal strike; a garbage strike; a strike by telephone operators; an air traffic controllers' strike; a civil aviation strike; a bus strike or a taxi strike. Any stay in Athens of more than three days will involve witnessing at least one demonstration and probably several. These are passionate but peaceful affairs and add to the general disruption which passes for daily Athenian life. Consulting one of the English-language publications might or might not tell you what they are about; most Athenians treat demonstrations as part of the urban landscape.

Former Prime Minister Andreas Papandreou and his Panhellenic Socialist Movement were involved in allegations of corruption during 1988 and 1989. His party (PASOK) has yet to recover from the scandals but the New Democracy Party, which defeated PASOK in 1990, has also experienced troubles.

The late 1980s and early 1990s saw a huge rise in inflation throughout the country; a shock for anyone who remembers the islands as a "cheap & cheerful" vacation destination. Inflation rose by 20 percent in 1986; by 16 percent in 1987; and by 12 percent in 1988. Although the islands are no longer the place for rock-bottom, cheap holidays, the drachma has fared fairly well against other currencies, and Greece remains good value for travellers.

GEOGRAPHY & POPULATION

Greece is one of the southernmost European countries, ensuring a high sunshine rate throughout much of the year. The combined population of Greater Athens and Piraeus at the last census was just over 3 million inhabitants. The most populated island is Crete, with just over half a million inhabitants, followed by Corfu (97,000), Lesvos (89,000), and Rhodes (88,000). The least populated islands covered in this book are the "Back Islands" of the Cyclades. Tiny Donoussa, Iraklia, Schinoussa, and Koufonissia have only 100 to 200 inhabitants each.

TIME ZONE

Greek time is two hours ahead of Greenwich Mean Time. So, when it is noon in Greece it is 10 a.m. in London, 5 a.m. in New York, and 8 p.m. in Sydney. Like the rest of the Common Market, the clock is advanced one hour during summer to give extended daylight hours.

CLIMATE

If you visit Greece in the summer months you'll want to bring lightweight, casual clothing. If you visit Greece during the winter months, bring the same kind of clothes you would wear during spring in the northern part of the United States or central Europe: that is, be ready for rainy, windy days and temperatures ranging between 40° and 60° F (3° and 16° C).

On the whole, islands are ill-equipped for visitors during the winter months. Heating can be basic or non-existent, boats infrequent, food tinned and amenities scarce. The tourist season is officially "over" in early October, when Olympic Airways lays on extra planes from the islands to Athens to cope with the hundreds of workers returning to the city for the winter. Should you find yourself on the islands during this period (the first week in October for the Sporades; the second week for the Cyclades), you will be treated to a curious spectacle: an emerging ghost-town. Cafés and shops close down daily, often locking their doors directly after you have left, and remaining closed for the next five months.

In general, the north coast of each island is subject to more gales and cooler temperatures than the protected south coast; be sure to check on a map exactly where a holiday resort is before making a final booking. Many travellers underestimate the differences in climate between individual island chains. The green, cool Ionian islands, for instance, are prey to rainy spells from mid-September through to the end of March. By contrast, the southern coast of Crete can offer swimming for the hardy as late as mid-December. A good rule to follow if planning to visit any island between mid-September through the end of April is this: the further south the island geographically, the better the sunshine rate.

CULTURE & CUSTOMS

SPELLING & PLACE NAMES

Syntagma Square in Athens is also known as Constitution Square. The island of Lesvos is known variously as Lesbos, Mytilene, or Mytilini. Corfu can be called by its Greek name Kerkira, or Kerkyra; Itaki by its English name Ithaca. Attempts have been made in this book to formalise a system which has no national standard. If you find a place-name which is unfamiliar, check on more than one map or ask at a local ticket office if the destination has another name or spelling.

TIPPING

Most restaurants and tavernas add a 15 percent service charge to the bill, so a tip is not expected, although it is customary to leave the small change on the plate after a bill has been paid. If the serving boy (*micro*) has been particularly good about clearing away empty plates, etc., reward him separately by placing change on the table rather than on the plate. Micros rely on tips as a supplement to rather meagre wages. Just as important as any gratuity, however, is your appreciation of the food. Greek restaurant owners are often proud when you tell them you like a particular dish.

SIESTA

Siesta is strictly observed on many islands, when, between the hours of 2 p.m. and 5 p.m., the driving of motorbikes and scooters in towns is prohibited. This provides a wonderful respite in even the noisiest of tourist towns, and is the ideal time to take a nap or extend a leisurely lunch into the afternoon. Most shops will close, perhaps to reopen again in the evening. Although the sun is fierce during these hours, anyone with a strong constitution and protective clothing will be rewarded if they choose this time to visit busy archaeological sites; crowds will have diminished considerably.

CLOTHING

Be aware of the social significance of the way you dress, and of how the Greeks perceive it. Greece, like any other country, has a set of codes, both stated and implicit, which defines the socially acceptable range of attire. The Greeks will not expect you as a tourist to dress as they do. However, in certain places and regions, you will encounter requirements or conventions concerning dress which do reflect on you as a visitor. To enter a church, men must wear long trousers and women, sleeved dresses. These will occasionally be provided at the church entrance if you do not have them. Not complying with this code will be taken as insulting irreverence on your part. It's also important to conform to the socially acceptable dress code of the region you are visiting. On Mykonos, for example, male and female tourists alike will shock no one by wearing shorts, a swimsuit or going bare-chested, even in many public places. But this same dress will be severely alienating if worn in a mountain village in Crete, less accustomed to tourists. The best approach is to observe what people around you are wearing and to dress accordingly.

NUDE BATHING

Nude bathing is another activity which merits discretion. Nude bathing is legal on very few Greek beaches, though socially acceptable on many. The main rule-of-thumb is this: if it is a secluded beach and/or a beach that has become a commonly accepted locale for nude bathing, you probably won't be bothered by, nor offend, anyone. Avoid stripping off on beaches near towns or principal harbours. If the island you are visiting has only recently joined the mainstream ferry route, also strip with discretion. In 1975, shortly after Ios, now one of the more carefree islands, joined the Mykonos/Naxos boat route, two young visitors were thrown into jail for a week, then taken to a Syros court in handcuffs, merely for removing their bathing trunks in public.

ELECTRICITY

220 AC is the standard household electric current throughout Greece. This means that appliances from the US require converters. Greek outlets and plugs are different from both American and most European types, so you'll probably need an adapter as well.

BUSINESS & BANKING HOURS

BUSINESS HOURS

The schedule for business and shop hours is a complicated affair, varying according to the type of business and the day of the week. The main thing to remember is this: if shopping for something important, buy it between 10 a.m. and 1 p.m. The store may or may not be open that afternoon; it may well open in the evening. Again, it may not. Athens is experimenting with "straight" hours during the winter to bring the country more in line with the EEC. Whether this will catch on and spread to the islands is anyone's guess.

Winter opening hours – Athens: Non-food shops: Monday, Wednesday: Open 9 a.m. to 5 p.m. Tuesday, Thursday and Friday: 10 a.m. to 7 p.m. Saturday: 8.30 a.m. to 3.30 a.m. Food shops: Monday 9 a.m. to 2.30 p.m. Tuesday to Friday: 9 a.m. to 6.30 p.m. Saturday: 9 a.m. to 3.30 p.m.

Summer opening hours – Athens: Monday, Wednesday, Saturday. Most businesses open 8 a.m. to 2.30 p.m. Tuesday, Thursday, Friday. Most businesses open from 9 a.m. to 1.30 p.m, then reopen from 5 p.m. to 8.30 p.m.

The shops in Athens' Plaka district remain open until 10 p.m. or longer to take advantage of anyone who wants to browse. Tourist shops (selling clothes, sandals, suntan oil) and kiosks will almost always be open until midnight on popular islands like Corfu, Rhodes, Paros, Mykonos and Kos.

Dry cleaners and specialty shops have yet another schedule of opening hours, which is not covered here. Chemists operate on a rota system so there will be at least one open for emergencies; check in the window of the nearest pharmacy for the list.

BANKING HOURS

All banks are open to the public from 8 a.m. to 2 p.m. Monday to Thursday; 8 a.m. to 1 p.m. Friday. In heavily touristed areas like central Athens and the popular islands, however, you may find at least one bank open on some summer evenings and/or weekends for currency exchange. This will always be in or around the main harbour area. On the small, rarely visited islands, expect only the minimum of banking facilities and travel with emergency supplies of cash.

Around Syntagma Square in Athens, at the time of going to press, these banks offered extended hours: General Bank of Greece, 1 Ermou St, tel: 324 6451, and the National Bank of Greece, 2 Karagiorgi Servias St, tel: 323 6481.

The East and the West Air Terminals in Athens have several banks each, all with extended opening hours:

EAST AIR TERMINAL

Agricultural Bank of Greece, tel: 962 2791. Open 24 hours, seven days a week.

Commercial Bank of Greece, tel: 961 3611. Open 8 a.m. to 8 p.m., seven days a week.

General Bank of Greece, tel: 961 3700. Open 7 a.m. to 9.30 p.m., seven days a week.

National Bank of Greece, tel: 961 2728. Open 7 a.m. to 11 p.m., seven days a week.

Agricultural Bank of Greece, tel: 984 1282.
Open 8 a.m. to 8.30 p.m., seven days a week.

Commercial Bank of Greece, tel: 981 1093.
Open 8 a.m. to 7 p.m., seven days a week.

Ionian Bank of Greece, tel: 982 1031.
Open 8 a.m. to 2 p.m. Monday-Friday.

National Bank of Greece, tel: 982 4699.
Open 7 a.m. to 11 p.m., seven day a week.

Athens is the headquarters for banks with international branches, and money can often be deducted straight from your account at home into your pocket in Greece by visiting the appropriate headquarters. The industrial disputes which plague Greece can lead to local banks locking their doors for days at a time. Knowing the Athens headquarters of your domestic bank can, quite literally, mean the difference between having money to eat and not having money.

American Express Bank, 31 Panepistimiou St, tel: 323 4781-6.

Arabian Express Bank, 369 Singrou Ave, tel: 942 9901.

Bank of America, 39 Panepistimiou St, tel: 325 1901-9.

Bank of Nova Scotia, 37 Panepistimiou St, tel: 324 3891-8.

Banque National de Paris, 5 Koumpari St, tel: 364 1880.

Bank Paribas, 39 Panepistimiou St, tel: 325 5021.

Barclays Bank International, 15 Voukourestiou St, tel: 364 4311.

Chase Manhattan Bank, 3 Korai St, tel: 323 7711-9.

Citibank, 8 Othonos St, tel: 322 7471.
• Kolonaki Sq, tel: 361 8619.

Credit Bank, 2 Stadiou St, tel: 322 0141.
• 9 Panepistimiou St, tel: 323 4351-5.

Credit Commercial de France, 20 Amalias Ave, tel: 324 1831.

Ergobank, 36 Panepistimiou St, tel: 360 1011.

Grindlays Bank, 7 Merlin St, tel: 362 4601.

Midland Bank, 1A Sekeri St, tel: 364 7410.

National Westminster Bank, 24 Stadiou St, tel: 324 1562-7.

Société Générale, 23 Ipokratous St, tel: 364 2010-9.

Trader's Credit Bank, 3 Santaroza St, tel: 321 2371.

Rush hours: One reason for experimenting with "straight" opening hours is to combat Athens' horrendous rush hours, which can take place up to four times a day: when businesses open, when they close for siesta, when they open again, and then when they close for the evening. The twin perils of traffic jams and pollution reached such heights in Athens that a law was introduced: on certain days of the week only cars with even-numbered license plates were allowed into the city centre; on other days only those cars with odd-numbered license plates. Rather than decrease the number of cars on the roads, however, the numbers have increased, as everyone who could afford the cost bought another car with the opposite type of license plate.

PUBLIC HOLIDAYS

1 January	New Year's Day
6 January	Epiphany
Shrove Monday	First Day of Lent
25 March	Feast of the Annunciation/ Independence Day
1 May	Labour Day and Flower Festival
variable	Good Friday
variable	Greek Orthodox Easter
15 August	Assumption of the Holy Virgin
28 October	Ohi Day (when Greece said "no" to Mussolini)
25 December	Christmas Day
26 December	Boxing Day

SEASONAL FESTIVALS

February-March (three weeks before Lent): Carnival season, with special festivities in Athens and on the islands of Skyros and Zakynthos.

June-September: Athens Festival at the Herod Atticus Theatre. Information and tickets from 4 Stadiou St, tel: 322 1459.

July: Rethymnon Wine Festival at the Municipal Garden on Crete. Information and tickets from 100 Kountouriotou St, Rethymon, tel: (083) 129148.

July-August: Dafni Wine Festival (on the outskirts of Athens). Information and tickets from 4 Stadiou St, tel: 322 7944.

July-August: Thassos Festival (ancient drama in an ancient theatre). Information and tickets from 2 Filellinon St in the town of Kavala, tel: (051) 223958.

September: Cricket season begins on Corfu

(dates subject to change each year)

There are smaller island festivals which occur most years during the summer, but details must be obtained locally. The festivals include the Rhodes Festival (May-October); the Iraklion Festival on Crete (June-August); a Music Festival on Ithaki (late-July); and the Hippokrateia Festival in Kos (August). Dates are subject to change.

RELIGIOUS FESTIVALS

The Greek Orthodox Church exerts enormous influence on contemporary life, both in Athens and on the islands. Sunday is the official day of rest, and even in mid-season (May & September) on some tourist-laden islands, shops and activities will be suspended on the Holy Day. Excursion boats to other islands might well be running to schedule, but what no one bothers to point out is that nothing on the destination island will be open when you arrive; enquire beforehand to avoid disappointment.

The most important holiday in Greece is Easter, celebrated by the Greek Orthodox calendar and usually several weeks later than Christian Easter. Traditional foods include *tsoureki*, plaited bread with red eggs inside, and *mayeritsa*, tripe and lettuce soup. It is advisable to find out before booking a spring holiday exactly when Easter might be, as services, shops and even airplane flights experience disruptions during the week before and the week after Easter.

On 15 August, the Assumption of the Virgin Mary, many islands hold a *paniyiri* (celebration) to mark the reception of the Holy Mother into heaven. Greeks make pilgrimages from all over the country to Tinos in the Cyclades where the icon of the *Panayia Evangelistria* is said to work miracles. Pilgrims flock to Patmos, too, where St. John is said to have written the book of Revelations. The most colourful festival of the Virgin, however, takes place on 15 August in the hillside town of Olympos on the island of Karpathos, where the women wear brilliant traditional dress and the *paniyiria* can last for days.

Other important celebrations include St. Spyridion in Corfu, when the relics of the patron saint are paraded around the streets (Palm Sunday and 11 August); the *Theophania* (Epiphany) on 6 January with a big ceremony in Piraeus and on Crete where the seas are blessed and boys dive for the cross thrown into the waves: the Feast of St. George on 23 April, where especially on Kos and Limnos the patron saint of Greece is remembered in festivities, and the celebration of St. John the Baptist on 29

August. Worthwhile festivals, with their origins in religion but now basically secular, are the spring Tavrus or Bull Festival at Agia Paraskevi on Lesvos; on 17 July, when the first grapes are ready for harvest, *Agios Sotiris* (celebrated on some Dodecanese islands on 12 August), when it is the custom to have fights with eggs, flour and yogurt and *Agios Demetrius* on 26 October, when the first wine is ready to drink.

Nearly every day is a cause for celebration for someone in Greece. Instead of marking birthdays, Greeks have *yiortes*, name days, which celebrate Orthodox baptismal names. When the day is to commemorate a popular name like John or Helen, practically the whole nation has a party. You'll hear locals say: "*Yiortazo simera*" (I'm celebrating today). To which you may reply: "*Xronia polla*" (Many years).

COMMUNICATIONS

MEDIA

THE PRESS

Kiosks on the major islands receive most British newspapers the day after publication; two days after weekends. The *International Herald Tribune* can sometimes be bought on the day of publication. Rhodes, Crete, Corfu and Kos produce local "What's On" guides (several languages in each publication) which can be found in kiosks or information centres.

English-language newspapers can be purchased around Syntagma Square in Athens from kiosks; again, the British press and a smattering of American papers are well represented. Several local publications provide news and information in English for both tourists and residents alike. The daily *Athens News* contains a smattering of world news taken from wire services, Greek news coverage plus interesting small ads. *The Athenian* is a monthly magazine providing literate coverage on various aspects of life in Greece (politics, culture, travel) and useful information on what's happening in the arts; a solid read with a wry approach. *Greece's Weekly* concentrates on business and finance for the English-speaking community. The Southeastern Review is Athens's best literary magazine. All these publications are readily available from kiosks in areas of Athens frequented by tourists. The tiny *Week in Athens* has been published for 41 years by the National

Tourist Organisation of Greece. It contains a list of useful addresses of amenities and entertainments. Pick up one free at any NTOG desk.

RADIO & TV

Athens, naturally, offers the best English-speaking communications. Most hotels now broadcast satellite TV. Channel 3 is Sky (movies and sit-coms); Channel 4 is Super (mainly music); and Channel 7 is CNN (news). There may be a fee for private TV if staying in a posh hotel; otherwise a communal set in the lobby is available free for visitors' pleasure.

The two state-owned and -operated TV stations in Greece are ERT 1 and ERT 2. These channels often transmit English-speaking movies and programmes with Greek subtitles.

ERT 1 and ERT 2 are the two Greek radio channels. ERT 1 is divided into three different "programmes". First (728 KHz) and Second (1385 KHz) both have Greek popular music and news, some foreign pop and occasional jazz and blues. Third Program (665 KHz) plays classical music. ERT 2 (98 KHz) is much like the first two programmes. News can be heard in English, French, German and Arabic on the First Program every morning of the week; in English twice a day on ERT 2 at 2 p.m. and 9 p.m. The BBC World Service offers news on the hour (plus other interesting programmes and features). To find out the best short wave (MHz) frequencies on which to pick up the BBC, ask at your hotel reception. The US Armed Forces Radio (AFRS) operates 24 hours at 1594 KHz and 1484 KHz with news on the hour.

LIBRARIES

The following libraries in Athens contain books in English, French, German, Spanish or, in the case of Greek institutes, perhaps all the above. Call for opening times (and/or an appointment) as hours are subject to change. A tip: in the case of the smaller libraries, be sure to take the complete address, i.e, 17 Valaoritou St. As with much of industrialised Athens, libraries do not necessarily look like libraries from the outside and specific places can be difficult to find.

American Library, American-Hellenic Chamber of Commerce, 22 Massalias, tel: 363 8114. Two libraries, one on the fourth floor; one on the seventh floor.

Benaki Museum Library, 1 Koumbari St, tel: 362 6462.

Blegen Library, American School of Classical Studies, 54 Souidias St, tel: 723 6313.

British Council Library, Kolonaki Sq, tel: 363 3215.

French Institute Library, 31 Sina St, tel: 362 4301.

Gennadius Library, American School of Classical Studies, 61 Souidias St, tel: 721 0536.

German Archaelogical Institute, 1 Fidiou St, tel: 362 0270.

Goethe Institute Library, 16 Omirou St, tel: 360 8114.

Italian Institute Library, 47 Patission Street, tel: 522 9294.

Loberdios Library, Othonos & Eleptheriou Venizelou, Kifisia, tel: 801 3861.

National Library of Greece, Panepistimiou, tel: 361 4413.

BOOKSHOPS

Most regularly-visited islands have at least one bookshop located near the harbour with books in English. Don't expect grand literature, however, as the stock-in-trade tends to be dire thrillers, international best-sellers, and bodice-ripping romances. Many island kiosks (as in Athens) sell second-hand paperbacks throughout the summer, probably rescued from beaches and hotels. These can be found in a heap on the pavement and are even more downmarket in quality than the bookshop books. Local guidebooks and maps tend to sell out by mid-August.

Athens has numerous bookstores which sell quality books in English. Distributors often import from America, so some books unavailable in Britain can be found on sale in Athens.

The Bookstall, 6-10 Har. Trikoupi, tel: 361 9933. Modern shop in swish complex; good on Penguin classics.

Compendium, 33 Nikis, in Plaka, tel: 322 6931. Friendly and helpful, owner is an ex-pat with good taste.

Eleftheroudakis, 4 Nikis, behind Syntagma Sq, tel: 322 9388. Most English-language books are upstairs in this comprehensive, convenient shop.

Kakoulides – The Book Nest, 25-29 Panepistimiou, tel: 322 5209. Upstairs in this old-fashioned shop in the Stoa Megarou Athinon arcade are shelves and tables piled high with books. Good for publications in French and other languages, too.

Pantelides, 11 Amerikis, tel: 362 3673.

POSTAL SERVICES

Signs denoting post offices are usually bright yellow, as are post boxes. Post boxes are tiny and can be hard to find; often they are on the outside walls of tavernas or shops obscured by flowers. Look carefully. Island post offices can be large and efficient (on Rhodes, there are separate mail slots to separate European destinations), or tiny and chaotic. If on a remote island, mail your postcards on the return journey to a larger island; it will arrive home quicker. Opening hours of post offices vary, but can most often be visited Monday to Friday between 8 a.m. and 1 p.m. The main post office in Syntagma Square, Athens, is open usually from 7 a.m. to 8.30 p.m. Monday to Saturday; and 9 a.m. to 1 p.m. on Sunday.

Stamps can be bought at post offices and most kiosks, although occasionally a service tax may be added by the kiosk. If sending the attractive, large-format postcards, additional postage may be required, so it's best to have them weighed first.

Parcels sent abroad must be inspected by the post office, so do not wrap them beforehand. Brown paper can be bought from the post office itself or from kiosks.The mail service is riddled with discrepancies: three parcels containing identical contents were sent to London at the same time. The sender was charged three different postal rates. Why? This is Greece. Give in gracefully.

TELEPHONE/TELEGRAMS

All large islands and most small ones have OTE offices (Greek Telephone Exchange) which are open most days and often well into the evening. OTE offices are the cheapest way to make local or international calls. To do so, walk in and wait for a booth to be free. A desk operator will switch on the phone, the meter registering zero units. After dialling, talk for as long as you like, either locally or internationally. At the end of the call, the desk operator will present you with a bill in drachmas. Connections from the islands vary, but persevere. Telegrams can also be sent from OTE offices. Two OTE offices in Athens are located at 15 Stadiou St, just behind Syntagma Square, open 9 a.m. to 10 p.m. Monday to Saturday; 9 a.m. to 8 p.m. Sunday, and at Omonia Square, open 24 hours.

Local and international calls can also be made from many kiosks. Although there is often a queue (island teenagers calling their friends), it is very romantic to talk to loved ones only a few feet from the sea and with a full moon.

The dialling code from Greece to the UK is 0044. From Greece to the USA or Canada it is 001. Calls made from hotels or pensions are often subject to extra tariffs, so it is cheaper to use OTE offices. Hotels, however, are likely to contain the only telex and fax machines around.

EMERGENCIES

SECURITY & CRIME

Crime is rare on the islands, and the petty theft which does occur might well be the result of other tourists, rather than locals. Although it is not advisable, luggage left on quaysides or temporarily in cafés will probably be left undisturbed. Should trouble arise, each island has a police number which can be rung in emergencies. Special officers known as "Tourist Police", whose duties are concerned solely with visitors, are also assigned to some islands and can even help with accommodation. Tourist Policemen usually speak English. The police numbers listed here are preceded by the code from Athens:

Ionian Islands:
Corfu – tel: (0661) 39503
Paxi – tel: (0662) 31222
Lefkas – tel: (0645) 95207
Cephalonia – tel: (0671) 22200
Zakynthos – tel: (0695) 22550

Saronic Gulf Islands:
Aegina – tel: (0297) 23333
Hydra – tel: (0298) 5220
Poros – tel: (0298) 22462
Salamis – tel: 465 1100
Spetsai – tel: (0298) 73100

Cyclades Islands:
Amorgos – tel: (0285) 71210
Anafi – tel: (0286) 61216
Antiparos – tel: (0284) 61202
Andros – tel: (0282) 22300
Folegandros – tel: (0286) 41249
Ios – tel: (0286) 91222
Kea – tel: (0287) 51205
Kimolos – tel: (0287) 51205
Kithnos – tel: (0281) 31201
Mykonos – tel: (0289) 23990
Milos – tel: (0287) 21378
Naxos – tel: (0285) 22100
Paros – tel: (0284) 21673
Santorini – tel: (0286) 22649
Serifos – tel: (0281) 51300
Sifnos – tel: (0284) 31210
Sikinos – tel: (0286) 51222
Syros – tel: (0281) 22620
Tinos – tel: (0283) 22255

Sporades Islands:
Alonissos – tel: (0424) 65205
Skiathos – tel: (0427) 21111
Skopelos – tel: (0424) 22235
Skyros – tel: (0222) 91274

Northeast Aegean Islands:
Hios – tel: (0271) 25914
Ikaria – tel: (0275) 22222
Lesvos – tel: (0251) 22776
Limnos – tel: (0254) 22200
Psara – tel: (0272) 61222
Samos – tel: (0273) 27980
Samothraki – tel: (0551) 41203
Thassos – tel: (0593) 22500

Dodecanese Islands:
Astipalea – tel: (0242) 61207
Halki – tel: (0246) 71213
Kalymnos – tel: (0243) 22100
Karpathos – tel: (0245) 22218
Kassos – tel: (0245) 41222
Kastelorizo – tel: (0241) 26068
Kos – tel: (0242) 22222
Leros – tel: (0247) 22221
Nissiros – tel: (0242) 31201
Patmos – tel: (0247)31303
Rhodes – tel: (0241) 27423
Symi – tel: (0241) 71238
Tilos – tel: (0241) 53222

Crete:
Agios Nikolaos – 17 Kon. Paleologou St,
tel: (0841) 22251.
Hania – 44 Karaiskaki St, tel: (0821) 24477.
Iraklion – Vas. Konstantinou St, tel: (081) 282243.
Rethymnon – 29 Iroon Politehniou Sq,
tel: (0831) 28156.
Sitia – 24 Mithonos St, tel: (0843) 22266.

Police stations in Athens/Piraeus:
24 hour Tourist Police number, tel: 171.
4 Leoharous St, tel: 323 0263.
58 Sokratous St, tel: 522 6067.
37 Iroon Politehniou St, tel: 412 0325.
East Air Terminal, tel: 969 9523.
West Air Terminal, tel: 981 4093.

LOSS/THEFT

If something of value has been stolen, contact the police number listed under the appropriate island or city. If something has been left in an Athens taxi or bus, call 523 0111.

PHARMACIES/DENTAL

Most large islands operate a roster for doctors and dentists. Any local "What's On" guide will have the emergency numbers, or ask in a tourist agency, an information centre or call the police number listed under the appropriate island.

In Athens, the doctor's roster can be obtained by dialling 105; the 24-hour pharmacy roster can be obtained by dialling 107.

LEFT LUGGAGE

There are no left luggage facilities at either of the Athens Air Terminals. Most hotels in Greece, however, will be willing to store locked suitcases for up to a week if you want to take any short excursions. This is a free service, and the hotel accepts no responsibility in the highly unlikely event of theft. Commercial left luggage offices operate in many harbour towns on the islands. For a small charge space can be hired by the hour, by the day, by the week or longer. Although contents will probably be safe, take any valuables with you.

GETTING AROUND

FROM THE AIRPORT

TO ATHENS

By taxi: From the East Terminal the taxi fare to Athens costs around 550 drachmas; from the West Terminal around 450 drachmas. Many charter flights to Athens arrive at the East Terminal in the early hours of the morning. From 1 a.m. to 5 a.m. taxis are allowed to charge "double time", i.e. 51 drachmas per kilometre. From 5 a.m. to 6 a.m. there is an additional charge of 30 drachmas. For each piece of luggage there is a 15 drachma charge.

By bus: From the East Terminal, Express lines A and B travel into Syntagma or Ormonia Squares every 20 minutes from 6 a.m. to midnight. The fare is 100 drachmas. From midnight to 6 a.m. the buses run every hour and the fare is 150 drachmas. From the West Terminal the fares and the hours are the same; the buses, however, are marked A and B with a diagonal slash through each letter.

TO PIRAEUS

By taxi: From the East and West Terminals to Piraeus the taxi fare costs under 1,000 drachmas. From the centre of Athens to Piraeus, expect to pay around the same.

By bus: From the East Terminal to Piraeus the Express line No 19 runs every 30 minutes from 6 a.m.

to 12 midnight. From 12 midnight to 6 a.m. buses run every 90 minutes. From the West Terminal, catch the same No 19 bus, as the Express line makes one continuous "loop". The journey is a slow one, but the only alternative is a taxi.

By metro: It is possible to get to Piraeus in about 25 minutes by catching one of the clean, tidy and safe metro trains. The stations nearest centre of Athens are Victoria, Omonia, Monastiraki, Thissio. The fare is cheap and the metro is open until around midnight.

DOMESTIC TRAVEL

Travelling on one of the domestic planes operated by Olympic Airways to an island is a delightful alternative to the ferryboat. The air fare, by European standards, is inexpensive, and the time saved is huge: it can take up to eight hours to sail from Piraeus to Mykonos; only 50 minutes to fly. The flights are fun, too; the planes too tiny (sometimes only 16 seats) to treat the journey as anything but a bus-ride in the sky. Carry your own luggage aboard, store it where possible, then grab a window seat for a magnificent view of low-lying hills, sparkling seas, and evocative islets crowned by chapels. Upon arrival, a modern or a dilapidated bus will transfer you to the principal harbour town. There is sometimes a fee, sometimes not.

There are drawbacks to inland air travel, however. Demand can be greater than the number of seats, and having a ticket doesn't guard against being unceremoniously bumped when you arrive at the West Terminal. (During the summer, Athenians with island homes "block book" seats, often more than two months ahead. Tourists rate as a low priority when it comes to check-in.) The domestic terminal itself is chaotic and confusing; check-in desks are unmarked and seem to appear or disappear at whim. Remote islands like Kassos can, at the height of the season, be almost impossible to reach, as planes are cancelled due to bad weather, industrial action or at the whim of the gods. When they do take-off, it is occasionally ahead of schedule, so be sure to arrive well in advance. Ferryboats are more reliable in every respect.

Having said that, if you approach domestic air travel as a treat rather than as a necessity and actually do achieve take-off, the experience is a delight. Early morning flights have the most advantages. Not only do you gain extra time to book on the next flight if you get bumped, but flying into the sun as it rises over the Aegean, or arriving on Mykonos in time to watch the revellers go to bed and the old ladies sweep the streets clean, is an island adventure on its own. Pick up a timetable (by mid-July all stocks in English will have run out) and reserve seats at any Olympic Airways office. The headquarters is a 96 Syngrou Avenue, tel: 929 2111. The most central office is at 6 Othonos St, Syntagma Sq, tel: 929 2489. Major credit cards accepted.

WATER TRANSPORT

FERRIES

Advanced ferry schedules are listed in the *Greek Travel Pages* which can be purchased in the bookstore Eleftheroudakis at 4 Nikis, behind Syntagma Square. Revised ferry schedules are published weekly, and given out at Tourist Information Offices. Most offices hang a schedule in a conspicuous place, so even though the desk itself might be closed the information is still obtainable.

Unless you want a berth or first class seat, there is no need to buy a seat in advance. Simply arrive at Piraeus a couple of hours before departure and cruise the various ticket agencies. Agencies handle different boats which are often sailing to the same destinations at the same times. Many agents will claim "their" boat is the quickest, most powerful, sometimes the only way to get to an island that day. Do some shopping around; it pays off. Cynical travellers will add at least one hour to the time any Greek claims it takes to sail to a specific destination.

Once aboard, position yourself on the top deck for sun-bathing *after* the boat has left the harbour and turned around; otherwise, you may find yourself in the shade. Food, bought beforehand, is a better idea than eating in one of the snack bars, although should you find yourself on a long cruise in an older ferry, dinner in the first-class dining room provides a touch of shabby ambience. Bring plenty to read, and prepare for a mild dose of sea-sickness on any journey longer than eight hours; the Aegean can be rough.

Although the situation is improving, catching a ferry on one island to sail to a distant island can be a frustrating experience. Ferries may arrive two, three, even five hours late, but to leave the port is to chance missing the boat entirely. Just occasionally, the boat can arrive early, and there is no guarantee it will wait until the scheduled departure time to leave. The only way to guarantee accurate, up-to-the-minute information on the erratic ways of ferryboats is to contact the Port Authority, which can (and does) monitor the movements of individual boats. Port Authority offices are usually located on the far end of the waterfront of each island's principal harbour, away from the cafés and boutiques. It would help to ask a Greek-speaking person to do the enquiring, as English is not widespread.

Port Authority telephone numbers are as follows (if dialling from Athens, locate the island area code in the "Emergency" section under island police stations).

Ionian Islands:
Corfu − tel: 39918
Ithaki − tel: 32909
Cephalonia − tel: 22224
Paxos − tel: 31259
Zakynthos − tel: 22417

Saronic Gulf Islands:
Aegina – tel: 22328
Hydra – tel: 52279
Poros – tel: 22274
Salamis – tel: 465 3252
Spetsai – tel: 72245

Cyclades Islands:
Andros – tel: 22250
Ios – tel: 91264
Kea – tel: 31344
Kythnos – tel: 31290
Milos – tel: 41607
Mykonos – tel: 22218
Naxos – tel: 22300
Paros – tel: 21240
Santorini – tel: 22239
Serifos – tel: 51470
Sifnos – tel: 31617
Syros – tel: 22690
Tinos – tel: 22348

Sporades Islands:
Skiathos – tel: 22017
Skopelos – tel: 22180
Skyros – tel: 91475

Northeast Aegean Islands:
Hios – tel: 23097
Lesvos – tel: 28647
Limnos – tel: 22225
Samos – tel: 27318
Samothraki – tel: 41305
Thassos – tel: 22106

Dodecanese Islands:
Astypalea – tel: 61208
Kalymnos – tel: 29304
Karpathos – tel: 22227
Kassos – tel: 41288
Kos – tel: 28507
Leros – tel: 22224
Nissiros – tel: 31222
Patmos – tel: 31231
Rhodes – tel: 27690

Crete:
Ag. Nikolaos – tel: 22312
Hania – tel: 22600
Iraklio – tel: 82002
Kasteli – tel: 22024
Sitia – tel: 22310

The telephone number for the Port Authority in Piraeus is 451 1311 or 452 7107 (Zea Marina). For more information on island-hopping by ferry, see the boxes "Island-hopping" and "Piraeus" in the text.

HYDROFOILS

Hydrofoils ("Flying Dolphins") are twice are quick and twice as expensive as ferryboats. A service between Piraeus and the Saronic Gulf islands continues throughout the year. Seasonally (from around May to September), hydrofoils connect islands in the Sporades and northern Dodecanese (Rhodes to Patmos, Samos, Kos). Modern hydrofoils show videos and have bar facilities, but rough seas and bumpy rides are common. As hydrofoils need a calm sea to travel, they are prone to cancellation due to weather or technical difficulties.

PUBLIC TRANSPORT

BUSES

Island buses can be converted school buses or modern coaches, or even farm equipment called into service to transport tourists. Some drivers ricochet through mountain roads at death-defying speeds; accidents, however, appear to be rare. Just stow your luggage carefully to avoid incident.

Almost without exception, a bus of some description will meet arriving ferryboats (even if a boat is delayed) to transport passengers up the hill to the island's Hora, or capital. Bus stops are usually in main squares or by the waterfront in harbours and vehicles may or may not run to schedule. A conductor dispenses tickets on the bus itself; rarely will the fare required and the stamped ticket be the same price. This isn't a con, but merely a practice. Island companies use pre-printed tickets until the supply is gone, which may take several years.

TAXIS

Taxis in Greece, especially in Athens, is a subject that merits a guidebook to itself. It may well be that your taxi "experience" will figure among the most prominent memories of your holiday. Perhaps the Greek taxi experience is best divided into three stages for analytical purposes.

First: getting a taxi. It's nearly impossible at certain times of the day, and probably worst before the early afternoon meal. When you hail a taxi, try to get in before stating your destination. The drivers are very picky and often won't let you in unless you're going in their direction. If you have to say it, say it loudly and clearly (and with the right accents) as they may well otherwise just pass you by. If you see an empty taxi, run for it; be aggressive. Otherwise you'll find that some quick Athenian has beaten you to it.

Second: the ride. Make sure the taxi metre is on when you start out, and not on "2" – that's the double-fare which is only permitted from 1 a.m. to 5 a.m. Once inside you may find yourself with company. Don't be alarmed. It is traditional practice for drivers to pick up two, three, even four individual riders, provided they're going roughly in the same area. In these cases, make a note of what the meter-count is. In fact, because taxis are so cheap they end up functioning as mini-bus services. (A series of recent strikes in Athens is trying to redress this situation, however.) Packed in with a Greek mother with her shopping bags overflowing with groceries, a chic businessman and a radical bohemian university student, you may find yourself in the middle (literally) of some rather interesting conversations. If, however, you are alone you may find yourself chatting with an ex-seaman who tells you a few yarns from his days in the United States, or perhaps with a driver who speaks no English at all.

Third: paying up. If you've travelled with company, make sure you aren't paying for that part of the trip that happened before you got in. Otherwise the meter will tell you the straight price which may be adjusted according to the following tariff regulations.

Some drivers will quote you the fair price, others will try to rip you off. If the price is clearly above the correct price, don't hesitate to argue your way, in whichever language, back down to a normal price.

Obviously these rules apply more to Athens than to the islands, although it's still necessary to be pretty aggressive on Crete and Rhodes. On the smaller islands, expect to share your taxi, not only with the aforementioned group of passengers, but also an animal or two.

In recent years various Radio Taxi services have started up in Athens. They can pick you up within a short time of your call. These taxis, however, are often more expensive than the regular ones.

PRIVATE TRANSPORT

CARS

Car hire and petrol is expensive in Greece, and taking your car to the islands is not recommended. Only Crete, Rhodes and perhaps Lesvos, Kos and Corfu could benefit from having a car at your disposal, otherwise it's more fun to rely on island buses and taxis. At island airports and in the ticket agencies on the waterfront are desks manned by the major car hire firms. Shop around for the best price.

The Automobile and Touring Club of Greece (ELPA) provides foreign motorists with assistance and information. Offices in Crete can be found in Hania at 1 Apokoronou & Skoula Sts, tel: (0821) 26059 and in Irakion at Knossos Ave & G. Papandreou St, tel: (081) 289440. In Athens ELPA offices are located at 2-4 Messoghion Ave, tel: 779 1615 and at 6 Amerikis & Panepistimiou Sts, tel: 363 8632.

Driving a car in Athens is unpleasant and confusing. Greek tempers are short and road-signs practically non-existent. Cars are, however, fun for day-trips out of the city. Avis, Hertz and Budget cars all have rental desks at both the East and West air terminals. Otherwise, head for Singrou Avenue in town, which is chock-a-block with car hire firms.

Avis, 46-48 Amaias Ave, tel: 322 4951-8.
Budget, 8 Singrou Ave, tel: 921 4771-3.
Hertz, 12 Singrou Ave, tel: 922 0102-4.
Just Rent A Car, 43 Singrou Ave, tel: 923 9104.
Speedo Rent A Car, 8 Singrou Ave, tel: 922 6102.
Thrifty Rent A Car, 24 Singrou Ave,
tel: 922 1211-3.

MOTORCYCLES, BICYCLES & SCOOTERS

On most islands you'll find agencies that rent small motorcycles, bicycles and various types of scooters. For a reasonable price they give you the freedom to wander independently and also to delight in the smell of a place, impossible on buses or in cars. For longer periods, rates are cheaper than for one-day rentals. Before setting off, however, make sure your vehicle actually works. Ask to take it for a test spin down the street (be on the look-out for lethal "staircase" alleys). Otherwise you may get stuck with a lemon or, worse, they may hold you responsible for its malfunctions when you return it. Above all, be careful. More than one holiday in Greece has been ruined by the bumps, scratches and bruises of a moped accident. Wear protective clothing and check that your holiday insurance covers any problems.

In Athens, motorbikes and bicycles can be hired from two companies: Meidanis Rent A Moto at 4 Dion, Areopagitou St, tel: 323 2346, and at Motorent, 5 Falirou St, tel: 923 4939.

WHERE TO STAY

HOTELS

The National Tourist Organisation of Greece governs the construction and classification of all hotels. The classification awarded is determined by the size of the rooms, size of public area including lobby, decor and furnishings of the rooms and services provided by the hotel. All hotel accommodation is divided into classes: deluxe (luxury class), then classes A-E. The price in each category is fixed, i.e., an A-class hotel will always cost more than a B-class hotel, even with seasonal variations in price. As the classifications are so formal, anyone who rates charm above lobby-space, or yogurt and honey above an all-inclusive breakfast, will probably be just as happy in a lower-class hotel as in one of the deluxe versions; almost all accommodation from C-class upwards can be guaranteed to have a high standard of cleanliness.

NTOG offices around the world can help with accommodation. See the section "Useful Addresses" for names and addresses of international NTOG offices. All NTOG offices receive pamphlets on each island chain which gives information on hotels in the A-C classes; these are available free to anyone who asks for them. The book Greek Travel Pages includes 124 pages of detailed information on accommodation supplied by the hoteliers themselves; pictures are included of many. Greek Travel Pages is available abroad from Timsway Holidays, Nightingales Corner, Little Chalfont, Buckinghamshire HP7 9QS England. In West Germany contact Ikon-Reisen, Schwanthalers. 31 - 8000 Munchen 2. To receive a copy in any other country write to BAS Overseas Publications Ltd, BAS House, 48-50 Sheen Lane, London SW14 8LP, England.

Hotel reservations can be made in writing directly to the hotel; in writing to the Hellenic Chamber of Hotels, 6 Aristidou St, Athens; or in person by calling in at the Hellenic Chamber of Hotels at 2 Stadiou and Karageorgi Servias St, inside the National Bank of Greece at Syntagma Square.

There is normally a 10 percent increase for a stay less than three nights and a larger increase for an extra bed in the room. Tax and VAT are added.

ATHENS

DELUXE CLASS

Astir Palace, Vas. Sofias & El. Venizelou corner, 10671 Athens. Syntagma Square area, tel: 364 3112. All rooms with TV and video, newsstand, sauna, health care, beauty parlour, conference and banquet facilities, gourmet restaurant, bar and coffee shop.

Athenaeum Inter-Continental, 89-93 Syngrou Ave, 11745 Athens, tel: 902 3666. Air-conditioned throughout, two bars, three restaurants, swimming pool, TV in all rooms with in-house movies, health studio, bank facilities.

Athens Hilton, 50 Michalakopoulou St, 11528 Athens, tel: 724 8322. Air-conditioned, central heating, American bar, restaurant, coffee shop, discotheque, bowling.

Grande Bretagne, Syntagma Square, 10563 Athens, tel: 323 0251. Lovely building with a distinguished history. 450 rooms plus 25 suites. Air-conditioned, central heating, two bars, three restaurants, convention and function facilities.

Ledra Marriott Hotel, 115 Syngrou Ave, 11745 Athens, tel: 952 5211. All rooms have individual climate control, radio and colour TV, in-room movies, mini-bar, rooftop swimming pool, hydrotherapy pool, three restaurants and a ballroom.

CLASS A HOTELS

Acropolis View, 10 Galli & Webster Streets, 11742 Athens, tel: 921 7303. Small hotel with roof garden, central heating, air-conditioning, bar, restaurant.

Electra Palace, 18 Nikodimou St, 10557 Athens, tel: 324 1401. Swimming pool and rooftop garden, cosy, nicely furnished bedrooms, air-conditioned throughout, pleasant bathrooms.

Golden Age, 57 Michalakopoulos St, 11528 Athens, tel: 724 0861. Near the Hilton Hotel, air-conditioned, mini-bar in every room, restaurant and taverna.

Novotel Mirayia Athenes, 4-6 Michail Voda St, 10439 Athens, tel: 862 7133. Underground car park, roof garden with swimming pool, mini-bar in rooms, satellite colour TV and radio in rooms.

Zafolia, 87-89 Alexandras Ave, 11474 Athens, tel: 644 9012. Bar, restaurant, roof garden, swimming pool, room service.

CLASS B HOTELS

Acropolis House, 6-8 Kodrou, Plaka tel: 322 2344. A favourite with academics and writers, this pension was once a family mansion. Warm, friendly atmosphere with good conversation in the lobby.

Adonis Hotel, Voulis & 3 Kodrou, Plaka, tel: 324 9737. Just across the pedestrian street from the Acropolis House, this sweet and functional pension serves breakfast on the roof which overlooks the Acropolis. The reception staff are unfailingly helpful and friendly.

Athenian Inn, 22 Haritos, Athens, tel: 723 8097. Just two blocks from fashionable Kolonaki Square, this family-run pension is pretty and rustic, with an open fire, paintings on the wall by local artists, and wall-to-wall carpets in the bedrooms.

Athens Gate, 10 Syngrou Ave, 11742 Athens, tel: 923 8302. Near the Temple of Oympian Zeus and not far from Syntagma Square, this modern hotel has a roof garden restaurant with a stunning view, spacious rooms (some with terraces offering the same panorama), and serving American-style buffet breakfasts.

Omiros Hotel, 15 Apollonos St, 10557 Athens, tel: 323 5486. In a street filled with hotels just on the edge of Plaka, this handy little place has the charm of an old world taverna and is efficient, too.

CLASS C HOTELS

Aphrodite Hotel, 21 Apollonos St, 10557 Athens, tel: 323 4357. A better-than-average C class hotel, with air-conditioning (uncommon even in many B class hotels), polite staff, room telephones, large lobby with bar and good, buffet-style breakfast for a small fee. The rooms on the top floors in the rear offer lovely views of tiled roofs and the Acropolis. Roof garden in summer.

Attalos Hotel, 29 Athinas St, 10554 Athens, tel: 321 2801. All rooms have a balcony, telephone, and some a view of the Acropolis. Roof garden bar.

Nicola, 14 Olenou Street, 11362 Athens, tel: 883 7911. Bar on a 24-hour basis, room service, roof garden, TV and video room.

Phoebus, 12 Peta St, Athens, tel: 322 0142. A family-owned, flower-filled hotel near the offices of The Athenian magazine in Plaka, the rooms are comfortable, but plainly furnished. As the hotel is tiny (only 23 bedrooms) and popular with returning visitors, it's best to book in advance.

Phaedre Hotel, 16 Cherefontos St, Athens, tel: 323 8461. The relatively large rooms in the front overlook towering palm trees and a lovely church; the scene is so tranquil during siesta it's impossible to believe the hotel is only a couple of blocks from the noisiest part of Plaka. But the olde worlde charm continues inside the hotel, too – unfortunately, none of the rooms has a private bathroom, just a sink.

A list of D and E class hotels can be obtained from offices of the National Tourist Organisation of Greece.

PRIVATE ROOMS

On the islands, the most widespread type of inexpensive accommodation is renting private rooms (*domatia*). These are rented out by local residents at prices controlled by the tourist police. In general, when looking for any kind of accommodation, the tourist police can be of considerable help. If you arrive without any accommodation and none seems to be available, inquire at their office. If you'd like to make a reservation or arrangement in advance call them and they'll often be able to help. For a list of police telephone numbers on individual islands, see the section "Emergencies".

Except at the height of summer, when rooms are scarce, domatia can be secured just by stepping off the ferryboat. Housewives meet any and all ferries until late into the evening. "Room? Room?" they will inquire, and a deal is struck there on the spot. The price is normally for the room itself, rather than per bed; a single, therefore, costs the same as a double. Within 10 minutes of the ferry departing the women and the rooms have disappeared. As most accommodation on the islands is clean and perfectly acceptable, upon arrival it might be an idea to take the first room offered for two nights (cheaper than one night) and shop around in the meantime. Men with rooms to offer, or when a car journey is involved, often bring their children along, a gesture which makes women travelling alone feel more secure.

PENSIONS

A pension tends to be a casual, family-run establishment, falling somewhere between a private room and a hotel. As the accommodation has been purpose-built, many rooms have balconies and, whenever possible, a sea view. As with hotels, they are divided into classes A-E, but rates tend to be less expensive than hotels. First class pensions are listed in the NTOG hotel guide and can be pre-booked directly. Lists of pensions in lower categories can only be obtained on the spot through the Tourist Police.

VILLAS & APARTMENTS

Self-catering is increasingly popular in Greece, especially for those holidaying with young children. Villas and apartments are clean, and comfortably, if sparsely furnished. These, too, are graded according to fixed-price categories. Expect to pay just under the same amount of money for a first class apartment as for a deluxe hotel room.

RENTAL AGENCIES

Accommodation Centre, 3 Filelinon St, tel: 322 0000. Flats in Athens.

Alexander Travel, 4 Stadiou St, tel: 322 7668. Flats throughout Greece, especially Skiathos and Corfu.

Ameridian Ltd, Room 63, 3 FilelinonSt, tel: 323 2608. Houses throughout Greece and villas in caves.

Corfu Sun Club, tel: (0661) 33855. Self-catering on Corfu.

Polytravel, No 60, 25th August St, Irakion, tel: (081) 282476. All types of accommodation throughout Crete.

Skopelos Tours, tel: (0424) 22721. Self-catering on Skopelos in the Sporades.

Ikos Travel, tel: ((0424) 65320. Self-catering on Alonnisos in the Sporades.

A certain portion of tourists who come to Greece decide to "rough it", although this type of holiday is now being discouraged by the NTOG. Those who want to camp at organised campsites with facilities will find scores of them all over the islands, some run by the NTOG, some by the Greek Touring Club, and many privately. The most beautiful campsites, however, are usually the ones you find on your own. While in most places it is officially illegal just to lay out your sleeping bag or pitch a tent, if you're discrete you'll probably not be bothered. That means asking permission if you seem to be on private property, avoiding "unofficial" campsites set up in popular tourist areas, and always leaving the place looking better than when you came. For a list of official sites, contact the NTOG.

A member's card is required in order to stay in a Greek Youth Hostel. An international membership card can be obtained by applying to the Greek Youth Hostels Association located at 4 Dragatsaniou St, 10559 Athens, tel: 323 4107.

ATHENS

Athens Youth Hostels are located at:
• 1, Agiou Meletinou & 57 Kipselis St, Kipseli, tel: 822 5860.
• Alexandras Ave & Drossi St, tel: 646 3669.
• 52 Peoniou St, Stathmos Larissis, tel: 883 2878.
• 75 Damareos St, Pangrati, tel: 751 9530.

Y.W.C.A. Youth Hostel, 11 Amerikis St, tel: 362 6180.

CRETE

Hania Youth Hostel, 33 Drakonianou St, tel: (0821) 53565.

Iraklion Youth Hostel, 24 Handakos St, tel: (081) 222947.

Malia Youth Hostel, Malia Beach (36 km. from Iraklion), tel: (081)285075.

Rethymnon Youth Hostel, 4 Therissou St, tel: (0831) 22848.

IONIAN ISLANDS

Kontokali Youth Hostel, Kontokali beach, Corfu, tel: (0661) 91202.

CYCLADES ISLANDS

Santorini Youth Hostel, Kontohori, Agios Eleftherios, tel: (0286) 22722.

Monasteries and convents can occasionally provide refuge for the adventurous and solitary traveller. Enquires must be conducted on the spot, or through a specific island's Tourist Police. Remember that you must dress and behave according to their rules; no shorts and skirts for women. The doors may be closed as early as sunset and some kind of donation may be expected.

Traditional settlements are villages recognised by the Greek government as forming an important part of the national heritage. Buildings in these villages have been restored and set up by the NTOG for tourist use. At the moment there are four on the islands: on Santorini, on Hios, on Kefalonia, and on the tiny islet Psara. For information write to the NTOG at EOT Diefynisis Ekmetalefseos, 2 Amerikis St, Athens 10564, tel: 322 3111-7.

FOOD DIGEST

Dining out in Greece is a social affair. Whether it is with family or *parea*, that special circle of friends, a meal out is an occasion to celebrate, a time for *kefi*. This may have something to do with the fact that eating out continues to be affordable and popular, not something restricted to those who have American Express cards. And the predominance of the taverna, that bastion of Greek cuisine, reflects this popularity. These casual eating establishments have more or less the same style and setting throughout Greece, and the menu is similar. Which is to say no frills, no packaging which tries to convince the "consumer" that this taverna is different from the others, special, distinct. The place, and your being there, is somehow taken for granted: you eat the good food at Yanni's or Yorgos', you enjoy yourself, and you don't pay an arm and a leg for it.

There is, of course, some variation. The taverna is by no means the only kind of eating establishment. You'll also encounter: the *estiatório*, a more conventional restaurant – fancier and more polished than the taverna, with linen tablecloths and higher prices; the *psistaria*, a barbeque-style restaurant which specialises in lamb, pork or chicken on a spit; the *psarotaverna* which specialises in fish; the *ouzeri* which is mainly an establishment for drinking, but which also serves *mezédes*, snacks of various types;

the *gyros* stand with *hiro* sandwiches and the ubiquitous *souvlaki* stand, sometimes a sit-down place with salads, sometimes a take-away on the corner.

There's also regional variety in Greek cuisine and you should keep an eye out for those specialties of the house which you haven't seen before. Another thing is how strikingly different the same dish can be when it's prepared well or prepared badly, for example, a *meletzánosaláta*, or stuffed tomatoes. It's worth shopping around in heavily-touristed areas for the best taverna, asking the locals where they eat. Even better – invite a Greek to dinner; the food is bound to improve immeasurably.

A few notes about Greek eating habits. The main meal is eaten at midday, between 1.30 p.m. and 2.30 p.m. and is usually followed by a siesta break lasting until 6 p.m. The evening meal can either be another full meal, or an assortment of *mezédes*. This is eaten late, between 9 p.m. and 11 p.m. (Breakfast in Greece is rather meagre, usually consisting of bread, butter, jam and coffee. Try ordering yogurt and honey as a delicious alternative.)

Greeks never simply "go out drinking". Even if an evening involves heavy drinking of retsina or ouzo, these will be accompanied by food – a habit which minimises the effects (and after-effects) of the alcohol. When it comes to ordering wine, check to see if they serve wine from the barrel (ask for *hima*). This is the inexpensive local drink not normally served to tourists. *Aspro* is white wine, *mavro* is red, and *kokkinelli* is rosé.

GREEK FOODS

Here is a partial list of the more popular foods you'll find in Greece.

STARTERS

Starters are usually eaten as appetizers with bread (*psomí*).

kdokithákia – deep-fried courgette (zucchini)
melitsánasálata – an aubergine (eggplant) dip
rossikisaláta – cold potato salad with lots of mayonnaise
taramasaláta – fish roe pate/dip
tzazíki – yogurt/cucumber dip, heavy on the garlic

VEGETABLES

anginária – artichokes
arakádes – peas
bámies – okra
dolmádes – stuffed grape leaves
fasolákia – snap beans
horiátiki – "Greek" salad
maróuli – lettuce
patzária – beetroot (beets)
yemistés – stuffed tomatoes or peppers
yígandes – large haricot beans

MEATS

Note the following terms: *psitó* – roasted; *sti soúvla* – barbecued on the spit; *tiganitó* – fried; *sto foúrno* – baked; *skáras* – grilled; *vrastó* – boiled; *kapnistó* – smoked

arní – lamb
biftéki – beefsteak
brizóla – pork or beef chop
keftédes – meatballs
kokorétsi – stuffed innards, spit-roasted
kotópoulo – chicken
loukaniko – sausages
mialó – brain
paidákia – lamb chops
sikóti – grilled liver
souvlaki – chunks of lamb or pork, spit-roasted

SOUPS & SPECIALITIES

avgolémono – chicken stock with egg and lemon
fasoláda – bean soup
moussaka – aubergine (eggplant) and lamb casserole
pastítsio – macaroni casserole
patsás – tripe stew sold at special stalls
salingária – snails fried in oil and herbs
stifádo – any kind of stew, stewed meat
souzoukákia – baked meat rolls
yiorvoulákia – meat-and-rice balls

SEAFOOD

astakos – lobster
bakaliáros – cod
galéos – shark meat
garídes – shrimp
glóssa – sole
gópes – small, fried fish
kalamária – squid
ksifias – swordfish
ktapódi – octopus
péstrofa – trout
sinagrída – red snapper

DESSERTS

Rarely will you find dessert served where you eat dinner. You'll find sweets instead at zacharoplastía (sweet shops) and some galaktopolía (dairy stores).

baklavá – fillo dough leaves, honey, nuts
kataifí – nuts and honey wrapped in shredded wheat
krema – plain custard
loukoúmi – Turkish delight
moustalevria – grape pudding (autumn)
rizógalo – rice pudding

SNACKS

kalambóki – corn on the cob, sold at stalls
kastana – roast chestnuts, sold at stalls
koulouria – sesame-sprinkled "pretzels"
kreatópita – meat pie
spanakópita – spinach pie
tirópita – cheese pie
tost – toasted sandwiches sold at stalls

OTHER USEFUL WORDS

aláti – salt & *pipéri* (pepper)
boukáli – bottle
potiri – glass
pirouni – fork
koutáli – spoon
mahiéri – knife
katálogo/lista – menu
to logariasmó – the bill

WHERE TO EAT

Island cuisine can be more than just moussaka. Stelios Platonos, the proprietor of the two excellent restaurants called Kalamaras in London's Notting Hill Gate, is passionate on the subject of Greek home cooking, and plans to open a food museum on his native island of Paros. But island cooking holds a few surprises. Seafood can be difficult to find, even impossible on some remote islands, and is quite expensive by local standards. The Aegean has been over-fished, and often the proceeds of a successful day are sent straight to Athens or the large island hotels. The most sensible thing to do is to walk into the café kitchens and see what's cooking. This is a respectable island practice, and guarantees better quality, although it must be said that in out-of-the-way tavernas, the evening meal might merely be luncheon dishes heated up. To enjoy the meal of a lifetime you must stay on one island for some time, and to strike up a friendship with a fisherman. The rewards will be worth it: the best of a daily catch often goes straight into the fisherman's family pot.

ATHENS RESTAURANTS

For an extensive listing of tavernas and restaurants in Athens, see The Athenian monthly magazine.

Apotsos, Penepistimious St, No 10 in the arcade, tel: 363 7046. Classic lunchtime place, good food; great decor. Open only at lunchtime. Closed Sundays.

Bajazzo, Ploutarchou and Dinokratous, Kolonaki, tel: 729 1420. Unusual food which combines nouvelle cuisine and traditional Greek dishes. Full wine list and expensive by Greek standards but cheap by world-wide standards for innovative, high-quality food. Open for lunch and dinner. Closed Sunday.

Gerofinikas, 10 Pindarou, tel: 362 2719. Cosmopolitan Greek cuisine with Constantinople specialities included. Fresh fish, lamb with artichokes and tantalising deserts. Pricey but recommended. Open lunch and dinner.

Eden, 3 Flessa St, Plaka, tel: 324 8858. Good vegetarian food, a nice change when you've had enough of standard taverna fare.

Kostoyiannis, 37 Zaimi (Pedion Areos), Exarchia, tel: 821 2496. Large selection of appetisers. Main dishes include rabbit stifado and quail. Good spiced quince with whipped cream and walnut cake for dessert.

Themistokles, 31 Vas. Georgiou, Pangrati, tel: 721 9553. Fine taverna fare on the first floor of an old Athenian dwelling.

DRINKING NOTES

Greek wines will never obtain the status of their French or Italian counterparts. But much local wine can be quite palatable. Some of the better Greek labels are: Rotonda, Cambas, Boutari, Calliga.

Retsina: the best-known Greek wine. Flavoured with the resin from pine trees and an acquired taste. Inexpensive.

Demestica: the popular alternative to retsina. White is the most common; also comes in red and rosé.

St. Helena: a reliable medium-dry white wine which can be found in many restaurants.

Cava Clauss: a full-bodied dry red wine, aged in oak barrels in the cellar of Gustav Clauss. Available in limited quantities of numbered bottles; try it if you get the chance.

Chateau Clauss: another vintage from the Achaia Clauss bottlers. Goodish dry red wine.

Nemea: a palatable red table wine; can be found on many menus.

Danielis: slightly spicy dry red wine, less common than Nemea.

Bon Viveur: a newish dry white wine with a fruity taste.

Patras: a robust white wine made from the grapes of the Patras region.

ISLAND WINES

Many islands bottle (or take from the barrel) wines which are sold only locally. Although island wines tend to be rough and ready, they're very cheap and certainly authentic. You may have to ask around for the following:

IONIAN ISLANDS

Corfu. Theotoki is the local wine (red or white); the speciality of the island is a very sweet orange liqueur called Kum Kwat.

AntiPaxi. The local grapes are much appreciated; ask for wine from the barrel.

Zakynthos. Try the wines made from grapes grown in Zakynthos's lush green vineyards: Comouto rosé or the white Verdea.

CYCLADES ISLANDS

Naxos. Ariadne wine is delicious; also white, red or rosé Promponas. Tastings are also held of the lemon-based local liqueur Kitrou.

Paros. Of the two major locals, Kavarnis is more expensive (and better) than Lagari. All in red, white and rosé.

Santorini. Two white wines: Visanto (sweet) and Nichteri (dry).

Serifos. A full-bodied retsina called Marko. Try it from the barrel.

SPORADES ISLANDS

Skopelos. Plums are the speciality here, and their dried-up cousins, prunes. Locally produced plum wine is delicious; from prunes disgusting.

DODECANESE ISLANDS

Rhodes. A visit to one of the numerous off-licences in Rhodes Town will find a whole range of locally-produced drinks; wines from Rhodes are consumed all over the Dodecanese. Ilios (named after the sun god) is the most popular, drunk by fishermen and tourists alike. Belvasia retsina is an alternative, as are the red Chevalier du Rhodes and the white Muscat or Grand Maitre. Rhodes champagne is exported to many islands and can also be found in Athens.

Samos. Samos is one of the few islands to export, not only to the mainland but also abroad. A number of drinks are produced locally, but the best-known Samian wine is the refreshingly light Samaina.

Nissiros. Produces a non-alcoholic drink called Sumada made from almonds.

Lesvos. Quite a few local ouzos; Epom is the principal distillers of wines.

CRETE

White wines include Regalo (dry) and Vilana (medium dry). Minos bottle a number of reds and whites of varying quality. Red wines include Castello, Mantiko and Saint Antonio. Also local variations on brandy, ouzo, and the very lethal raki.

THINGS TO DO

CRUISES

Apparently one in six of all visitors to Greece embarks on an Aegean cruise. Cruises can range from one-day trips to the Saronic Gulf islands, to 21-day packages on a "floating hotel" departing from Piraeus and taking in Gibraltar, Morocco, and Barbados. Many people elect for the seven-day excursion, which offers an opportunity to see a couple of islands in the Cyclades, a few Dodecanese islands, and a stop-over in Turkey or Morocco for good measure. Accommodation, prices and standards vary widely and it might be an idea to shop around for a good price.

Ticket agencies in Athens are the places to visit, with cruise opportunities prominently displayed in windows. (Although, if you have ever been at Mykonos harbour when the ships arrive, and watched the frantic preparations of shop managers adjusting their prices upwards, it may change your mind about a cruise entirely.)

Sun Line are one of the most comprehensive companies and are accustomed to dealing with foreigners. Details can be found from any travel agent or by contacting Sun Line's headquarters at 3 Iasonos St, Piraeus, tel: 452 3417.

A more casual atmosphere can be found aboard the boats used by Viking Tours, a long-established company with a fine reputation. Only 36 passengers can be carried in Viking's 118-ft ships, so the feeling is more like travelling on a private yacht than being aboard a mammoth ship. It's the type of holiday where you make new friends – and keep them. For more information contact Viking at 3, Filellinon St, in Athens.

EXCURSIONS

If a tourist island boasts a major attraction, it has scores of package trips to view it/visit it/swim off it. It's even possible to make a day trip to Athens from Skiathos, in the far-flung Sporades. Ticket agencies promote excursions aggressively, so you can pick and choose at your leisure. Unless you enjoy the company of gregarious strangers, the site is of premier importance, or if time is limited, it's often nicer to make your own way to attractions as local transport is usually available, too.

If embarking on an excursion, be sure to check that you will not be arriving at a destination during siesta or on a Sunday; if so, there may not be a great deal to do upon arrival.

A tip: lots of "excursion" boats offering daytrips to neighbouring islands leave and depart at the same time as regular ferryboats. The difference? Excursion boats are twice as expensive.

SOUND & LIGHT SPECTACLES

Throughout the summer, Athens, Corfu and Rhodes offer "sound and light" shows projected onto the frontages of their ancient ruins. These performances are perfect for children, and the lights are exciting to watch from the comfort of a nearby terrace-top. The words, however, are dire. Try attending a show in a language other than your own.

Athens: 9 p.m. (English); 10.15 (French – except for Tuesdays and Fridays); 10 p.m. (German – Tuesdays and Fridays only). Tickets available at the Pnyx before the show. Information from 332 1459

Corfu: 9.30 p.m. (English – except Saturdays and Sundays) 9 p.m. (French – Sundays); 9 p.m. (Greek – Saturdays). Ticket price includes Greek folk dances. Reduced rates for students. Information from (0661) 30520.

Rhodes: The spectacle at the Palace of the Knights is performed several times each evening in English, French, German and Greek. Information from (0241) 23255.

TOUR GUIDES

A tour of the island Kalimnos is fondly remembered by one traveller as the highlight of her trip to Greece. The guide, an ebullient former seaman, arrived at her hotel in a battered '68 Chevy, and for the rest of the morning kept up a steady stream of repartee and island facts in a Greek/Australian accent.

A tour guide is a good idea for anyone who wants to study an island in detail, who has no transport, or who enjoys the idea of spending several hours in close proximity with a local. Whether all the "facts" are actually true remains anyone's guess, but an entertaining companion can be worth the price. Guides generally hire themselves out by the half day, full day or even week; enquire at the Tourist Police

or ask around at various ticket agencies. There are no set fees and few regulations governing the tour guide business, so negotiate everything in advance, including petrol and lunch.

CULTURE PLUS

MUSEUMS

Museums and archaeological sites permit the taking of photos if a portable camera is used. Foreign students are allowed into most sites for half the price on production of their student cards. If an archaeological site is particularly crowded, try walking around it backwards, against the crowds. All opening hours are subject to change without notice and most island attractions are closed on Mondays and afternoons. Please check before setting out.

ATHENS

The Acropolis, tel: 321 0219. Open daily 8 a.m. to 5 p.m. Saturdays, Sundays & holidays 8.30 a.m. to 3 p.m. Entrance fee.

Acropolis Museum, on the Acropolis, tel: 323 6665. Open daily 8 a.m. to 5 p.m., Saturdays, Sundays & holidays 8.30 a.m. to 3 p.m., Mondays 11 a.m. to 5 p.m. Entrance fee.

Ancient Agora Museum in the Stoa of Attalos, entrance from Thission Sq. & 24 Andrianou Sts, tel: 321 0185. Open daily 8.30 a.m. to 3 p.m. Closed Mondays. Entrance fee.

Athens City Museum, 7 Paparigopoulou St, tel: 323 0168. Open Mondays, Wednesdays, Fridays 9 a.m. to 1.30 p.m. Entrance fee. Admission free on Wednesdays.

Benaki Museum, Vas. Sophias Ave, tel: 361 1617. Open daily 8.30 a.m. to 2 p.m. Closed Tuesdays. Entrance fee.

Byzantine Museum, 22 Vas.Sophias Ave, tel: 721 1027. Open daily 8.30 a.m. to 3 p.m. Closed Mondays. Entrance fee.

Cycladic Arts Museum, 4 Neof. Douka St, tel: 723 4931. Open daily 10 a.m. to 4 p.m., Saturdays 10 a.m. to 5 p.m. Closed Tuesdays & Sundays. Entrance fee.

Epigraphical Museum, 1 Tossitsa St, tel: 821 7637. Open daily 8.30 to 3 p.m. Closed Mondays. Admission free.

Museum of Greek Popular Art, Plaka, tel: 321 3018. Open daily 10 a.m. to 2 p.m. Closed Mondays. Entrance fee.

Hellenic Theatre Museum & Studies Centre, 50 Akademias St, tel: 362 9430. Open daily except Saturdays, 9 a.m. to 3 p.m. Mondays 5 p.m. to 8 p.m. Sundays 10 a.m. to 1 p.m. Entrance fee.

Historical and Ethnological Museum, Stadiou St, tel: 323 7617. Open Tuesdays to Fridays 9 a.m. to 2 p.m., Saturdays & Sundays 9 a.m. to 1 p.m. Closed Mondays. Entrance fee.
Admission free on Thursdays.

Kanellopoulos Museum, Theorias & Panos Sts, Plaka, tel: 321 2313. Open daily 8:45 a.m. to 3 p.m. Sundays & holidays 9.30 a.m. to 2.30 p.m. Closed Mondays. Entrance fee.

Keramikos Museum, 148 Ermou St, tel: 346 3552. Open daily 8.30 a.m. to 3 p.m. Closed Mondays. Entrance fee.

Keramikos Archaeological Site, Ermou & Pireos corner, tel: 346 3552. Open daily 8.30 a.m. to 3 p.m. Closed Mondays. Entrance fee.

Municipality of Athens Tradition & Folk Art Centre, 6 Hatzimihali St, Plaka area, tel: 324 3987. Open Tuesdays & Thursdays 9 a.m. to 9 p.m., Wednesdays, Fridays, Saturdays 9 a.m. to 1 p.m. & 5 p.m. to 9 p.m., Sundays 9 a.m. to 1 p.m. Admission free.

National Archaeological Museum, 1 Tossitsa St, tel: 821 7717. Open daily 8 a.m. to 5 p.m., Saturdays, Sundays & holidays 8.30 a.m. to 3 p.m., Mondays 11 a.m. to 5 p.m. Entrance fee (includes fee to the exhibits from Fira & the Numismatic Museum).

National Gallery and Alexandros Soutsos Museum, 46 Vas. Sophias Ave, tel: 721 1010. Open daily 9 a.m. to 3 p.m. Sundays & holidays 10 a.m. to 2 p.m. Closed Mondays. Entrance fee.

National History, 13 Levidou St, Kifissia, tel: 808 0254. Open daily 9 a.m. to 1 p.m. & 5 p.m. to 8 p.m. Closed on Fridays. Sundays & holidays an entrance fee is charged.

Numismatic Museum, 1 Tossitsa St, tel: 821 7769. Open daily 8.30 a.m. to 1.30 p.m. Sundays & holidays 9 a.m. to 2 p.m. Closed Mondays. Admission free.

Roman Agora, end of Eolou St, tel: 321 0185. Open daily 8.30 a.m. to 3 p.m. Closed Mondays. Entrance fee.

Temple of Hephaistos and Ancient Agora, tel: 321 0185. Open daily 8.30 a.m. to 3 p.m. Closed Mondays. Entrance fee.

Temple of Olympian Zeus, Olgas and Amalias Ave, tel: 922 6330. Open daily 8.30 a.m. to 3 p.m. Closed Mondays. Entrance fee.

Temple of Dionyssos, D. Areopagitou Ave, tel: 323 6665. Open daily 8.30 a.m. to 3 p.m. Closed Mondays. Entrance fee.

War Museum of Greece, Vas. Sophias Ave, tel: 729 0543-4. Open daily 9 a.m. to 2 p.m. Closed Mondays.

PIRAEUS

Maritime Museum of Piraeus, Akti Themistokleous, tel: 451 6822. Open daily 9 a.m. to 12.30 p.m. Sundays & holidays 10 a.m. to 1 p.m. & 5 p.m. to 8 p.m. Closed Mondays, Tuesdays & Fridays. Admission free.

Piraeus Archaeological Museum, 31 Char. Trikoupi St, tel: 452 1598. Open daily 8.30 a.m. to 3 p.m. Closed Mondays. Entrance fee.

SITES NEAR ATHENS

Daphni Monastery, tel: 581 1558. Open daily 8.30 to 3 p.m. Closed Mondays. Entrance fee.

Epidavros Archaeological Site and Museum, tel: 0753 22009. Open daily 8 a.m. to 5 p.m. Saturdays, Sundays & holidays 8.30 a.m. to 3 p.m. Museum open Mondays 11 a.m. to 5 p.m. Archaeological site closed Mondays. Entrance fee.

Elefsis Museum, tel: 554 6019. Open daily 8.30 a.m. to 3 p.m. Closed Mondays. Entrance fee.

Kaissariani Monastery, tel: 723 6619. Open daily 8.30 a.m. to 3 p.m. Closed Mondays. Admission free.

IONIAN ISLANDS

CORFU

Archaeological Museum, tel: (0661) 30680. Open daily 8.30 a.m. to 3 p.m. Closed Mondays. Entrance fee.

Museum of Asiatic Art, tel: (0661) 23124. Open daily 8.30 a.m. to 3 p.m. Closed Mondays. Entrance fee.

SARONIC GULF ISLANDS

AEGINA

Temple of Afaia, tel: (0297) 32398. Open daily 8 a.m. to 5 pm. Saturdays, Sundays & holidays 8.30 a.m. to 3 p.m. Entrance fee.

Island Museum, tel: (0297) 22637. Open daily 8.30 a.m. to 3 p.m. Closed Mondays. Entrance fee (including fee to the Temple of Apollo).

CYCLADES ISLANDS

ANDROS

Archaeological Museum, tel: (0282) 23664. Open daily 8.30 a.m. to 3 p.m. Closed Mondays. Entrance fee.

Museum Basil & Elisa Goulandris (Modern Art), tel: (0282) 22650. Open daily 10 a.m. to 1 p.m. & 5 p.m. to 8 p.m. Closed Mondays. Admission free.

DELOS

Archaeological Site, tel: (0289) 22259. Open daily 8.30 a.m. to 3 p.m. Closed Mondays. Entrance fee.

Island Museum, tel: (0289) 22259. Open daily 8.30 a.m. to 3 p.m. Closed Mondays. Entrance fee.

MILOS

Archaeological Site & Museum, tel: (0287) 21620. Open daily 8.30 a.m. to 3 p.m. Closed Mondays. Entrance fee.

The Catacombs, tel: (0287) 21620. Open daily except Wednesdays & Sundays 9 a.m. to 2.30 p.m. Entrance fee.

SANTORINI (THIRA)

Akrotiri Thira Archaeological Site, tel: (0286) 81366. Open daily 8.30 a.m. to 3 p.m. Closed Mondays. Entrance fee.

Archeological Site, tel: (0286) 22217. Open daily 8.30 a.m. to 3 p.m. Closed Mondays. Admission free.

Island Museum, tel: (0286) 22217. Open daily 8.30 a.m. to 3 p.m. Closed Mondays. Entrance fee.

NORTHERN AEGEAN ISLANDS

SAMOTHRAKI

Archaeological Site, tel: (0551) 41474. Open daily 8.30 a.m. to 3 p.m. Closed Mondays. Entrance fee.

Island Museum, tel: (0551) 41474 Open daily 8.30 a.m. to 3 p.m. Closed Mondays. Entrance fee.

DODECANESE ISLANDS

KOS

Asclepieion & other Archeological Sites, tel: (0242) 28763. Open daily 8.30 a.m. to 3 p.m. Closed Mondays. Entrance fee.

Island Museum, tel: (0242) 28326. Open daily 8.30 a.m. to 3 p.m. Closed Mondays. Entrance fee.

Kos Castle, tel: (0242) 28326. Open daily 8.30 a.m. to 3 p.m. Closed Mondays. Entrance fee.

Restored Ancient Dwelling, tel: (0242) 28326. Open daily 8.30 a.m. to 3 p.m. Closed Mondays. Entrance fee.

LESVOS

Eressos Archaeological Museum, tel: (0251) 22087. Open daily 8.30 a.m. to 3 p.m. Closed Mondays. Admission free.

Mytilini Archaeological Museum, tel: (0251) 22087. Open Wednesdays & Thursdays 3 p.m. to 6 p.m. Saturdays & Sundays 9 a.m. to 6 p.m. Entrance fee.

Theofilos Art Museum, tel: (0251) 28179. Open daily 9 a.m. to 1 p.m. & 4.30 p.m. to 8 p.m. Closed Mondays. Entrance fee.

PATMOS

Island churches and other monuments, admission free.

Monastery of St. John & Library, Vestry, tel: (0241) 21954. Open daily 8.30 a.m. to 3 p.m. Closed Mondays. Admission free.

RHODES

Rhodes Acropolis, Theatre and Stadium, tel: (0241) 21954. Open daily 8.30 a.m. to 3 p.m. Closed Mondays. Admission free.

Acropolis of Ialyssos, tel: (0241) 21954. Open daily 8.30 a.m. to 3 p.m. Closed Mondays. Entrance fee.

Acropolis of Lindos, tel: (0241) 21954. Open daily 8.30 a.m. to 3 p.m. Closed Mondays. Entrance fee.

Decorative Collections, tel: (0241) 21954. Open daily 8.30 a.m. to 3 p.m. Closed Mondays. Admission free.

Island Museum, tel: (0241) 21954. Open daily 8.30 a.m. to 3 p.m. Closed Mondays. Entrance fee.

Kamiros Archaeological Site, tel: (0241) 21954. Open daily 8.30 a.m. to 3 p.m. Closed Mondays. Entrance fee.

Palace of the Knights, tel: (0241) 21954. Open daily 8.30 a.m. to 3 p.m. Closed Mondays. Entrance fee.

Perimetre of the Medieval Walls, tel: (0241) 21954. Open to visitors accompanied by a guide on Tuesdays & Saturdays from 3 p.m. to 5 p.m. Visitors should gather in the courtyard of the Palace of the Knights. Entrance fee.

CRETE

Ag. Nikolaos Museum, tel: (0841) 22462. Open daily 8.30 a.m. to 3 p.m. Closed Mondays. Entrance fee.

Aghia Trias Archaeological Site, tel: (081) 226092. Open daily 8.30 a.m. to 3 p.m. Closed Mondays. Entrance fee.

Gortys Archaeologicial Site, tel: (081) 226092. Open daily 8 a.m. to 5 p.m. Saturdays, Sundays & holidays 8.30 a.m. to 3 p.m. Entrance fee.

Hania Museum, tel: (0821) 20334. Open daily 8.30 a.m. to 5 p.m. Sundays & holidays 8.30 a.m. to 3 p.m. Mondays 11 a.m. to 5 p.m. Entrance fee.

Iraklion Archaeological Museum, tel: (081) 226092. Open daily 8 a.m. to 5 p.m. Saturday, Sundays & holidays 8.30 a.m. to 3 p.m. Mondays 11 a.m. to 5 p.m. Entrance fee.

Iraklion Harbour Fortress (Koules), tel: (081) 286228. Open daily 8.30 a.m. to 3 p.m. Closed Mondays. Entrance fee.

Knossos Archaeological Site, tel: (081) 231940. Open daily 8 a.m. to 5 p.m. Saturdays, Sundays & holidays 8.30 a.m. to 3 p.m. Entrance fee.

Mallia Archaeological Site, tel: (0841) 22462. Open daily 8.30 a.m. to 3 p.m. Closed Mondays. Entrance fee.

Phaestos (Festos) Archaeological Site, tel: (0892) 22615. Open daily 8 a.m. to 5 p.m. Saturdays, Sundays & holidays 8.30 a.m. to 3 p.m. Entrance fee.

Rethymnon Museum, tel: (0831) 29975. Open daily 8.30 a.m. to 3 p.m. Closed Mondays. Entrance fee.

Tylissos Archaeological Site, tel: (081) 226092. Open daily 8.30 a.m. to 3 p.m. Closed Mondays. Entrance fee.

Zakros Archaeological Site, tel: (0841) 22462. Open daily 8.30 a.m. to 3 pm. Closed Mondays. Entrance fee.

OTHER ARCHAEOLOGICAL SITES

St. Titus, Gournia, tel: (081) 226092. Open daily 8.30 a.m. to 3 p.m. Closed Mondays. Admission free.

OUTDOOR MOVIES

One of the delights of an island evening is to sit under a starry sky and enjoy an outdoor movie. Like an American drive-in without the cars, Greece's outdoor cinemas do not attempt to compete with mainstream movie houses, screening instead old Westerns, Hollywood war movies and films you've never heard of. Usually in English with Greek subtitles, the noise in the theatre (Greeks talk through screenings) often makes the movie dialogue incomprehensible but doesn't spoil the evening out a jot. Take snacks, a blanket or warm jacket and wear lots of anti-mosquito spray.

NIGHTLIFE

Most island nightlife consists of strolling from taverna to *zacharisplastí* to a café on the promenade. Having said that, discos abound on any island with a sizable influx of tourists. The best are out of town and out of doors; dancing under the stars is an unforgettable Greek experience. Canny managers of discos located some distance from the port hire a nightly mini-bus which transports revellers to the premises. Discos on small islands are the most fun when, around midnight, the Rolling Stones give way to traditional island music and older folks join young foreigners on the dance floor. For a more sophisticated evening out, both Rhodes and Corfu have casinos.

GREEK FOLK DANCES

Athens, Corfu and Rhodes have regular performances of Greek folk dancing during the summer
months. In Athens, the renowned Dora Stratou
Group perform at the Philopappou Theatre most
nights at 10.25 p.m. On Wednesdays and Sundays
there is an extra performance at 8.15 p.m. Information from 324 4395. Performances are held each
evening at 9 p.m. on Corfu at the Old Venetian
Castle. The ticket price includes the Sound and Light
spectacle. Information from (0661) 39730. On
Rhodes, the Nelly Dimoglou Group holds sway at
the old and attractive Rodini Theatre most evenings
at 9.15 p.m. Information by calling (0241) 27524.

SHOPPING

WHAT TO BUY

Most Greek tourist tat is instantly forgettable; it
also takes up room on ferries and airplanes. Much
better to concentrate on small local items like
sponges from Kalimnos, leather bags from Rhodes,
hand-made pottery from Sifnos, herbs from Symi,
and extremely attractive silver jewellery from a
number of islands. Much of this jewellery is made by
local craftmen, and styles range from the traditional
to the fashionable.

Other good buys include baskets, copper pots and
other copperware, honey, olive oil, and the ubiquitous loukoumia (Turkish Delight), made on Syros
but exported to other islands too. The Dodecanese
islands are particularly rich in fur coat shops and are
also a source of inexpensive booze, both local and
imported.

Hydra, Mykonos and Paros have some of the most
fashionable boutiques to be found in Greece. Much
of their stock out-rivals Athens; but not, unfortunately London, Paris or New York.

Bargaining is expected in market places and stalls.
In these places, even if an item has a price tag, try
offering a lower price. Even better, show interest and
then walk away. (You can always return if the ploy
doesn't work. It usually does.) Bargaining is unac-
ceptable in department stores, chain stores and most
boutiques.

Department stores implement a complicated service system not recommended for anyone in a hurry.
If you happen to go to a large stationers to purchase
a notebook, a pencil, a couple of envelopes and

perhaps a birthday card, you could find yourself
standing in six different queues: one for each
department (where an assistant writes a receipt for
each item), one to pay the cashier the total amount,
and one for delivery of the goods. If you're lucky,
all four items will have arrived from their various
departments (only a few steps from each other) at the
delivery desk, wrapped or placed into four separate
bags with four separate receipts taped on top. This
curious approach to consumerism is often accompanied by sullen silence on the part of the sales
assistants.

PERIPTERA (KIOSKS)

Always open days, nights, holidays and Sundays, life
in Greece would be unmanageable without a
neighbourhood *periptera*. Although they may appear
limited by their diminutive structures, kiosks are
really multi-purpose powerhouses. Besides filling the
function of newsagent/tobacconist, these businesses,
many family-run, also double as mini amusement
parks with kiddie rides, sporting goods stores,
ironmongers, locksmiths, and for many customers
with problems, the proprietor may dispense psychiatric or medical advice. Here, too, is a quick place
to buy tourist requisites: shampoo, nail clippers,
postcards.

There are over 3,000 kiosks in Athens alone. It
is not unusual for a *periptera* to work shifts of 12
hours in conditions which vary from furnace-like in
summer to chill and damp in winter. The kiosks
started as gifts from the government to wounded
veterans of the Balkan and First World Wars. Many
people remark on the similarity between the architecture of kiosks and that of military guardposts
such as those used by the honour guard in front of
Parliament on Syntagma Square. In a symbolic way
the *periptera* are also guard houses where old soldiers
prolong their duty, emerging from the military into
the commercial sector, watching over and serving the
community.

SPORTS

Many of the larger hotels have tennis courts and
facilities for water-skiing. Major beaches can provide
surf boards, water bikes, snorkelling and windsurfing
equipment; there's even scope for parascending on
Crete, Rhodes, Kos and Skiathos.

GOLF

Greece has a few golf courses in the entire country. In Athens, the course is at Glyfada (tel: 894 6875). Rhodes' golf course is at Afandou (tel: [0241] 51255). Corfu's Ermones Bay golf club (tel: [0661] 94220) is particularly nice. Lessons and rental equipment available at all courses.

YACHTS

The NTOG publishes an excellent booklet called Sailing the Greek Seas. Included is information on weather, coastal radio telephone stations, entry and exit regulations. The pamphlet is particularly detailed on marinas, bunkering ports and supply stations. There are four marinas within striking distance of Athens. Information on services or facilities may be obtained by calling:

Vouliagmeni marina – tel: 896 0012
Zea marina – tel: 451 3944
Alimos – tel: 982 8642
Flisvos – tel: 982 8537

If you prefer to charter a yacht, the NTOG can provide lists of yacht brokers and consultants. All charter agreements have to be made in the manner and on the official form prescribed by the Greek government. The following organisations can also offer help and advice:

Greek Yacht Brokers & Consultants Association, 36 Alkyonis St, 175 61.

P. Faliro, tel: 981 6582.

Greek Bareboat Yacht Owners Association, 56 Vass. Pavlou St, Kastela, Piraeus, tel: 452 5465.

Hellenic Professional Yacht Owners Association, 43 Freatidos St, Zea Marina, 185 36 Piraeus, tel: 452 6335.

Anyone planning to sail independently around the islands is advised to become familiar with the list of Port Authorities (see "Getting Around"). The Port Authority Harbour Police are the only people who can provide up-to-the-minute information on conditions concerning a specific island. Fuelling facilities and other provisions are available at: Adamas (Milos); Aegina; Agios Nikolaos (Kea); Agios Nikolaos (Crete); Argostoli (Kefalonia); Corfu Port; Ermoupoli (Syros); Hania (Crete); Hios; Hydra; Kalymnos; Kamares (Sifnos); Kapsali (Kythera); Kastelorizo; Kastro (Andros); Katapola (Amorgos); Kos; Lakki (Leros); Lefkas; Linaria (Skyros); Mirina (Limnos); Mytilini (Lesvos); Mykonos; Naxos; Parikia (Paros); Pigadia (Karpathos); Poros; Mandraki (Rhodes); Skala (Patmos); Skiathos; Skopelos; Spetses; Tinos; Vathi (Ithaki); Zakynthos.

SPECIAL INFORMATION

Islands for photographers: Santorini, Crete, Nissiros, Delos, Symi, Skyros.

Islands for hikers: Crete, Cephalonia, Hios, Samothraki.

Islands for gays: Mykonos.

Islands for children: Crete, Skiathos, Rhodes, Pserimos.

Islands for fun-lovers: Mykonos, Corfu, Paros, Kos, Crete.

Islands for privacy-seekers: The "Back Islands", Pserimos, Telendos, Astypalea, Ithaki.

Islands for academics: Lesvos, Crete, Rhodes, Kos, Patmos, Aegina.

Islands with spas: Kythnos, Lefkas, Andros, Nissiros, Ikaria.

Islands for the disabled: For a list of hotels with facilities suitable for handicapped people, write to the NTOG Information Office, 2 Amerikis St, Athens.

LANGUAGE

USEFUL WORDS & PHRASES

yes	*né*
no	*óhi*
okay	*en dáksi*
thank you	*efharistó*
(very much)	*para polí*
excuse me	*signómi*
it doesn't matter	*dhen pirázi*
it's nothing	*típota*

certainly	*málista*	telephone	*tiléfono*
good day	*káli méra*	bank	*trapeza*
good evening	*káli spéra*	marketplace	*agora*
good night	*káli níhta*	pharmacy	*farmakío*
goodbye	*addio*	doctor	*yatros*
Greetings!	*yá sou, yá sas*	hospital	*nosokomío*
	(plural or formal)	police	*astinomía*
"health to you!" (a toast)	*yá sou, yá sas*	station	*stathmós*
	(plural)	boat	*karávi, vapóri*
bon voyage	*kaló taksídhi*	bike/moped	*podílato/motopodílato*
welcome	*kalós ilthathe*	on foot	*me ta pódhia*
good luck	*kalí tihi*	ticket	*isitirio*
How are you?	*ti kánis, ti kánete*	road/street	*thromos/othos*
	(plural or formal)	beach	*paralía*
fine (in response)	*kalá*	church	*eklisia*
so so (in response)	*étsi kétsi*	ancient ruins	*arhéa*
pleased to meet you	*hárika*	centre	*kentro*
Have you...?	*éhete...?*	square	*platia*
Is there...?	*éhi...?*	sea	*thálassa*
How much does it cost?	*póso káni?*		
It's (too) expensive	*íne (polí) akrivó*		
How much?	*póso?*		
How many?	*pósa?*		
Do you have a room?	*éhete éna domátio?*		
Can I...?	*boro na...?*		
When?	*póte?*		
Where is...?	*póu ine...?*		
Do you speak English?	*milás/miláte angliká?*		
	(sing./plural or formal)		
Do you understand?	*katálaves?*		
What time is it?	*ti ora íne?*		
What time will it leave?	*ti ora tha figi?*		
I don't	*dhen (plus verb)*		
I want	*thélo*		
I have	*ého*		
today	*simera*		
tomorrow	*avrio*		
now	*tóra*		
here/there	*edho/eki*		
near/far	*konda/makria*		
small/large	*mikro/megalo*		
quickly	*grigora*		
slowly	*argá*		
good/bad	*kaló/kakó*		
warm/cold	*zestó/krio*		
shower with hot water	*douz me zestó nero*		
hotel	*ksenodhohio*		
bed	*kreváti*		
key	*klidhi*		
entrance	*isodhos*		
exit	*eksodhos*		
toilet	*toualéta*		
women's	*ginekón*		
men's	*adrón*		
store	*magazi*		
kiosk	*periptero*		
open/shut	*aniktos/klistós*		
post office	*tahidromio*		
stamp	*grammatósima*		
letter	*gramma*		
envelope	*falelos*		

NUMBERS

1	énna
2	dio
3	tria/tris
4	téssera
5	pendhe
6	éksi
7	eptá
8	oehtó
9	ennea
10	deka
11	éndeka
12	dódeka
13	dekatria
14	dekatessera
20	ikosi
21	ikosi énna
30	triánda
40	saránda
50	peninda
60	eksinda
70	evdhominda
80	ogdhonda
90	enneninda
100	ekató
150	ekatopeninda
200	diakóssia
300	triakóssia
400	tetrakóssia
1,000	hília

DAYS OF THE WEEK

Monday	*theftéra*
Tuesday	*tríti*
Wednesday	*tetárti*
Thursday	*pémpti*
Friday	*paraskeví*
Saturday	*sávato*
Sunday	*kiriakí*

UNTRANSLATABLE WORDS

kéfi – to be in good spirits, having a good time with your paréa

paréa – one's group of close friends, your "gang"

kaimós – the opposite of kefi, one's long-suffering or sadness

palikári – a good fellow (honourable, brave, intelligent, etc)

filótimo – adjective meaning literally "love of honour"

mángas – a "toughie," a "cool dude," macho

re – short for moré, meaning baby, kid, dummy; a word thrown in when addressing a buddy in the typically male Greek rough-affectionate manner

malákas – literally "masturbator"; often combined with re (re malákas); can be directed to one's friends affectionately or to others more antagonistically

paidhia – the "boys," fellows, guys

alítis – a bum, roughly the opposite of palikári

lipón – well, so, now then

ella! – Come! Come on!

oríste (?) – Can I help you?

po po po! – Well well! What have we here!

ópa – Look out!; also, at a music taverna for instance, "way to go!" "all right!" etc.

THE LANGUAGE OF GESTURES

Greek is a gestural language; you don't speak it with your hands in your pockets or with your head still. The body and its movements are signs which form an integral part of the communicative process. You can learn this aspect of Greek only through close observation. Two of the most common of these gestures are those indicating "yes" and "no". "No" is often communicated by jerking the head and chin up and back sharply. This is a very slight movement, but emphatic. Sometimes, in fact, only the eyebrows or eyes make this upward gesture. The gesture indicating "yes" is a rather gentler one, a slow downward angling of the head.

FURTHER READING

HISTORY

Booth, C.D. and I.B. *Italy's Aegean Possessions.* London: 1928.

Cheetham, Nicholas. *Medieval Greece.* New Haven, 1981.

du Boulay, Juliet. *Portrait of a Greek Mountain Village.* Oxford: Clarendon Press, 1974.

Finley, M.I. *The Ancient Greeks.* Harmondsworth/ Penguin, 1963.

Hamilton, Edith. *Mythology.* New York: New American Library, 1969.

Hopkins, Adam. *Crete: Its Past, Present and People.* London: Faber & Faber, 1977.

SPECIAL TRAVEL BOOKS & GUIDES

The Aegean Islands: The Cyclades, or Life Among the Insular Greeks. London: Argonaut,1965.

Constantine, David. *Early Greek Travellers and the Hellenic Idea.* Cambridge: CUP, 1984.

Dubin, Marc. *Greece on Foot.* Leicester/London: Cordee, 1986.

Durrell, Lawrence. *The Greek Islands.* London: Faber and Faber.

Ellingham, Mark. (ed.) *The Rough Guide to Greece.* London: Harrap Columbus,1988.

Freeley, John. *The Cyclades.* London: Jonathan Cape, 1986.

Karpodini-Dimitriadi, E. *The Greek Islands.* Athens: Ekdotike Athenon S.A., 1987.

Let's Go Greece. Harvard Student Agency, 1986.

Stavrolakes, Niki. *Poros.* Athens: Lycabettus Press.

Stone, Tom. *Patmos.* Athens: Lycabettus Press.

Vanderpool, Catherine. *Hydra.* Athens: Lycabettus Press.

Zenfell, Martha Ellen. *Guide to the Greek Islands.* London: Robert Nicholson,1986.

FOREIGN WRITERS & GREECE

Andrews, Kevin. *The Flight of Ikaros.* Harmondsworth/Penguin, 1984.

Boleman-Herring, Elizabeth. *The Other Side of the Road.* Lycabettus Press, 1988.

Durrell, Lawrence. *Prospero's Cell, Reflections on a Marine Venus, Bitter Lemons.* London: Faber & Faber.

Fowles, John. *The Magus.* London: Cape, 1977.

Gage, Nicholas. *Eleni*. London: Collins, 1983.

Kitroeff, Alex. *The Bananaless Republic*. The Athenian Press, 1988.

Levi, Peter. *Hill of Kronos*. New York: Penguin, 1984

Miller, Henry. *The Colossus of Maroussi*. New York: New Directions, 1958.

Renault, Mary. *The Last of the Wine*. London: Sceptre, 1986

USEFUL ADDRESSES

TOURIST INFORMATION

National Tourist Organisation of Greece overseas offices can be found at the following places:

United Kingdom & Ireland. 195-197 Regent St, London W1R 8DL, tel: 734 5997.

USA. 645 Fifth Avenue, Olympic Tower, New York, N.Y. 10022, tel: 421 5777;
• 611 West Sixth St, Los Angeles, California 90017, tel: 626 6696;
• 168 North Michigan Ave, Chicago, Illinois 60601, tel: 782 1084;
• Building 31, State St, Boston, Mass, tel: 227 7366.

Canada. 1233 rue de la Montagne, Montreal QC, Quebec H3G 1Z2, tel: 871 1535;
• 80 Bloor Str West, Suite 1403, Toronto ONT M5S 2V1, tel: 968 2220.

Australia & New Zealand. 51-57 Pitt Str, Sydney, N.S.W. 2000, tel: 241 1663.

Germany. Neue Mainzerstr, 22,6 Frankfurt/Main 1, tel: 236 562;
• Pacellistr, 2,8000 Munchen 2, tel: 222 035;
• Neuer Wall, 35,2000 Hamburg 36, tel: 366 910.

Austria. Karntner Ring 5,1015, Wien, tel: 525 317.

Belgium. 62-66 Blv. de l'Imperatrice, 1000, Bruxelles, tel: 513 0206.

Denmark. Vester Farimagsgade 3, DK 1606, Kopenhagen, tel: 1-123 063.

Finland. Stora Robertsgatan 3-5 C38, 00120 Helsingfors 12, tel: 0-655 223.

France. 3 Avenue de L'Opera, Paris 75001, tel: 260 6575.

Italy. Via L. Bissolati 78-80, 00187, Roma, tel: 4744 301;
• Piazza Diaz 1, Ang. Via Rastrelli, Milano, tel: 860 470.

Japan. 3-16-30 Nishi Azabu, Minato-Ku, Tokyo 106, tel: 4031 812.

Netherlands. Leidsestraat 13, NS Amsterdam, tel: 2542 12.

Norway. Ovre Slottsgatan 15B, Oslo 1, tel: 426 501.

Saudia Arabia. Embassy of Greece, Madina Road, City Centre, P.O.B. 13262, Jeddah 21493, tel: 667 6240.

Spain. Alberto Aguilera No 17, Madrid 28015, tel: 248 4889.

Sweden. Grev Turegatan 2, Box 5298, 10246 Stockholm 5, tel: 203 802.

Switzerland. Gottfried Kellerstr 7, CH 8001 Zurich, tel: 251 8487.

IN GREECE

The 24-hour Tourist Police number in Athens is 171.

The Athens headquarters of the National Tourist Organisation of Greece is located at 2 Amerikis St, tel 322 3111-19. Visiting hours are from 12 noon to 2.30 p.m., Monday to Friday. There is also an information desk at the East Air Terminal which is open during the day and displays ferryboat sailings even when closed. Most general literature (maps, hotel information, etc.) can be obtained from the two information bureaus located in Syntagma Square, which also post daily sailings of ferries from Piraeus.

Inside the General Bank of Greece, 1 Ermou St, tel: 325 2267-8. Open Monday to Friday 8 a.m. to 6 p.m., Saturday 9 a.m. to 1 p.m; National Bank of Greece, 2 Karageorgi Servias St, tel: 322 2545. Open Monday to Friday 8 a.m. to 2 p.m., then 3.30 p.m. to 8 p.m. Saturday 9 a.m. to 2 p.m; Piraeus. Marina Zeas, NTOG building, tel: 413 5716/4134709.

ISLANDS TOURIST OFFICES

At least one third of all the islands operate unofficial tourist information centres from June until September. These are prominently sited in the centre of the main harbour town and often located in picturesque buildings, i.e. a windmill on Paros, a clocktower on Symi. They serve the usual function of all tourist information centres, and some can even help with accommodation. These information centres are not to be confused with the numerous ticket and tourist agencies at every port and promenade. These are run by private individuals, usually to promote excursions and activities of their own. Although they may be helpful and provide details when asked, information from tourist agencies will never be comprehensive. Occasionally, this will be the only office on an island where anyone speaks English. Most islands also devote a special section of the police force to deal solely with visitors and their requirements. This division of the police force is called the Tourist Police. They, too, can help with accommodation. For a list of Tourist Police telephone numbers on the islands, see the section on "Emergencies". The larger islands have proper, authorised tourist information centres. Although opening times vary with the island and the season, a weekday visit in the morning between 9 a.m. and 1 p.m. is sure to find them open.

Corfu. The Governor's House, Diikitirion Kerkyras, tel: (0661) 30298/30360.

Cephalonia. Information Office, Argostoli, tel: (0671) 22847.

Syros. Ermoupolis, tel: (0281) 26725/22375.

Kos. Information Office, Akti Koundourioti, tel: (0242) 28724/24460.

Rhodes. Archbishop Makarios & Papagou St, Rhodes Town, tel: (0241) 23655/23255/27466. City of Rhodes Information, tel: (0241) 35945. Lindos Information Office, tel: (0244) 31428.

Samos. Central Tourist Office, tel: (0273) 28582/28530.

Crete. Hania: 40 Kriari St, tel: (0821) 26426/42624.

Iraklion. 1 Xanthoulidou St, tel: (081) 228203/228225. Information office tel: (081) 228203.

Rethymnon. El. Venizelou Av, tel: (0831) 29148/24143.

EMBASSIES & CONSULATES

United Kingdom. 1 Ploutarhou St, Athens, tel: 723 6211-9.

United States of America. 91 Vas. Sofias Ave, Athens, tel: 721 2951-9.

Australia. 37 D. Soutsou St, Athens, tel: 644 7303.

Canada. 4 I. Genadiou St, Athens, tel: 723 9511-9.

New Zealand. 15-17 An. Antosha St, Athens, tel: 641 0311-5.

France. 7 Vas. Sofias Ave, Athens, tel: 729 0151-6.

Germany. 10 Vas. Sofias, Maroussi, tel: 36941.

Argentina. 59 Vas. Sofias Ave, Athens, tel: 722 4753.

Austria. 26 Alexandras Ave, Athens, tel: 821 1036.

Belgium. 3 Sekeri St, Athens, tel: 361 7886-7.

Brazil. 14 Filikis Eterias Sq., Kolonaki, tel: 721 3039.

China. 2a Krinon St, Paleo Psihiko, tel: 6723282.

Cyprus. 16 Irodotou St, Athens, tel: 723 7883.

Denmark. 15 Filikis Eterias Sq, Kolonaki, tel: 724 9315.

Finland. 1 Eratosthonous St & Vas. Konstantinou Ave, Athens, tel: 751 5064.

India. 4 Meleagrou St, Athens, tel: 721 6227.

Ireland. 7 Vas. Konstantinou Ave, Athens, tel: 723 2771.

Israel. 1 Marathonodromon St, Paleo Psihiko, tel: 671 9530-1.

Italy. 2 Sekeri St, Athens, tel: 361 1722-3.

Japan. 2-4 Messogion Ave, Athens, tel: 775 8101-3.

Luxembourg. 11 Stissihorou St, Athens, tel: 721 7948.

Malta. 2 Efplias St, Piraeus, tel: 418 1501.

Morocco. 14 Mousson St, Paleo Psihiko, tel: 647 4209.

Netherlands. 5-7 Vas. Konstantinou Ave, Athens, tel: 723 9701-4.

Norway. 7 Vas. Konstantinou Ave, Athens, tel: 724 6173-4.

Portugal. 44 Karneadou St, Athens, tel: 729 0096.

Spain. 29 Vas. Sofias Ave, Athens, tel: 721 4885.

Sweden. 7 Vas. Konstantinou Ave, Athens, tel: 729 0421.

Switzerland. 2 Iassiou St, Athens, tel: 723 0364-6.

Turkey. 8 Vas. Georgiou II St, Athens, tel: 724 5915-7.

ART/PHOTO CREDITS

INDEX

A

Achillion 86
Adamas 137
Aegina 101–103
Agathonisi 215
Agnik 239, 240
agriculture 87
Akrotiri 115, 236
Alimia 202
Alínda 214
Alonissos 153, 155
Amorgos 122, 123
Anafi 119
Andros 134, 135
Ano Méra 131
Ano Palalókastro 238
Ano Zákros 242
Anogia 227
Antiparos 127, 128
Antipaxos 89
Apollon 125
Apolonía 138
Archangelos 193
Argenti Museum 172
Argostóli 93
Arkádi Monastery 233
Arkoi 215
Asklépieion 209
Assos 93
Astipalea 205–207
Athens 79
Ayia Galíni 230
Ayia Rouméli 234
Ayias Efstratios 168, 169
Ayii Déka 229
Ayios Nikólaos 239, 240
Ayiossos 169, 170, 171

B

Back Islands 123, 124
Batsí 134
Benaki 77
Bouboulina, Laskarina 106
bouzouki 263
Brooks, Rupert 156
Byrokastro 143

C

Cape Sounion 76
Cephalonia 92, 93
Colossus of Rhodes 184
Commonwealth Cemetery, Crete 236
Corfu 32, 83–86
Crete 223, 242
    Ayios Nikólaos (Agnik) 239, 240
    Haniá 235, 236
    history 38–40
    Iráklion 226, 227
    Knossos 228
Cyclades Islands 113–143
    Amorgos 122, 123
    Anafi 119
    Andros 134, 135
    Antiparos 127, 128
    Back Islands" 123, 124
    Donoussa 123
    Folegandros 119, 120
    history 34, 35
    Ios 120–122
    Iraklia 123
    Kea 143
    Kimolos 139
    Kithnos 142, 143
    Koufonissia 123
    Milos 137–139
    Mykonos 128, 129, 131
    Naxos 124–126
    Paros 126, 127
    Santorini 115, 116
    Schinoussa 123
    Serifos 140–142
    Sifnos 139, 140
    Sikinos 120
    Syros 131, 132
    Tinos 132–134

D

Daphni Monastery 76
Dapia 106
Delos 130
Diktaian Cave 240
Dodecanese Islands 181–217
    Alimia 202
    Astipalea 205–207
    Halki 202
    history 37, 38
    Kalimnos 211–213
    Karpathos 199, 200
    Kashellorizo 201, 202
    Kassos 200, 201
    Kos 207–209, 211
    Laros 213–215
    Lipsi 215
    Nissiros 205
    Patmos 216, 217
    Pserimos 211
    Rhodes 183–195
    Symi 203
    Telendos 213
    Tilos 202, 203
Donoussa 123

Doxarás, Panayiótis 94
Durrell, Lawrence 84, 291

E & F

Eántio 101
Elaphonísi 237
Embonas 191
Epta Piges 192
Erectheum Temple 73
Eressós 170
Ermoúpolis 132
Evans, Sir Arthur 228
Faltaits Museum 154
festivals 210
Festos 230
Firá 115
Folegandros 119, 120
Fowles, John 106

G & H

Gaios 89
Glóssa 153
Gortyn 229
Goulandris Museum 113
Halki 49–51, 202
Haniá 235, 236
Herod Atticus Theatre 75
Hios 172, 173
Hippocrates 208
Hora, Ios 121, 122
Hora, Kithnos 142
Hora, Naxos 125
Hrissopigi, Monastery 140
Hydra 104–106

I

Idaian Cave 227
Ierápetra 231, 242
Ikaria 173, 174
Ionian Islands 81–94
    Cephalonia 92, 93
    Corfu 83–86
    history 32
    Ithaki 90–92
    Lefkas 89, 90
    Paxos 89
    Zakynthos 93, 94
Ios 120–122
Ioulis 143
Iraklia 123
Iráklion 226, 227

K

Kaisariani 75
Kalimnos 211, 213
Kalithéa 192
Kapsás Monastery 242
Karpathos 199, 200, 210
Kassos 200, 201
Kastelliorizo 201, 202

Kastro, Skiathos 151
Katholikó Monastery 237
Kazantzákis, Nikos 231
Kámeiros 190
Kástro, Sikinos 120
Káto Zákros 242
Kea 143
Kerameikos Cemetery 75
Khrysoskalitissa Convent 237
Kimolos 139
Kithnos 142, 143
Klima 137, 138
Knossos 228
Kos 207–209, 211
Koufonissia 123
Koukoukanariés 151
Kritinia Castle 191
Kritsá 240

L

Lakki 213, 214
Lantas 230
Lasíthi Plain 240
Lató 241
Lefkas 89, 90
Lefkes 127
Leros 213–215
Lesvos 169–171
Limnos 167, 168
Lindos 193–195
Lipsi 215
Livádi 140

M

Mandraki, Nissiros 205
Mandraki, Rhodes 185–187
Marathi 215
Markopoulo 92
Matala 230
Mállia 239
Megísti 201
Miller, Henry 103, 291
Milos 137–139
Mirtía 231
Mírina 168
Mírties 212
    monasteries
    Arkádi 23
    Hrissopigi 140
    Kapsás 242
    Katholikó 237
    Nea Moni 173
    Panahrandou 135
    Panormítis 203
    Préveli 230
    Profitas Elias 116
    St John the Theologian 217
    Taxiarhon 141
    Toploú 241, 242
    Tsambika 193
    Vronda 175
    Zoödóchou Pigís 104, 135
Monolithos 116
Mouliki 101

Mount Profitas Elias 116
Móhlos 241
Mólivos 169
Museum of Cycladic and Ancient Greek Art 77
music 263–265
Mykonos 128, 129, 131
Mylopotas 121
Myrivilis, Stratis 170
Mytilíni 169, 170

N

National Archaeological Museum 76
Naxos 124–126
Náoussa 127
Nea Moni, Monastery 173
Nidri 89
Nissiros 205
Northeast Aegean Islands 163–175
  Ayios Efstratios 168, 169
  Hios 172, 173
  history 35, 36
  karia 173, 174
  Lesvos 169–171
  Limnos 167, 168
  Psara 171, 172
  Samos 174, 175
  Samothraki 165–167
  Thassos 165

O & P

Odysseus 90, 91
Oia 115
Olympos 199, 200, 210
Palace of the Grand Masters 188
Palaiochora 103
Palatanos 214
Paleokastrítsa 85
Paleópolis 135
Panahrandou, Monastery 135
Panayia 210
Panayía Kerá 240
Panormítis Monastery 203
Paroíkia 126
Paros 126, 127
Parthenon 73
Patheni 215
Patmos 216, 217
Paxos 89
Perasta 201
Petaloudes 190
Petra 170
Phaistós 230
Phodele 232
Pighadia 199
Piraeus 77, 253, 275, 276
Pithagório 175
Plaka, Milos 137
Polirinía 238
Polyrrhénia 238
Poros 103, 104
Poseidonis Temple 76
Pothea 212
Préveli Monastery 232
Profitas Elias Monastery 116

Psara 171, 172
Pserimos 211
Pythagoras 175

R

Rethymnon 233
  Rhodes
    East Coast 191–193
    New Town 185–187
    old city 187–189
    West Coast 189–191
Rodini Park, Rhodes 187

S

sailing 251–253
Salamína 101
Salamis 101
Samaria Gorge 234
Samos 174, 175
Samothraki 165–167
Santorini 31, 115, 116
Sappho 170
Sappho's Leap 90
Saronic Gulf Islands 99–106
  Aegina 101–103
  history 34, 35
  Hydra 104–106
  Poros 103, 104
  Salamis 101
  Spetsai 106
Schinoussa 123
Serifos 140–142
Seven Springs 192
shipping 275–277
Sifnos 31, 139, 140
Sikinos 120
Sitia 241
Skala 216
Skiathos 151, 152, 257
Skopelos 152, 153
Skyros 149, 154, 155, 156, 269
Solomás, Dionysios 94
Spetsai 106
Spilean Cave 127, 128
Spinalonga 43, 241
Sporades Islands 149–156
  Alonissos 153, 155
  history 34, 35
  Skiathos 151, 152, 257
  Skopelos 152, 153
  Skyros 149, 154, 155, 156, 269
St John the Theologian, Monastery 217
Symi 203
Syros 131, 132, 276

T

Taxiarhon Monastery 141
Telendos 213
Temple to Aphaía 102
Thassos 165
Theophilos 170
Therma 166
Thirá 116
Tilos 202, 203
Tinos 132–134, 210
Toploú Monastery 241, 242
Tower of the Winds 75
Tripiti 138
Tsambika Monastery 193
turtles 95

V–Z

Vale of Klima 137, 138
Varthí, Kalimnos 212
Vathí, Ikathi 91
Vathí, Samos 175
Venizélos, Eleftherios 236
Venus de Milo 137
Vourkári 143
Vronda Monastery 175
Youra 155
yachting 251–253
Zakynthos 93, 94, 95
Zoödóchos Pigís, Monastery 104, 135